1-14-58

Great
Enterprises

"In a great city filled with great businesses, people like to be associated with great enterprises."

—Expansion Report of 1919

Great Enterprises

100 Years of the YMCA of Metropolitan Chicago

by **Emmett Dedmon**

RAND McNALLY & COMPANY

NEW YORK   CHICAGO   SAN FRANCISCO

To

the thousands who have served
and are not named in this history
but without whom there would have been no history
this centennial volume
is gratefully dedicated

Contents

CONTENTS

List of Illustrations

Credits for the illustrations are given in parentheses following the listing

List of Illustrations

Great
Enterprises

CHAPTER 1

"Our Object Is to Do Good"

To America in 1850 the West was the land of opportunity—and Chicago the first stop on the road to fortune. Pioneers crowded into the young city by schooner, stagecoach, and wagon train, booming the population so quickly that there was no time for Chicago to pave its streets, finish its buildings, or worry about its morals. Buildings were put up in a day, often consisting of no more than a thin wall of slats and a tar-paper roof. There were few street lamps. And the only means for crossing the Chicago River was a rope ferry.

In 1840 the population of Chicago had been less then 5,000. By 1850 this figure had increased to 29,963. The census of 1860 recorded a population of 109,260—more than twenty times as great as it had been twenty years earlier.

Most of these newcomers were young men. "Long John" Wentworth, who was to be elected mayor of Chicago in 1858, had written to his sister Lydia about the new city shortly after

A view showing the Chicago skyline and lake front in 1858, the year in which

he arrived twenty-two years earlier. "I have no recollection of ever having seen a man over fifty years of age," he wrote. "Most of us are under thirty. I seldom see a child."

The census of 1850 confirmed Wentworth's impressions. More than 50 per cent of the male population of Chicago was between fifteen and thirty-nine. Few of these brought families with them. Most were crowded into boardinghouses or improvised second-story dormitories above the wooden stores that were jammed together along the muddy streets of the central business district. Even less fortunate newcomers were forced to spend their nights on the dirt floor of a saloon, where space for a man to lie down and throw a blanket over him might command a premium price.

There was plenty of money to be made and much of it was spent freely. "The young men are mostly those who have made a fortune out of nothing and are consequently quite dis-

the Young Men's Christian Association of Chicago was organized.

sipated," Wentworth added in his letter to his sister. The *Chicago Times* editorialized on the situation under the heading, "These Rowdy Boys." "What can be done with these rowdy boys?" the editor asked rhetorically. "Cannot some effectual means be devised to give them steady employment and proper moral instruction? Will someone propose what shall be done? Who will suggest?"

The situation was at its worst in the winter, when the closing of navigation on the Great Lakes threw thousands of men out of employment and many others came to the city from the forests of Michigan and Wisconsin where lumber operations were suspended until the return of mild weather. Added to this was a tremendous transient population—"birds of passage, mostly vultures," as one chronicler put it—who were in the city only long enough to assemble supplies for the trip farther west, or to make a quick killing by speculating in real estate.

To meet the needs of the young men who were not content to squander their money in the gambling halls and saloons of Randolph Street (where shootings were so common that one section was known as "Hairtrigger Block"), several societies providing facilities for self-improvement had been organized. Among these were the Chicago Lyceum, which sponsored debates and lectures; the Mechanics Institute, which had its own technical library of 7,000 volumes and a public reading room; and the Young Men's Association, organized by the grain merchant Walter Newberry and others during the great temperance revival of 1841. The purpose of the Young Men's Association, according to its founders, was to provide "a place of resort" where young men could "spend a leisure hour . . . in quiet and rational amusement." As the years passed, the YMA, as it was frequently referred to in the papers, took on something of the nature of a fashionable club; success in one of its keenly contested elections was a recognized mark of social prestige.

None of these organizations did more than provide a refuge for young men for whom the gambling houses and saloons had no appeal. They had no program for changing the conditions among which the city's young men were forced to live and which fostered the growth of vice. Among the Chicagoans dissatisfied with this stopgap approach to the problem was the Rev. Luther Stone, editor of the religious paper, *Watchman of the Prairies*. Rev. Stone published a series of articles calling for the establishment of an organization to look out for the interests and well-being of young men new in the city. Such an organization, he suggested, might be patterned after the YMCA's already founded in such eastern cities as New York, Boston, and Buffalo. In a series of articles, he explained that the YMCA stood for Young Men's *Christian* Association and differed in its program from Chicago's Young Men's Asso-

18

ciation, which had no religious purpose. It was not long before he had persuaded a group of earnest young laymen to meet with him and discuss the founding of a Young Men's Christian Association in Chicago.

The Young Men's Christian Association movement had been started in London in 1844 by George Williams, then a clerk for a London dry-goods firm. There were many parallels between the situation faced by Williams in 1844 and that confronting Chicagoans in the 1850's. Williams had been only twenty when he came to London. With eighty other young men, he had lived in a barnlike dormitory maintained by the store for its employees on a vacant upper floor. Living conditions in this company dormitory were only slightly better than they were to be in the unruly barracks over the stores of Chicago. Williams, a conscientious Sunday School worker, soon found others in the dormitory as lonely as he was for a better kind of companionship. As a result, he and eleven of his friends held a meeting to form "a society for improving the spiritual condition of young men engaged in the drapery and other trades." They quickly found others to join them and adopted a constitution formally identifying themselves as "The Young Men's Christian Association" and their purpose as "the improvement of the spiritual condition of young men engaged in the drapery and other trades, by the introduction of religious services among them." A year later their goal had broadened to that "of improving the spiritual and mental condition of young men in houses of business." By 1846 it had become "the spiritual and mental improvement of young men by any means in accordance with the Scriptures."

The growth of the new movement was spectacular. Within a year eighteen different groups had been organized in London. Prominent businessmen had been persuaded to accept the prin-

George Williams founded
the YMCA movement in London
in 1844 when he was a clerk
for a London dry-goods firm.

cipal offices, and twenty-two ministers were serving as vice-presidents. By 1851 the idea had been brought to America and the first YMCA's organized in Montreal and Boston.

Although conditions in Chicago were similar to those in London, the first attempt to organize a YMCA in the city was not to meet the speedy acceptance it had in England. The group of young men whom the Rev. Luther Stone had interested in the YMCA organized the first Chicago Association at a meeting over Olmsted's dry-goods store at 121 West Lake Street on January 25, 1853. Samuel Dexter Ward, thirty-one-year-old layman of the Second Presbyterian Church, was elected president; Cyrus Bentley, then thirty-three, an active Baptist layman, was named secretary. A Board of Managers of forty-four members—two from each Episcopal, Methodist, Congregational, Baptist, and Presbyterian church in the city—was elected to conduct the affairs of the organization. Rooms for meetings were opened with the name of Harmony Hall at 48 (now 172) North Clark

Street. The program of the Association was very limited, consisting for the most part of special services for young men held in the city's churches and addressed by the ministers.

In the summer of 1854, when a national convention of Young Men's Christian Associations was held at Buffalo, New York, the Chicago Association sent two delegates—Cyrus Bentley and E. P. Montgomery. Both returned from the convention full of enthusiasm for the Y program, but they had little chance to apply what they had learned. Chicago was in the midst of one of its worst epidemics of cholera, brought on by overcrowding and lack of proper sanitation. In July of 1854 more than 1,400 deaths had been attributed to the disease. Many young men fled the city, taking their families with them. Such public meetings as were not forbidden were sparsely attended. By fall the momentum which had led to the organization of the YMCA in Chicago had been lost. The membership was dispersed, and the churches were faced with new problems of their own brought on by the toll of the cholera epidemic.

Another factor which prevented an active resumption of the YMCA program was the competition of the Young Men's Association. The YMA, noting with a certain nervousness the advent of another organization of similar name, had drafted Samuel Dexter Ward as its own president and with him two other key officers from the YMCA. This action deprived the new organization of its best leaders and it disappeared from the Chicago scene. When the first compilation of YMCA's in the United States was made in 1856, no organization was listed at Chicago. Only Quincy, which had organized in 1853, was included from Illinois.

Meanwhile, Chicagoans returned to their first interest—making money. The cholera epidemic was soon forgotten and the city continued its phenomenal expansion. Fortunes were made overnight in real estate. The city continued to be the great reception funnel for homesteaders en route to the western prairies. And from these same prairie farms—over the rails built to the west by William B. Ogden—came great trainloads of grain to be transshipped by schooners to the East. More than 13,000 ships a year made port at Chicago, and the river sky was a crowded pattern of masts and sails. Making money was the goal of every Chicagoan. Even a devout young man from Northfield, Massachusetts, named Dwight L. Moody came to Chicago with the expressed determination of making $100,000. This was a modest ambition. Most Chicagoans talked of millions, and one Chicago paper was to boast that Chicago had more millionaires than any other city in the United States.

A contemporary lithograph showing the raising of the block between Clark and La Salle to a higher street grade in 1861. Second building from the right

Two forces were to distract Chicagoans from this pre-occupation with money. One was financial panic, which throughout history has often served as an unconscious instrument of moral enlightenment. The other force was the great religious revival of 1857-1858, which began as a by-product of the country's financial disaster but was to be carried on with a force and vitality of its own.

The prosperity which Chicago had enjoyed during the 1850's was but an exaggerated version of a national credit expansion sustained by the development of the West. Optimism, untempered by business judgment, produced an inevitable over-expansion and unwise speculation in railroads and real estate. In October of 1857, those railroads which had been founded

(with sign advertising PRINTING) is 132 West Lake Street, where the YMCA of Chicago was organized in 1858 by Cyrus Bentley and others.

by wildcat promoters on inadequate capital began to collapse. Within a month fourteen railroads suspended, became insolvent, or protested their obligations. Orders were canceled, goods piled up that could not be shipped, and thousands of men were thrown out of work.

New York City, as capital of the money market, was hardest hit by the panic. In the downtown financial district, noon prayer meetings were started at the Dutch Reformed Church at the corner of Fulton and Williams streets. These meetings were soon taken over by laymen who were members of the YMCA and who met together to consider ways of easing the hardships of those thrown out of work. At Broadway Tabernacle, the evangelist Charles G. Finney inaugurated a series of revival meetings which attracted national attention and spread the revival movement to Chicago and other cities.

The newspapers of the time gave many columns of space to accounts of this religious revival. In Chicago, the *Democratic Press* on March 13, 1858, carried a front-page story on the subject. ". . . A large class of our readers, we are assured," the paper said in the personal editorial style of the day, "will be interested in such details as we have been able to collect . . . of the extent to which Chicago has shared in the general religious awakening that has been one of the marked events of the year, throughout the entire country, East and West." Mayor John Wentworth commented in his newspaper, *The Chicago Democrat*, that "So far as the effects of the present religious movement are concerned, they are patent to all. They are to be seen in every walk of life, to be felt in every phase of society. The merchant, the farmer, the mechanic—all who have been within their influence—have been incited to better things; to a more orderly and honest way of life. All have been more or less influenced by this excitement."

Among those "influenced by this excitement" was a group of young Chicagoans who had met on November 9, 1857, to form the Chicago Young Men's Society for Religious Improvement. They held weekly meetings devoted to a study of the Scriptures and other religious activity. All young men were invited to attend. Throughout the winter of 1857–1858, the society met and discussed methods by which its influence might be widened. One of the members was Cyrus Bentley, who had been secretary when the first attempt was made to form a Young Men's Christian Association in Chicago. To Bentley and others, the time seemed right, in view of the widening interest in religion, to try again.

On Monday, March 22, 1858, notices appeared in the Chicago newspapers of an organizational meeting to be held that evening at 132 Lake Street over the store of A. D. Titsworth & Company. After the Scripture reading and prayer, those at the meeting passed a resolution favoring the organization of a YMCA in Chicago "on a similar basis with YMCA's now existing in the United States and British provinces." A committee "from each evangelical denomination represented" was appointed to work out a plan of organization and report back the following Monday. A series of preliminary meetings followed and a constitution was adopted.

The language of this first constitution indicates the nature of the program which the founders wanted to carry out. The preamble said:

We the subscribers, actuated by a desire to promote Evangelical religion, and to stimulate vital piety among young men, resident in, or visiting this city or vicinity, and impressed with the importance of concentrated and united effort in accomplishing that object, and desirous of forming an association in which we may together labor for the great end proposed, hereby agree to adopt for our Government the following Constitution:

The first article of the constitution reiterated this purpose in language more familiar to those acquainted with the broad program of the YMCA today. It defined the object of the Association as: ". . . the improvement of the spiritual, intellectual, and social condition of young men." Although this language suggests a purpose comparable to that of the modern YMCA, it is to be noted that no mention is made of any physical program. And the constitution's provision for membership qualifications made it plain that the dominant interest of the founders was in a purely religious program.

Four types of members were provided for: *Active*—which was to include only those belonging to some evangelical church; *Associate*—all those elected on grounds of "good moral character" although they might not belong to any church (but who were denied voting privileges); *Life*—those in the first two categories who contributed $20 to the work of the Association; and *Honorary*—members who might be elected by the Board of Managers.

The word "evangelical" had a very specific meaning to the authors of the first constitution. It meant, according to the first annual report, that although "distinct and different in many of their views of religious truth, they (the members) harmonize in the great central evangelical doctrine of justification by faith in Christ alone."

Following the adoption of the constitution, an election was held and Cyrus Bentley was named first president of the new Young Men's Christian Association of Chicago. He was installed in office on June 21, 1858, closing his inaugural address with these words:

Cyrus Bentley,
first president of the
Young Men's Christian Association
of Chicago.

"Moved by the reports that are borne to us of the benign results achieved by the Young Men's Christian Associations of other cities, we have spontaneously come up hither from the various churches of the city, without any reference to sect or denominational preferences, and organized this Association, for the avowed purpose, under God, of rescuing and saving vast numbers of young men in our city from the temporal and eternal ruin to which they are exposed. On the banner we this night unfurl to the breeze of Heaven is emblazoned this grand purpose of our combined energies under the Almighty, 'The Salvation of Young Men'."

To make this program effective, the Association assumed responsibility for the noon prayer meetings in Chicago. These meetings had been transferred from the First Presbyterian Church to Metropolitan Hall at the invitation of Edwin S. Wells, thirty-year-old proprietor of a boot-and-shoe shop who owned the lease on the hall and offered it free to the Association.

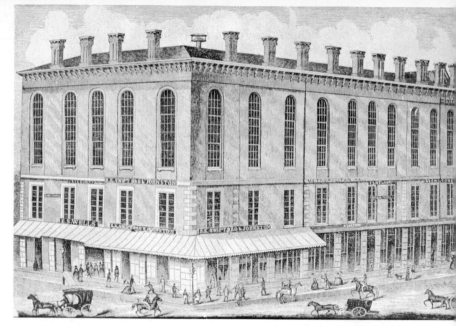

Metropolitan Hall, where noon prayer meetings were held after hall was made available by Edwin S. Wells, whose shop may be seen at the left.

Wells' soon became one of the active leaders of the Chicago Association, and the noon prayer meetings in Metropolitan Hall were for many years the best-known feature of Association work.

Other plans were also under way. Rooms were rented at 205 West Randolph Street and fitted up as a library. Chauncey Hutchins was named chairman of the library committee, but he found himself with few funds to buy books. He published an appeal for donations in the *Democratic Press and Tribune* on November 5, 1858, but there were so few books in the homes of Chicagoans that most families had none to spare. A short time later, the Board of Managers authorized President Bentley to write "at Association expense" to publishers in Boston, New York, and Philadelphia, seeking contributions for the library. At the end of the first year, only 140 books had been received

—one of them being an English volume described in the minutes of the Board of Managers as "over 200 years old and as good as it is aged." Although the first annual report could claim proudly that the books were all "pure, healthful, and religious literature," Bentley was forced to add realistically that "We cannot but at the same time express our regrets that . . . many of the excellent authors of the present as well as the past time, are not yet represented upon our shelves."

The rooms on Randolph, although adequate for the library, were not too practical for meetings. In April of 1859, the Association moved to larger quarters in the new block of the Methodist Episcopal Church at the corner of Clark and Washington streets. Here the members had the use of a reading room and library on the second floor, a lecture hall on the third floor, and a small meeting room where the Board of Managers held their sessions. Gas was still being used for illumination, and the first annual report makes a point of the fact that both the lecture hall and reading room were well lighted. Regular meetings of the Association were held in the lecture hall and Saturday night prayer meetings in the Board of Managers' room. The Association also held three prayer meetings each week at the city's fire houses—one each in the North, West, and South divisions. The first annual report speaks bluntly of the difficulties encountered in this widespread evangelistic program. "These meetings, though shunned at first," the report concluded, "have been many times largely attended by firemen and were often occasions of deep interest to all present."

The work of the Chicago Association during this first year was carried on exclusively by committees and volunteers. As with any volunteer effort, some members were more conscientious in performing their duties than others. In his first report, President Bentley noted that most committees raised from the general membership of the Association had "discharged their duties nobly and well." He then added, with what sounds like a trace of impatience with his Board, that "This may be said of nearly, if not quite all, of the committees raised from the Board of Managers."

The committee work provides an accurate portrait of the YMCA of Chicago as it sought to make its influence felt in the rapidly growing city. Among the committees on which Y members served were:

Committee to Aid Members and Strangers in Selecting Suitable Boarding Places. This committee was charged with "preparing a list of boarding places in which young men might find homes in Christian families and thus be brought under such genial influences as would overcome any desire to associate with the dissipated and profane during their hours of leisure."

Committee to Aid Members and Strangers in Procuring Places of Employment. This committee, the report said candidly, had "through no fault of its own accomplished but little. The past year has perhaps been unprecedented for the difficulties attendant upon securing a place of employment for young men. Owing to the extreme financial embarrassments that have prevailed among a large portion of our business community, a great number of young men have been thrown out of employment—and the demand for employees has almost entirely ceased."

Committee on Attendance upon the Sick. This was considered one of the most important works of the Association. Through it, the members hoped to redeem those whose health had been ruined by debauchery. Cards were distributed in all public places asking the proprietors of hotels and boardinghouses to notify the YMCA of any young man in need of medical attention or other care. This work was also particularly demanding on the members. A picture of what they might find on answering a call for help is easily visualized behind the euphemisms and ornate language characteristic of the time. Many times, Bentley said in a report, the members of this committee had stood "by the bedside of the sick and dying, and patiently lingered at the couch of the young man, who without the restraining influences of Christian associations and counsels of pious friends, had plunged from steep to steep of dissipation, until debauch succeeding debauch had dethroned reason and reduced man made in the image of God to a level with the brutes."

Bentley was not content with alleviating pain and suffering. He frequently reminded the membership that the YMCA had an equal responsibility to prevent young men from falling into bad habits. "Our object is to do good," he said, "to throw around

Methodist Episcopal Church block at Clark and Washington. From 1859 to 1867 the YMCA of Chicago rented quarters here on the second and third floors.

Serving on the "Committee on attendance upon the sick."

In the reading room.

the young man, whether a resident in our midst or coming a stranger to our city, those influences that shall turn his steps from snares laid for his feet throughout the highways and by-paths of our city into the higher and serener paths of sobriety and religion."

During this early period, the members of the Board of Managers had dual responsibilities. They served both upon the general membership committees and upon six management committees established by the by-laws. These management committees were those for the library, a finance committee, a committee on printing and publishing, a committee on lectures and meetings, a committee on rooms and reception, and a committee on statistics which had the formidable assignment of endeavoring "to ascertain how many young men are communicants in the several evangelical churches in the city, the number of young men who attend divine worship, and also the number of those who desecrate the Sabbath; it shall also collect such other facts as may serve to show the moral and religious condition of young men in this city."

Because the Board of Managers was drawn from among the busiest men in Chicago—both in business and in good works—the demands of the young Association frequently proved more than Board members could yield the time for. One requirement, for example, was that two members of the committee on rooms and reception were required to be in the rooms each evening except Saturday. Only the most devoted could adhere to such a schedule. As a result, there was a frequent turnover in the membership of the Board. (Another factor was the Board's policy of automatically dropping any member who was absent from three consecutive meetings without a proper reason.)

Despite the many personnel changes in the Board of Managers, the new Association achieved a large measure of stability during its first year. The report of the finance committee in 1859 showed expenditures, (mostly for the remodeling, furnishing, and upkeep of the new rooms in the Methodist block) of $1,544.40. Receipts were $1,791.25. There remained, the treasurer noted, "this day in the Treasury, with every debt paid, [a balance of] $246.85."

Among the sources of revenue during the first year were two lectures by the Rev. Henry Ward Beecher which the YMCA sponsored in conjunction with the once-hostile Young Men's Association. Funds were also raised from lectures by the Rev. Dr. Nathan L. Rice (who was asked to repeat "his able

Young Men's Christian Association.

Mr. L W Dudley

The Board of Managers, will
meet for the transaction of business at the rooms
of the Association *Monday* Evening
August 9th at 8 o'clock.
Your punctual attendance is requested.

Wm Ross Denniston

Rec. Sec.

Mr H. W. Dudley
With Hinsdale & Babcock
Chicago

An announcement of the third meeting of the Board of Managers.

discourse in refutation of the prevailing error and delusion of the age—spiritualism.")

In addition to these fund-raising enterprises, a series of free lectures by the clergymen of the city was presented at the Association's lecture hall. These lectures by the clergy were evidence of a cordial relationship between the YMCA and most of the city's ministers. The report of the lecture committee, for example, pointed out that "our invitations to these Reverend brethren were all, with perhaps a single exception, promptly and cordially accepted." But if the members of the clergy were willing to work individually with the Association, they were still wary of co-operating as a group with an organization which paid so little attention to doctrinal and theological distinctions.

In September of 1858, the Board of Managers appointed a committee to invite all the Christian ministers of the city to hold a prayer meeting in the Association rooms "on any afternoon they see fit." However, the chairman of the committee reported back that (as the recording secretary digested it) ". . . certain difficulties . . . seemed to lie in their path and to prevent action on the part of the committee." When President Bentley asked the Rev. E. F. Dickinson of the Chicago Home of the Friendless his opinion of the matter, Rev. Dickinson gave (again according to the secretary's view) "satisfactory reasons why the ministers could not be brought together, whereupon the committee was discharged and the subject dropped." However, in 1860, individual ministers did agree to preach under YMCA auspices when the Association acquired the use of the famous Wigwam (where Lincoln had been nominated) for a series of Sunday afternoon services.

Some churches formed individual YMCA groups within their denomination, but these appeared only briefly and apparently were rapidly absorbed by the Chicago Association. However, the officers of the YMCA missed no opportunity to assure the churches that the work of the Y and its lay evangelists was to supplement and not to supplant the work of the organized denomination.

"Our organization is not intended, nor does it practically interfere with the denomination or the church," Bentley said in a report. "None of us undervalue the names by which we are respectively called. . . . Like the cylinder . . . which has drawn upon its circumference in separate and distinct sections the various colors of the rainbow—presenting here, isolated and in bold contrast to the other, the Presbyterian's favorite blue— then the rubric red of the Episcopalian, and still further on the water color of the Baptist, and so on, when turned quickly by a single hand, presents naught but the purely white—so Christians of different denominations, when moved by the arm of a common faith, symbolize that beautiful unity and harmony that will prevail, by and by when we shall all see eye to eye. Neither do we hold ourselves as superior to, or independent of, but as auxiliary to the church organization."

The acceptance which the YMCA gained during the first year was reflected in the growth of the membership. The Association had been founded with 151 members—140 active, 9 associates and 2 life. At the end of the first year, the active members had been increased to 293, the associates to 48, and the life members to 14 for a total of 355 members. This growth occurred during a period when the major emphasis was more on winning converts than on getting new members. Most of those who joined, it should be remembered, were more than names on a roll. They were active workers, pledged to win others to a Christian way of life. For this reason, the Association played a role in the life of Chicago beyond what might have been expected of a less dedicated organization of the same size.

The members of the YMCA used every means possible to bring its work to public attention—including on occasion reminders to the editors of the city's newspapers. On February 1, 1859, a long letter appeared in the *Press and Tribune* outlining the many activities of the Chicago Association. The correspondent added this tart observation: "It is a little singular that, while your paper, as well as others in the city, is eager to report to your readers everything of interest transpiring in our midst, whether judicial, political, or religious, all have seemed to overlook the operations of one of our most beneficent enterprises. I refer to the Young Men's Christian Association." The letter closed with the expressed wish that "the few hints above thrown out may excite an interest in this enterprise not heretofore felt on the part of the Christian public, as well as in your own corps editorial." The editor did not wait until the next day to reply but published his answer in the same issue. "Whenever the members of the Association bring to bear upon this branch of their duties a modicum of the practical sense which they evince in their individual business operations," he wrote, "none again will fancy that it is his duty to lecture an editor through his own columns and at his own expense, for not giving them a large space in the public eye."

Having replied in kind, the editor was apparently satisfied —and convinced. Two months later, in reporting the move of the Association to "new and commodious apartments in the Methodist Church block," the *Press and Tribune* referred to the YMCA as ". . . a most flourishing and useful organization." By the time that Cyrus Bentley was elected to serve a second year as president, the same editor was commenting that "The Association enters upon its second year under the most favorable auspices, and we believe is destined to accomplish much good in our city."

It was a prophetic understatement.

Illustration advertising
a YMCA lecture.

CHAPTER 2

"Some of Our Most Sterling Young Men"

ONE OF the greatest influences in the early history of Chicago was the Puritan tradition brought to the Midwest by the emigrants from upper New York and the New England states who became the leaders in Chicago's business community. These Anglo-Saxo-Yankees, as the newspapers described them, brought with them a concept of duty as sternly applied in business as in religion.

These were the men who worked the longest hours, drove the hardest bargains, kept the sternest personal discipline—and built the fortunes out of which the great business institutions of Chicago have emerged. When these men chose to devote themselves to good works, they did so with the same firmness of purpose they applied to business. The results were likely to be as impressive as in the accumulation of the personal fortunes that had been their objective in coming to Chicago. Through the pattern set by these business pioneers, Chicago has been to a greater degree than most cities the beneficiary of enlightened private philanthropy. When the business community has chosen to do so, it has pushed reform and good works at a breakneck speed. And, although these efforts have been sporadic, they have been so well organized and efficiently planned that the results have endured far beyond the time in which they were accomplished.

In 1860 the Young Men's Christian Association of Chicago chose as its president one of these Anglo-Saxo-Yankees— John V. Farwell. The time required a man of firm purpose if the Association was to survive. The nation was divided in the Civil War and it appeared that many of the leaders in the Y would be called into the army. There are frequent references in the minutes of the Board of Managers to the resignation of young men "who left for the war." Political issues—and slavery in particular—proved a divisive influence in the Association that was often more powerful than pleas for religious unity. Because much of the Association's work was directed toward the winning of converts, the membership rolls grew slowly. Members' dues were not enough to meet the expenses of the Association and there were continual problems over finances.

John V. Farwell, however, had that resiliency in the face of hardship characteristic of the pioneer. As a boy of thirteen he had walked beside the prairie schooner that had brought his family from Steuben County, New York, to a homestead on the Rock River. He had walked, that is, until a hair-covered trunk toppled off the tailgate of the wagon and "landed its iron-bound corner" on the toes of his foot. He tried to keep walking despite the injury but was forced to an uncomfortable bed in the wagon by a combination of "fever and the ague." Finally a doctor was found who, with the aid of "a very bitter dose of herb medicine," reduced the swelling in the foot and young Far-

John V. Farwell,
one of the Anglo-Saxon-Yankees
who brought the Puritan tradition
to Chicago and who labored as
hard at good works as at building
one of the great business houses
of early Chicago.

well was able to resume his marching. When he was twenty he left the Rock River farm to come to Chicago. He had $3.00 in his pocket and a Bible which his mother had given him with this admonition: "Study and obey the teachings of this book, choose your companions from those who love it, and you must succeed. You will be known by the company you keep."

Farwell's first job in Chicago was as bookkeeper in the City Clerk's office. As he told it later, he made "millions on paper, with my bookkeeping, and quite a little sum in real cash, in reporting the Council proceedings for a weekly paper." His reporting—"in facsimile," as he described it—was much too accurate for the comfort of the aldermen in the Council and he was dismissed from his job in the Clerk's office. After this misadventure he eventually secured a job as a clerk and bookkeeper with the merchant firm of Cooley, Wadsworth and Company. In ten years he was a partner in the firm and two years later its name was changed to Cooley, Farwell and Company. It included among its officers a third partner named Marshall Field. Later, when Marshall Field left to head his own store, the firm became simply John V. Farwell and Company.

This financial independence lay far in the future when young John Farwell arrived in Chicago. His first year he made a salary of only $96. But of this amount, he gave $50 to help build the first Methodist church to be erected of brick in the city. He was to be no less generous with the Young Men's Christian Association in the years he was connected with it. Yet equally as important as his financial support was Farwell's partnership with another of the Anglo-Saxo-Yankees, a man who was to apply to religion the same genius for success that he had originally intended to apply to the accumulation of $100,000. His name was Dwight L. Moody.

Moody had come to Chicago in 1856 and taken a job in a shoe store. The same year he organized a small Sunday School class in an empty building on North Wells Street. In 1858 he moved his Sunday School activities to North Market Hall, then police headquarters for the North Division of the city. His first class at the Market Hall Sunday School consisted of some sixty children, described later as "mostly from saloons . . . and so noisy that few even of the most zealous in such works would have thought it possible to succeed in the enterprise."

A mutual interest in Sunday School work brought Moody and Farwell together. Both attended the Methodist Sunday School, and Farwell noticed with annoyance that Moody was invariably late. When he complained to the class leader (whom he described with affection in his autobiography as "a converted drunkard from Galena"), Farwell was told that Moody spent the time before class going up and down the streets trying to get others to attend. This information so impressed Farwell that he sought out Moody to apologize. The two men soon became friends and co-workers; as Farwell's daughter, Abby, was to describe it, "from that time on father had such a love for Mr. Moody as existed only between David and Jonathan."

Within a short time Farwell had become superintendent of the North Market Hall Mission Sunday School and Moody had transferred a portion of his energies to the "committee to visit the poor and sick" of the YMCA. In 1861 Moody quit his job as a salesman at Buel, Granger and Hill (where he saved $7,000 toward the $100,000 goal he had set for himself) to become the librarian of the YMCA. On May 13, 1861, the Board of Managers passed a resolution authorizing the employment of Moody "as librarian with the understanding that he shall act as agent for the Association and City Missionary for the coming year at a salary of $———." The minutes mention no salary, a mystery which was explained later by Farwell. "Moody never would take a salary," Farwell wrote, ". . . as it would hamper him as a free hand. He spent all his accumulations in business on his mission work, and was discovered sleeping on benches and eating crackers and cheese in the YMCA union prayer meeting room. It was then that I urged him again to take a salary, which he refused, on the basis that he had only one source for orders in his ministry."

Farwell in his autobiography provided a modest outline of how he aided in making Moody's ministry possible. "He never wanted for anything after that," Farwell recalled, "and when I had finished a block of dwellings on the North Side and his small home became too small for his family, I gave him rent-free one of them, and friends furnished it in good style, including a portrait of himself and wife, and surprised him by introducing him to a home of his own."

Farwell pursued his own religious work as actively as he supported Moody's. "My father did enough work during the

Dwight L. Moody (in cap) with boys from the North Market Hall Mission. Man in top hat is identified as John V. Farwell. Urchins are identified only by such names as "Red Eye," "Butcher Kilroy," and "Billy Bucktooth."

week to kill an ordinary man," Farwell's daughter wrote. "He was at the store almost every night until nine o'clock. Sunday was really his busy day. This was his Sunday program: At nine o'clock he talked to the men at the Bridewell; at ten, Presbyterian church; after dinner he went to the North Market Hall Mission Sunday School. In the evening he attended the Methodist Church, which was just across the street on the corner of Harrison Street and Wabash Avenue. My mother's church was the Second Presbyterian, and he was as interested in that as if it was his own church."

The war provided additional challenges for both Moody and Farwell. But it also provided opportunities for service which the two men were to exploit thoroughly and which were to make the YMCA known throughout the front lines as the soldier's friend. It was also the start of a tradition that was to be carried on by the YMCA in future years when the United States again found itself at war.

Union recruits were being trained at Camp Douglas on Chicago's South Side. Moody enthusiastically set about organizing prayer meetings and other work to make the soldiers conscious of the Young Men's Christian Association of Chicago. Every evening eight or ten prayer meetings were held in camp barracks under the auspices of the YMCA. Within a few months, Moody had secured $2,300 in donations for a camp chapel— the first building of its kind to be erected on an army base through public subscription. The Chicago Association also issued an army hymnbook that was distributed to the soldiers and included an invitation for them to call upon the YMCA for any religious or hospital supplies which they might require. Moody and his co-workers spent many hours visiting with the recruits; when they found the soldiers gambling, they proposed an exchange of hymnbooks for the cards. Under Moody's persuasive exhortations, the soldiers usually agreed to the exchange; soon the YMCA found itself with a storeroom of surrendered playing cards. After the battle at Fort Donelson, when Camp Douglas was converted into a prisoner-of-war camp for Confederate soldiers, the Y carried on its work among the prisoners just as it had done before.

There were many evidences of the popularity of this program. On November 10, 1862, the Board of Managers elected as an active member Levi Verness, a soldier from Baraboo, Wisconsin, who wrote that he wanted to go to the war as a member of the YMCA. He paid his dues, according to the minutes, "for this and the next year, then left for safekeeping if he should return, a certificate of deposit for $10 in a bank in Madison, Wisconsin, but if he should never return, he wished the Association to use it in doing good." On December 18 of the same year, the Association received a contribution of $10 from James Brown of Company H, Thirty-second Regiment of the Ohio Volunteers. He described himself as "not a Christian" but said he wanted to make the Association a present of $10 "to be used in doing good."

Another service of the Chicago Association was the sending of "delegates" to regiments at the front which had no chaplains. During the war, 219 of these volunteer missionaries went out from the YMCA of Chicago to act as spiritual counselors and sometimes as hospital aids for the troops. Chief among them was the indefatigable Moody, whose visit to the Nineteenth Illinois Infantry, encamped at Elizabethtown, Kentucky, was described by a soldier correspondent in the regimental paper, the *Zouave Gazette*. Since Moody arrived, the paper reported, he had "labored unceasingly both day and night to distribute books, papers, tracts, hymnbooks, etc. Many of the boys have signed the temperance pledge and commenced to lead a different life. The secret of Mr. Moody, both here and among the soldiers and at home, is that he makes a personal application of the gospel truths to those he meets and living a life devoted to his Master, his advice and example convinces (sic) and converts."

Farwell was equally busy in activities connected with the war. When a group of members enlisted in the Chicago Dragoons, Farwell presented the company with a stand of colors on behalf of the YMCA. The flag was described in the following morning's *Tribune* as "of rich blue silk, five feet wide by six feet long with a heavy silk fringe in red, white, and blue.

On one side, in the center of an oval, is a mounted dragoon, in gold, on a cloud background. Above the figure appears the motto, 'We Will Pray For You' surrounded by thirty-four stars [representing the states of the Union]. On the reverse side, in a similar oval, is an American Eagle, with the motto, 'In God Is Our Trust'."

In November of 1861 Farwell went to New York City, where he met with delegates from fifteen other YMCA's to consider ways of extending and improving relief work among the soldiers. Out of this meeting came the U. S. Christian Commission with a central board of twelve members to "take charge of the whole work" and act as a clearinghouse for all religious work in the armed forces. Its various divisions were patterned after those of the U. S. Sanitary Commission, which had been organized earlier in Washington to assist in purely medical relief work. Farwell was elected a member of the central committee and also president of its Chicago branch. Other Chicago members active in the Christian Commission work were Benjamin F. Jacobs, Tuthill King, and Moody. Bentley, still an active Y member, was to become one of the leaders in the work of the Sanitary Commission.

In theory, relief work at camps and hospitals some distance from the front lines was to be under the charge of local YMCA's, "if practical." Relief near the battle areas was to be under the direct control of the Christian Commission. In practice, this distinction meant little. In 1862, when the Chicago Christian Commission sent out twenty-six men and four women as delegates to the camps, battlefields, and hospitals in the West, most of these were drawn from the membership of the YMCA.

When the Union army engaged the Confederate forces at Fort Donelson in February of 1862, the YMCA of Chicago sent a committee headed by Moody directly to the battlefield to

Coffee wagon used by U. S. Christian Commission in Civil War.

care for the sick and wounded and to relieve their suffering. The following April, after the battle at Shiloh, the Sanitary Commission appealed directly to the Chicago Association to send nurses and supplies. Again under the direction of Moody, a group of volunteers went directly to the front-line area on a special train chartered by the Commission.

Farwell saw to it that the soldiers were well supplied with "creature comforts" as well as what he described as "spiritual food." At one time he bought up all the codfish available in Chicago, saying that it was the best cure known "for the prevalent bowel complaint in the army in the South." When a Tennessee cold wave caught the soldiers in the army under General George Henry Thomas unprepared, Farwell bought up every woolen glove and mitten in Chicago to send to them. Neither of these purchases fell within the orbit of either the

Christian Commission or army regulations, but they were enthusiastically received by the soldiers.

The Chicago Association also participated in recruiting troops for the Union cause. In 1862 it joined with the Board of Trade in raising companies for an all-Chicago regiment. There was some opposition to this direct support of the fighting. When Farwell announced to a membership meeting that the Association was going to help the Board of Trade recruit a regiment, an anti-war member raised the shout of "Humbug!" Patriotic feeling was so high that the objector was seized, lifted along by the crowd, and among cries of "Put him out!" and even "Hang him!" was roughly hurried down the stairs and dumped onto the sidewalk.

On August 23, 1862, just one month after the recruiting began, the regiment was complete. Company E, one of those raised by the YMCA, gained a premium for being the first filled to the maximum and in camp. Company B of the regiment called itself the Havelock Guards. The *Tribune* described the company as composed of "some of our most sterling young men and its officers [who] are all members of the evangelical churches of this city: Capt. Jacob S. Curtis being connected with the Third Presbyterian, 1st Lt. D. W. Perkins with the First Presbyterian, and 2nd Lt. D. W. Whittle with the First Congregational." The *Tribune* explained that "as a large number of the rank and file of this company are professing Christians, they have, therefore, fitly chosen the name Havelock." Although the newspaper did not explain the origin of the name Havelock, it was unquestionably a tribute to the British general, Sir Henry Havelock, a man of deep religious piety who had led the expedition for the relief of Lucknow during the great Sepoy mutiny in India just a few years before. When the chaplain of these same Havelock guards resigned later in the war, Lieutenant Whittle organized a YMCA group within the company that cared for the religious needs of the regiment for the balance of the war.

This regiment—officially designated as the Seventy-second but known to most Chicagoans as the first Board of Trade regiment—played an important role in the war in the West. It fought at the siege of Vicksburg and again at Natchez and at Franklin. In one attack at Vicksburg, the regiment lost 130 men killed and wounded. Later the regiment was shifted north and participated in the battle in which General John B. Hood was defeated at Nashville.

The YMCA of Chicago also recruited a company for the Eighty-eighth Illinois Volunteer regiment, famous as both the second Board of Trade regiment and the "Pet and Pride" regiment because of the large number of its members from fash-

A winter chapel and headquarters of the U. S. Christian Commission.

ionable families. The Eighty-eighth was a fighting regiment; during its entire period of service it was seldom away from the front lines or on garrison duty. Among the principal battles in which it saw action were the Chickamauga campaign, Missionary Ridge, the capture of Atlanta, and the battles at Stones River, Franklin, and Nashville.

With so many members away at war, the Association sought to strengthen itself by extending membership privileges to women. On May 13, 1861, the Board of Managers recommended admitting women as auxiliary members, and an amendment to the constitution providing for such membership was approved by the Association. Two years later another amendment permitted their election as auxiliary life members.

The women were to play an important part in Association work—particularly in fund-raising and relief work among the families of men away at war. Some of these activities are recorded in the minutes of the Board of Managers. One report mentions the receipt of "$100.45 from a fair held by three young Misses on Wabash Avenue"; on another occasion $37 was received from a similar fair. On July 18, 1862, a "Floral Festival" sponsored by the auxiliary members and committee of church women netted $456.63 for Association work—less, the report notes, "$5 counterfeit money." A postscript to this entry indicates how meticulous the Board of Managers was in caring for the funds entrusted to it. The counterfeit money was carried on the books until December 8, 1862, when a motion was made and passed directing the treasurer "to redeem of B. F. Jacobs the sum of $5.00 counterfeit money, that was received at the Floral Festival last summer and been held by him ever since."

The major fund-raising effort in which the women members participated was the Second Sanitary Fair, sponsored by the Northwest branch of the U. S. Christian Commission and U. S.

Sanitary Commission to raise funds for relief and for operating the Soldiers' Home, established to help soldiers en route to and from the front at the suggestion of the YMCA. Before the fair could be held (in May of 1865) the war was over. But aided by the presence of such war heroes as Generals Grant and Sherman, the fair brought in receipts in excess of $240,000, which were divided among the work of both the Christian and the Sanitary Commission.

An annual report issued after the war took official notice of the good will which resulted from these many services of the YMCA of Chicago and other Y associations. "The day has long since gone by, when honest distrust attached to the question of their [the YMCA's] utility," the report asserted. ". . . The spirit and letter of their workings, as manifested in the U. S. Christian Commission during the war, swept away any lingering doubt from the minds of all who had previously regarded them as useless appendages to the church of Christ."

These war services, demanding as they were, did not slow the Chicago Association in its pursuit of its long-range goals. In fact, it was during these war-busy years that the Association, under the leadership of Farwell and Moody, was extending its activities into ever wider areas of community service and laying the organizational plans that were to be the basis of its future greatness.

One of Farwell's early actions as president was to persuade the state legislature to issue a charter giving the Chicago Association exclusive rights to use the name of "Young Men's Christian Association" in the city. Other groups of announced Christian purpose had grown out of the revival movement of 1858 and some of these had adopted names similar to that of the YMCA. The result was a confusion of activity that prevented any organization from accomplishing its purpose. It was to eliminate this confusion and to assure contributors that their money would be handled responsibly that a charter—good for a thousand years—was granted to the Chicago Association on February 22, 1861.

The charter, signed by Gov. Richard Yates, provided that "Cyrus Bentley, J. P. Babcock, William Blair, E. S. Wadsworth, Tuthill King, Peter Page, Orrington Lunt, J. V. Farwell, Hugh T. Dickey, Henry W. Hinsdale, W. W. Boyington, T. M. Eddy, Robert Boyd, and their associates are hereby created a body corporate under the name of the 'YOUNG MEN'S CHRISTIAN ASSOCIATION' and by that name shall be recognized in all courts of justice and equity in this state for the term of one thousand years." A second section granted the Association the right to hold real estate for its own use without being liable for taxation. A third provision governed the sale or transfer of property owned by the Association.

The extension of YMCA activities into more and more areas of the city resulted from two factors: one was that as Chicago was predominantly a young men's city, there were few problems that were not in some way related to an organization dedicated to the betterment of young men; the second was that the evangelistic aims of the Y's founders led them to seek converts for the Christian way of life among all classes of society.

One of the greatest services rendered by the early Association was that of relief. This program had begun in 1861 when the Board of Managers established a relief committee for the purpose of "aiding the worthy poor" of Chicago. Two years later, this committee reported it had raised more than $6,000 in one year and provided relief for more than 1,600 families. All of this was accomplished through volunteer committees, many of them drawn from Sunday School teachers who were associated with missions sponsored by the YMCA.

To expedite the distribution of this aid, a series of store sheds for supplies were established in different districts of the city and a volunteer superintendent was placed in charge of each district. Before he could authorize aid, however, he was required to make a personal visit to the family applying for it. If the superintendent felt the family belonged to the class of "worthy poor," it was given the right to draw "one-half ton of coal, one-third cord of wood, or other supplies not exceeding three dollars in value." The Puritan precept that "God helps those who help themselves" was strongly reflected in the rules governing distribution of relief goods. "Our mission is not only to relieve suffering, but to improve the morals of those who are aided by us," the committee said in one of its reports. Among other things, families on relief were required to "abstain from liquor and tobacco" and "to keep children in school unless apprenticed." The manual for relief workers added that "families often need advice and counsel as much as material aid. . . . Especially insist upon cleanliness both of person and house as an indispensable condition on which aid is given." This combination of material aid plus stern Puritan counsel proved so successful that the Chicago Association was to be charged with the responsibility of acting as trustee for much of the city's private relief funds for nearly two decades.

The committee on employment, which had such an inauspicious first year, was also showing gains. In 1863 an informal employment agency was established at the Association rooms by J. M. Chapman and J. M. Cutler, two members who gave fifteen minutes a day to act as a clearing agency for employers and job applicants. During the first year, positions for more than five hundred young men were found.

That so much was being accomplished was a direct reflection of the zeal of John V. Farwell, who had served as president until 1862, and Dwight L. Moody, who continued to serve in many capacities without pay. Farwell's final report as president indicates the financial tightrope the members were walking. Receipts for the year had been $445.70 and the expenditures exactly the same, "leaving no balance in the Treasury." Farwell was not downhearted. In fact, he felt that having come out even, the Association was now in a strong enough position to start paying Moody a salary.

"Brother D. L. Moody," Farwell commented in his annual report, "without an official action on the part of the Association, has given his entire time and energies in executing the several plans of doing good referred to herein, and to his efforts mainly are we indebted for their practical execution. Not having raised

Only known view of North Market Hall. The Hall stood on Michigan Street—now Hubbard—facing south between Clark and Dearborn streets.

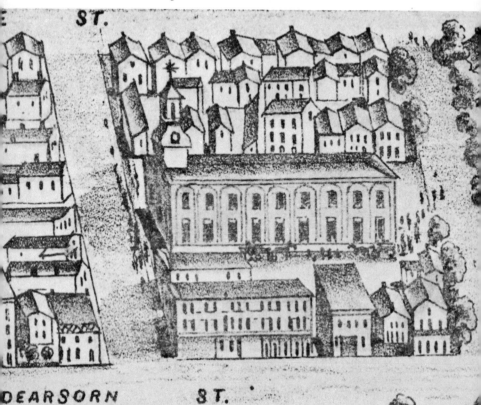

any funds outside of membership dues, we have not been able, as an Association, to make him any remuneration. 'Trust in the Lord and do good, and verily thou shalt be fed' has been literally acted upon and fulfilled in this case, but our duty as an Association has not been fulfilled, though it has been and still is his desire that no pecuniary obligation should rest upon it on his behalf. . . . I scarcely deem it necessary to recommend his continued employment as city missionary, for which service he is eminently qualified and that some systematic plans be carried out to meet the expense of such an engagement."

Moody's increasing role soon resulted in another extension in Y activities—this time into Sunday School mission work. In 1861 the Chicago Association took over formal sponsorship of Moody's North Market Hall Mission, which had grown from sixty noisy pupils to an enrollment of more than two hundred. Two years later the Association took over the West Market Mission Sunday School. Moody also revitalized the noon prayer meetings. He personally walked the street in front of Metropolitan Hall inviting strangers to the meetings; there were few who stopped to talk with him who could resist his persuasive and earnest invitation.

Farwell was succeeded as president by Dr. J. H. Hollister. In 1863 the presidency was taken over by Benjamin F. Jacobs, prominent real estate man who was one of the Y's founders and who was winning fame for his ideas in the field of religious education and Sunday School work. Edwin S. Wells, who had given the use of Metropolitan Hall for the prayer meetings, was named president in 1864, and the following year the Association chose as president Henry Weld Fuller, brother of Melville W. Fuller who was later chief justice of the U. S. Supreme Court. All of these men were leaders in their own churches as well as in the work of the Association. Their identification with the

Dwight L. Moody on the platform.
He came to Chicago
hoping to make $100,000, but gave
up this ambition and used
up his savings while serving the
YMCA without salary.

Y program brought about an even closer relationship between the lay evangelists of the Association and the city's clergy.

By 1862, the confidence of the clergy in the Y was such that they appointed a committee to ask the Association to take over both the printing and distribution of religious tracts and other religious papers for the churches. The offer was accepted and a committee of ministers established to select the tracts for distribution. By November of 1863 the YMCA of Chicago had distributed more than 675,000 tracts, and its workers had made more than 100,000 personal calls in passing out this literature. The work grew so rapidly that it became necessary to hire a full-time supervisor—the first full-time professional worker to be hired by the Association. (Moody, although working for the Association, still refused to accept a salary.) To direct the tract distribution, the Board of Managers selected Frank Malaby Rockwell, a twenty-five-year-old lay evangelist from Vermont, who was hired at a salary of $500 per year. In 1866 this sum was raised to $1,200 per year and Rockwell was known as superintendent of the City Mission Department.

This tract work was but one aspect of the co-operation between the clergy and the officers of the Chicago Association. It was an important gain for the struggling young YMCA when on November 9, 1863—only five years after its founding—the city's ministers sat down to dinner in the Tremont House for a special report on Y work. After the reports were given, the ministers present adopted a resolution praising the YMCA for what it had accomplished, assured it of their "hearty co-operation," promised "to render such aid as may be consistent with our varied duties," and vowed to commend the YMCA "to the sympathy and aid of our churches."

The pledge of co-operation from the churches, the extension of its program into more and more areas of the city, and the good will created by its manifold war activities encouraged the Association to make even larger plans for the future. And the president whom they named to translate this program into aggressive action was that "other Yankee"—Dwight L. Moody.

The printing and distribution of tracts was an important part of the religious program of the YMCA of Chicago.

CHAPTER 3

"Our Hall Is Burning"

THE GROWTH of the Chicago Association during its early years was difficult to measure. Membership figures told only a part of the story. Much of the program was evangelistic and many of those whom the YMCA helped were converts who made a direct affiliation with the churches and did not become active Y workers. The most direct evidence of the rate of growth during these years is the often-mentioned need for larger quarters to accommodate the many projects being undertaken by the Association.

In April of 1864, while still occupied with the complex demands of the war years, the Board of Managers devoted most of its monthly meeting to "the subject of procuring a permanent building and grounds as a home for the Association." As a result of this meeting, a committee of Benjamin F. Jacobs, P. L. Underwood, Charles Covell, and Moody was named "to inquire on what terms grounds could be purchased and the feasibility of erecting a suitable building." In May of 1866, John V. Farwell was named chairman of the building committee and a specific plan of action was outlined to give the Chicago Association a building of its own.

The boldness of the plan may be measured by the fact that only one building (a small two-story structure in Baltimore) had ever been erected for the specific use of a YMCA. The Baltimore building had cost $7,000 when it was erected in 1859 and contained only a meeting hall and library; the Chicago building, by contrast, was to cost $200,000. The Chicago Association hoped to achieve this grandiose plan by combining an appeal for civic betterment with a profitable business proposition—an approach that was sure to appeal to the Anglo-Saxo-Yankees who were the leaders in the community. The money was raised through the sale of the $200,000 in stock to a group of sixty-one stockholders. The stock certificates were to earn 6 per cent interest, based on funds to be earned from rental of office space in the new building. Farwell took $30,000 of the stock himself and other large amounts were purchased by Cyrus Hall McCormick, the inventor of the reaper; lumber merchant T. M. Avery (later founder of the Elgin National Watch Company); and George Armour of the grain firm of Armour and Dole, who had been an active worker in the YMCA Sunday Schools. Farwell, in addition to his stock purchase, donated as land for the new building the site of his former family home at 148 Madison Street. The city government had originally intended to erect a reservoir for its water supply at this location, but Chicago had grown so fast that the plan for the reservoir became obsolete before it could be executed. Another contribution of Farwell's was to push through the state legislature a bill amending the charter and permitting the Chicago Association to hold property under the stock plan without being burdened by high taxes. Under this amendment, a separate Board of Trustees was established to control all real estate held by the Association and Avery named as its first chairman. This plan was to prove so sound that it is still retained as a basic part of the organization of the YMCA of Metropolitan Chicago.

Construction of the new building created additional interest in the YMCA. In 1867 it was necessary to hold two annual meetings—one for members in the South Division and another for the West Division. The return of soldiers from the war stimulated the membership drive. The minutes reveal that at one meeting 334 new members were elected and at the next meeting 518.

The relief work continued to be a major part of the Association program. In the ninth annual report in 1867, O. C. Gibbs reported as chairman of the relief committee that aid totaling $24,325.38 had been granted to 3,815 applicants the previous year. The relationship of this relief work to the spiritual goals of the Y was expressed by Moody. "Opportunities have been afforded for reaching a large number of people with the gospel of peace, otherwise almost unapproachable," he said, "simply because its forerunners were bread, coal, and clothing. The heart as naturally opens to such kindness as flowers to the sunshine; and when Christianity thus opens human hearts, its power with God and men is recognized and felt."

A breakdown by nationality of those given relief reflects the changing nature of Chicago's population during these years and reveals how the YMCA was helping immigrants of all nationalities adjust to their new environment. Of the 3,815 families given relief, only 1,500 were United States citizens. In addition to giving this material aid, the Y distributed over 42,000 copies of religious papers in foreign languages.

The operating budget of the Association in its first post-

Chicago in 1858, looking south from the Courthouse. Arrow indicates early home of John V. Farwell, site of the first building of the YMCA of Chicago.

war year was only $8,000 (less than one-third the relief expenditures); of this amount $1,307 was a deficit. The deficit would have been larger if it had not been for contributions of $2,866.18 which came from collections taken in the city's churches—a good index of the close cooperation of the churches and the YMCA at the time.

This same year the Association performed one of the noblest services in its history, literally stepping in to aid the "untouchables" of another of Chicago's cholera epidemics (which still appeared recurrently because of the lack of a good water system and adequate sanitation). The Association was asked to nurse and minister to those whom no others would help. With the aid of other volunteers from the Chicago Theological Seminary and Hahnemann Medical College, Y workers nursed more than sixty families stricken with the disease; where necessary, they performed the last rites for the dead. As a result of the experiences of Association members during this epidemic, the Board of Managers passed a resolution calling upon the state legislature to establish a separate Board of Health in Chicago with powers similar to those of the Board of Health in New York. Other Chicago groups joined with similar appeals. As a result of this mobilizing of public opinion, the legislature on March 9, 1867, passed an act creating the present board and giving it power to eliminate many of the hazards which had caused the epidemics in the early history of Chicago.

A less successful effort approved by the Board of Managers was the attempt in 1866 to establish a Boarding House for Working Girls. A home was found and rented which would provide rooms for thirty-five young women; but after six months of operation the home was abandoned because of its high costs and the difficulties of managing it properly.

Throughout these years, the Chicago Association insisted

upon specific church affiliation as a condition of active membership. In May of 1867 instructions were given that no name proposed for membership would be acted on by the Board of Managers until proof of church membership in an evangelical denomination was provided. The same year, the Rev. Robert Collyer, the pastor of Unity Church who was one of the city's most prominent clergymen and a member of the Christian Commission, asked that members from his congregation be admitted on an equal footing with those of other churches. However, the Board held firmly to the position that evangelical church membership was a prerequisite for anyone wishing the voting privileges of an active member.

Another request, more sympathetically received by the Board of Managers, was a letter from J. W. Moon in regard to forming "an auxiliary association of colored men." Major D. W. Whittle, who had become an evangelist after serving in one of the Y's companies during the war, moved that the president be instructed "to tell Mr. Moon that the Association is open to them and that we will do all that we can for them," a motion which was quickly approved by the Board.

Another new project was the publication in 1867 of *Heavenly Tidings,* a four-page digest of the "most choice and pithy" selections from the various religious papers of the country. This was so well received that it became, as the annual report observed with something less than originality, "a household favorite," and was sold in bulk quantities to associations in other cities.

The chief pride of the young Association, however, was its new building—the only one of its kind in the world, and named Farwell Hall after its principal benefactor. Five stories in height and covered with a handsome marble façade, it had been designed by an Association member, W. W. Boyington, one of

Farwell Hall, at 148 Madison, was the first building in the world with full YMCA facilities. It was destroyed by fire January 8, 1868.

the city's leading architects, who had also designed the new Chicago Water Works, Crosby's Opera House, the Sherman and Grand Pacific hotels, and several of the city's churches.

An idea of the grand dimensions on which Farwell Hall was erected may be gained from the size of the auditorium. There were seats in the main auditorium for 3,500 people—just a few hundred less than the capacity of the Civic Opera House that was to be built a half a century later. The ground floor, beneath the hall, had space for five street-front stores. A library, reading room, a smaller lecture room, and rented offices were located on the other floors. Remarkable evidence of the importance of the new building in the life of Chicago is the fact that the tenants in one wing of the second floor were the police, fire, and health departments of the city government. On the top floor was a long dormitory with space for forty-two young men "who could not afford more ample accommodations." On the same floor was a large hall fitted up as a gymnasium. Although the national YMCA convention of 1860 had recommended gyms for all associations as "a safeguard against the allurements of objectionable places of resort, which have proved the ruin of thousands of the youths of our country," the Chicago Association was not yet ready to embark on any secular seas. Rather, it preferred to lease the gymnasium to the Metropolitan Gymnastic Club, which operated it separately from the YMCA.

When the building was dedicated on September 29, 1867, it represented an investment of $199,000, but it was expected that surplus earnings from rental space would retire all the stock in about ten years. After this period, the Association said it expected the receipts "to be devoted to a free library [Chicago had no public library as yet] and other benevolent purposes." The size of the achievement represented by the Chicago Association building did much for the reputation of Chicago. A New York minister, speaking at the dedication, noted that the clock had passed 9:00 P.M.—which in his own city was "a signal for the congregation to go home." However, he said, that "in this wonderful city where they eat, drink, and I suppose sleep by steam, perhaps they do not need so much sleep." Being something of a punster, he went on to observe that the name of the hall was "indeed a happy one" for it sounded "Far" and "Well" and "so it must through all time to come."

The omens, however, were not as favorable as they appeared to the dedication speaker. Only a few months later, Farwell Hall was hit by one of the many fires that broke out in Chicago in the 1860's when it was still a city of slats, tar paper, and wooden shingles. On the morning of January 7, 1868, fire destroyed most of Farwell Hall and a number of buildings around it. One wing of the building was saved, but the main portion, which represented most of the Association's interests, was demolished by the flames.

The drama of these hours, as the members saw their accomplishments destroyed by the fire, is recorded in a remarkable entry in the otherwise tersely unemotional minutes of the Board of Managers:

"We were called upon in the Providence which God permitted to visit us to 'pass under the rod' and literally to obey the voice of the prophet, 'Glorify ye the Lord in the fires,' " the secretary wrote. "At a quarter past nine the cry of fire in Farwell Hall rang sharply through the office, seeming at first as the cry of one who mocketh, but soon realizing as true in the awful conflagration which swept in an hour to the object of our prayers and labors for years. But in the hour of the fierce, fiery elements, God's hand was manifest in kindness, for no flame kindled upon the person of our young men in the work and no life was lost. Many friends came to the rescue of such effects as could be saved and we succeeded in securing all the Association records, part of the library and rooms furniture, with nearly eight hundred volumes of the most valuable works in our library. When the flames were fiercest, a call for prayer was sounded and a daily prayer meeting, which has never been suspended for one day since its organization, gathered in the lecture room of the Methodist Church at the usual hour for prayer and praise. Most earnestly and humbly we bowed before the great and all-wise Giver, blessing the hand which took as well as gave. The test of our faith was also the test of our friends, and until the flames had wrapped our building as a winding sheet, we had never known how many and how true were those who loved our Association. Scores wept as though their own homes were burned."

Two visitors to Chicago at the time were to record the remarkable courage of the Y's members in the face of this adversity. David MacRae, a visitor from England, wrote in his book, *The Americans at Home,* that "The secretary (Mr. Moody) and other officials, as soon as they found the building was doomed, ran about asking the merchants in the city for subscriptions. 'Our hall is burning, sir, the engines are at work but there is no hope. We shall want a new one. Let us have money to begin at once!' Thousands upon thousands of dollars were subscribed without a moment's hesitation and it is said that before the fire was out, enough money had been raised to build a new hall in a style of even greater magnificence than the first. This is only a specimen of the lightning Christianity of Chicago." F. Barham Zincke, another English visitor, added in his recollections that the fire "gave the merchants of the place an opportunity for exercising the liberality which is one of the characteristics of America and in no higher degree than in Chicago. . . . In a few hours after the occurrence, enough had been subscribed to rebuild the hall!"

The raising of funds for the second building was not quite as easy as it appeared to the English visitors. But enough money was subscribed to reconstruct the main portion of the building, and a year later—on January 19, 1869—the second Farwell Hall was ready for use. The new building was constructed on a more modest scale than its predecessor, as the Association was still obligated to the stockholders in the first building. The auditorium was reduced by almost a third in size and the new building contained neither a gymnasium nor a dormitory. Even with this retrenchment, it was an impressive structure. The *Chicago Times* described the hall—which seated about 2,500—as "the largest in the United States, the nearest approach thereto being the Tremont Temple of Boston." The hall was lighted by two hundred gas jets, including two groups of jets suspended from enormous reflectors in the ceiling. It was decorated with Biblical frescoes painted by Jevne and Almini, the artist-lithographers whose famous scenes of Chicago were to become rare collector's items. The new Farwell Hall was a source of great civic pride, just as the first hall had been. *The Times* called it a "modern Pantheon" where "Arminianism and Calvinism sit side by side."

The impatient Moody and Farwell were urging further expansion almost as soon as the second building was finished. Farwell in particular was dissatisfied with the facilities for the library, which now housed an extensive collection of religious literature. In June of 1869 he guaranteed with his personal note a loan of $100,000 from the Northwestern Mutual Life Insurance Company to the young YMCA for the erection of a library building adjacent to second Farwell Hall. A portion of the building was given over to stores and offices; it was expected that the rent from these would provide the funds to repay the loan.

While Farwell's business acumen and reputation were providing the basis for the expansion of the Y's physical properties, Moody was busy in other ways. As a fund raiser, he had no equal. His was the persuasive voice which enlisted other Chicagoans in the projects for which Farwell's gifts were the initial impetus. Moody also led the Association into an aggressive program of evangelistic work.

One of the organizations created under Moody's influence was the Yokefellows. This group of young men—organized in 1870 during Moody's final year as president—included the most devout of the Association's members. They met for tea every Sunday and Monday evening. Then, after prayer together, they went out individually to saloons, boardinghouses, and street-corner gathering places to invite any young men they could find to attend worship services at Farwell Hall. In the articles of association which the Yokefellows forwarded to the Board of Managers, they described their work as that of "inviting all persons who can be reached, within a circuit of one mile of Farwell Hall, to attend the Sunday evening and other religious services, unless they are known to be regular attendants at other evangelical places of worship; and to be ready at the call of duty for every good work." Another article in their agreement was obviously intended to prevent their earnestness from being diverted to matters of theological doctrine. "No questions shall be discussed at any meeting touching points of doctrinal differences," the article read, "nor shall any religious ordinance be practiced which would involve the conscientious withdrawal of any member from participation therein."

The Yokefellows were active from 1870 to 1876, when they were disbanded as part of the YMCA and the various members reorganized within their own denominations. In 1878 they

A Yokefellow at work.

were again organized as part of the YMCA. By providing experience in personal evangelism, the Yokefellows served as an unofficial training school for young men wishing to make a career of religious work. In the six years following their reorganization, sixteen of the Yokefellows entered YMCA secretarial work, five entered theological seminaries, and two entered the foreign mission field.

One of those who became a missionary was David D. Jones, a pioneer in the China field. He traveled to China by way of his native Wales. In a letter published in the weekly Y *Bulletin* on May 8, 1880, he told of paying $10 toward his passage on a sailing vessel and working during the four-month ocean voyage for the rest of his fare. He had arrived in Hong Kong with only $1.50 in his pocket. While in Chicago, Jones had founded a Chinese Sunday School under the sponsorship of the YMCA. Because of language difficulties, the school provided each child with his own teacher—mostly women recruited from the city's churches. In 1882 the average attendance had grown to about forty-five teachers and fifty-five pupils. Five other Sunday Schools patterned after this one were also founded for Chinese children. When Jones returned from his mission work for a visit five years later, he was to find an audience of more than 125 children, to whom he addressed a sermon on Christianity in their native language.

Moody, as he saw more and more of his young men take up general evangelistic or mission work, became restless despite the growth of the Association under his leadership. He felt that evangelism was his first calling and that the objectives of the Young Men's Christian Association limited, by their nature, the area in which he could win converts for the religion whose power he so deeply felt and believed. Meanwhile, his fame as an orator and evangelist was spreading. He had made one trip to England in 1867 for a series of revival meetings and had been invited to return in 1871. At the same time, the Chicago Association was faced with so many financial problems that he was reluctant to leave it in a time of distress.

Minutes of the Board of Managers for the year 1871 reveal the subject of finances so dominated the thinking of the members that weekly meetings were held on the subject—and so little hope could be recorded that the secretary was reduced to "Ditto."

April   3—Meeting was spent in conversation on financial condition of the Association.

June   5—Meeting spent in Finance discussion.

June 12—Meeting spent in Finance.

June 19—Ditto

June 20—Ditto

June 26—Ditto

July   3—Ditto

The Board, apparently having exhausted all avenues of relief, then adjourned for the summer. The next entry in the minutes was eloquent in the brevity with which it spoke of the next tragedy to hit the Chicago Association. It read only:

Oct. 8, 1871—The Association buildings were burned in the Great Fire.

The great Chicago fire, which burned for two days and two nights, had swept across the entire business section of Chicago and the residential section on the near North Side. The flames destroyed 2,124 acres of buildings, burned 17,450 homes, made 90,000 people homeless, and destroyed property worth $200,-000,000—one-third of the total wealth of Chicago. Among the buildings to fall in flames and ashes was the second Farwell Hall.

For the third time in less than five years, the members of the YMCA of Chicago were faced with the task of finding money for a new building. And on this occasion they had to find these funds in a city that had lost one-third of all its resources.

True to its purpose, the Y turned to helping others before it considered its own problems. Soon after the fire, a committee of members was appointed to aid in the distribution of supplies and food to victims of the fire. The tireless Farwell was treasurer; the other members of the committee were Moody, Jacobs, Whittle, the Rev. C. E. Cheney, and the Rev. Robert Patterson. As it had in the past, the Association acted as co-ordinator and trustee for supplies from many sources. Its work was done so efficiently that on December 16, 1871, the committee was able to publish a notice acknowledging receipt of $16,533.12 in cash and 959 packages of clothing and supplies. The committee added

"Serving Out Rations to the Destitute" after the Great Fire of 1871.

that "so abundant (had) been the supply of clothing that all
deserving persons coming under their supervision have been
supplied, or will be supplied, from contributions already made;
so that it will not be necessary to trespass further upon the
generosity of the Christian public for clothing." A postscript
to this relief work was written a year later, when the Boston
YMCA suffered the loss of its building in a fire. The Chicago
Association, still with no building of its own, offered the Boston
Association the right to draw up to $5,000 from Chicago relief
funds, of which $1,000 was accepted.

One unexpected consequence of the fire was to persuade
Dwight L. Moody that he could make no immediate contribu-
tion to the material problems to be faced in the wake of the
catastrophe and that he was free to accept the call to come to
Great Britain for a series of evangelistic meetings. His friend
John V. Farwell was to write later that the Chicago fire "was
the climax which persuaded him to go to Great Britain. I did all
I could to persuade him to stay in Chicago and help build up
from the ruins of the fire along religious lines, but to no effect.
. . . With his own home, that of the YMCA and of his Sunday
School and the Union Church all in ashes, all barriers were
burned away which stood in the way of an invitation to come
to England to take up evangelistic work, which had been given
him before then while on a visit there." In later years, Moody
explained why he welcomed the opportunity to devote his full
time to evangelism. "A man cannot be an evangelist and a general
secretary without spoiling his work in both positions," he told
a national YMCA convention. "The secretary, in order to succeed, must take up the work for young men and decide to do
this one thing. On this account, I gave up the secretaryship to
become an evangelist. You cannot do both." (Although Moody's
title had been president, his services to the Chicago Association

had actually been comparable to those of the modern general secretary as they concern the day-to-day operation of the Association.)

Moody's leaving meant that new leaders would have to be found in Chicago to replace him and that an additional burden would fall on the other members of the volunteer committees of the Board of Managers. The remaining members briskly faced up to this challenge. On November 16, 1871, Major Whittle reported that his committee had secured rooms on the West Side at 97 Randolph Street in Rice and Jackson's Building and had ordered shelving put in for library purposes. The Association had no intention of being content with makeshift provisions, however; the Board of Managers under President Turlington W. Harvey was already making plans to raise funds for a third building.

Before any new obligations could be assumed, it was necessary to dispose of the stock commitments from the first building. This stock represented an investment of more than $200,000 on which stockholders had been promised 6 per cent interest. The Board decided to ask these stockholders to surrender this stock without compensation, and a committee headed by Frank G. Ensign was appointed to see if this could be done. The committee functioned so diligently and persuasively that more than $150,000 of these stock certificates were given back to the Association so that it could embark upon a new building program. Of the balance outstanding, about half the sum represented stock held by owners who had perished in the fire or who could not be found.

Property in downtown Chicago had zoomed so much in value that the Board of Trustees was able to finance the third building—also named Farwell Hall—by making a loan secured by the value of the property on which the building stood. This

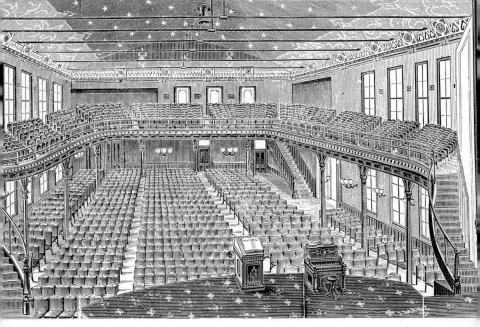

Auditorium of the third Farwell Hall, dedicated November 28, 1874. It had a seating capacity of 2,000.

loan was augmented by generous contributions from Farwell and from Cyrus H. McCormick, Jr., who was moving toward a position of leadership in the Association.

The third Farwell Hall was dedicated on November 28, 1874, before an audience of 1,000 ("the majority of whom were ladies," the following morning's *Tribune* noted). The Association *Bulletin* of the following February contained a detailed description of the hall—and of the conditions governing those who would be permitted to use it. "No political meeting or entertainment connected with any lottery gift or presentation enterprise, or an immoral or sensational character, will be permitted to be given or take place in this hall," the *Bulletin* said. It described the hall as having a seating capacity of 2,000 persons, 1,200 on the main floor and 800 in the balcony. Lighting was provided by a "sunburner having 117 jets of gas, as well as other gas jets around the sides." There was a wide stage with dressing rooms at either side, and the hall was a principal stopping place for lecturers and concert artists on the lyceum circuit in those days. Within a few months of its opening, the hall was rented for six months in advance—though one promoter had to be cautioned "to omit anything which might be considered in the nature of dancing from his program of entertainment."

The cost of erecting the new building was almost $150,000, and the repayment of the loan covering the cost of its construction went very slowly. But in 1877 Dwight Moody returned to Chicago for a series of evangelistic meetings with his singing colleague, Ira Sankey (whom he had first met at a national YMCA convention). At the close of the meetings, Moody made an appeal for funds to pay off the debt on Farwell Hall. Through these public appeals, Moody raised enough money to free the Chicago Association of the main burden of its debt, enabling

The library of the third Farwell Hall in the 1880's, when it was known as the Madison Street Department.

The reading room provided current newspapers and periodicals.

it to devote more of its energies to an expansion of its program.

Moody did not restrict his aid to the Chicago Association. C. Howard Hopkins, writing in the official *History of the YMCA in North America*, says Moody "unquestionably raised more money than anyone else in the 19th century to refinance or build YMCA's and laid the foundation for the 'short term' financial canvass." In 1876 Moody had raised money to pay off the mortgage on the New York YMCA building and an additional $50,000 for a Bowery branch. He twice raised money to preserve the property of the Brooklyn Association. At other times he raised more than $83,000 in San Francisco and more than $200,000 (in two campaigns) to get the Philadelphia Association out of debt.

The growth of the YMCA of Chicago was part of the growth of the Young Men's Christian Association movement in all parts of America during these years. When the Chicago Association erected the original Farwell Hall, the building was the

Comfortable furnishings gave the parlor at Farwell Hall a homelike appearance.

only completely equipped (with gymnasium and dormitory) YMCA building in the world. When the third Farwell Hall was erected eight years later, there were fifty YMCA buildings throughout America. With this growth in the Association movement, there became an increasing demand for trained men who could devote full time to directing its programs. The age of specialization was coming into being. And in Chicago, fastest-growing city in the world, there was a pressure for another kind of specialization. Chicago was no longer just a city of young men. The young men of ten and twenty years before were now family men. The city had grown so huge that no one organization could deal with all the problems that were produced by an emerging urban society. The time had come to specialize in program as well. The next step for the Chicago Association was to decide how this specialization should be achieved. It was to be a difficult step.

CHAPTER **4**

"For Young Men and for Them Only"

MOODY'S TENURE as president had lasted from 1865-1870, twice as long as any of his predecessors in the office. In this time he left so strong an imprint on the Chicago Association that his ideas continued to dominate its program even after his departure. Throughout the 1870's there was a continuing emphasis on general evangelistic work. "Even if our gymnasium is crowded, and our musical and literary entertainments are intensely interesting, unless souls are converted we fail in the great aim of our Association," members were told in the *Bulletin* of March 7, 1880. During the summer of 1881, the Association sponsored 500 open-air evangelistic meetings with a total attendance of over 125,000. The *Bulletin* each week carried a column of verses for the hymns to be sung at the largest of these meetings on the lake front. Another feature of the *Bulletin* was the lesson to be discussed at Benjamin F. Jacobs' meeting for Sunday School workers that attracted 500 teachers each week.

MEETINGS FOR THE WEEK ENDING MAR. 20, 1880.

Noon-day Prayer Meeting in Lower Farwell Hall, No. 150 Madison Street, or Arcade Court, every day at 12 M. for 45 minutes.   Entrance through book store.   Prayers and remarks limited to three minutes.

LEADERS:

MONDAY,	- -	Rev. Burke F. Leavitt.
TUESDAY,	- - -	Rev. W. H. Parker.
WEDNESDAY,	- -	Charles Chappell.
THURSDAY,	- -	Edward Dack.
FRIDAY,	- -	W. O. Lattimore.
SATURDAY,	- -	To be supplied.

N. B.—Requests for prayer may be sent by mail or otherwise, addressed, Noon-day Prayer Meeting, No. 150 Madison Street, Chicago.

L. F. Lindsay leads the S. S. Teacher's Meeting, in Farwell Hall, Saturday noon, Mar. 13.

S. S. Lesson, MAR. 14.   Matt., vii, 15-29.

15. Beware of false prophets, which come to you in sheep's clothing, but inwardly they are ravening wolves.
16. Ye shall know them by their fruits.   Do men gather grapes of thorns, or figs of thistles?
17. Even so every good tree bringeth forth good fruit; but a corrupt tree bringeth forth evil fruit.
18. A good tree cannot bring forth evil fruit, neither can a corrupt tree bring forth good fruit.
19. Every tree that bringeth not forth good fruit is hewn down, and cast into the fire.
20. Wherefore by their fruits ye shall know them.
21. Not every one that saith unto me, Lord, Lord, shall enter into the kingdom of heaven; but he that doeth the will of my father which is in heaven.
22. Many will say to me in that day, Lord, Lord, have we not prophesied in thy name? and in thy name have we cast out devils? and in thy name done many wonderful works?

23. And then will I profess unto them, I never knew you: depart from me, ye that work iniquity.
24. Therefore whosoever heareth these sayings of mine, and doeth them. I will liken him unto a wise man, which built his house upon a rock:
25. And the rain descended, and the floods came, and the winds blew, and beat upon that house; and it fell not: for it was founded upon a rock.
26. And every one that heareth these sayings of mine and doeth them not, shall be likened unto a foolish man, which built his house upon the sand:
27. And the rain descended, and the floods came, and the winds blew; and beat upon that house; and it fell: and great was the fall of it.
28. And it came to pass, when Jesus had ended these sayings, the people were astonished at his doctrine:
29. For he taught them as one having authority, and not as the scribes.

EVENING MEETINGS, AT 7:45 P. M.

SUNDAY and TUESDAY,	Gospel Temperance	W. O. Lattimore.
MONDAY,	Strangers' Meeting,	A. T. Hemingway.
MONDAY, Tuesday and Thursday,	Chinese Night School.	W. O. Robinson, Supt.
THURSDAY,	Lecture,	Rev. Geo. C. Needham.
FRIDAY.	Gospel Temperance,	W. H. Murray.
FRIDAY.	Lyceum,	O. W. Muller, Pres.
SATURDAY,	Commercial Travelers,	J. H. Chapman.
SATURDAY.	Bliss Choir.	F. B. Williams.

MEETINGS FOR RAILROAD MEN.

At the R. R. Reading Room, cor. Canal and Kinzie Sts., Sunday at 3 P. M., Tuesday evening, Cottage Prayer Meeting.   At the R. R. Reading Room, 634 South Canal St.   Gospel Meeting, Sunday, 7:45 P.M.
At the R. R. Reading Room. 4645 State St. (Rock Island Shops.) Gospel Meeting, Sunday, 3:30 P.M.

BIBLE STUDY and MISSION WORK.

YOUNG MEN'S BIBLE CLASS. Every Sunday, from 3 to 4 P. M., in Association Parlor, Mr. W. A. Morgan. Entrance from Arcade Court.
CHINESE SUNDAY SCHOOL. Every Sunday, at 2:30 P. M., in Lower Farwell Hall. Wm. Picket, Supt.
COUNTY HOSPITAL. Visitation of the sick Sunday, at 9 A. M.; Service at 10 A. M.; Preaching at 3 P. M. by Mr. Alfred Rowland.
HOSPITAL for Women and Children, cor. Adams and Paulina Sts.; Service Sunday at 4 P.M. by F. M. Carharf.
POOR HOUSE. Service and S. S. every Sunday at 3:00 P. M.
HOUSE OF CORRECTION. Service, Sunday at 2:00 P. M.
JAIL. Visitation every Sunday at 9:00 A. M.

A typical week's program from the *Bulletin*, March 20, 1880.

In continuing to emphasize general evangelism, the Chicago Association was pursuing a course independent from that recommended by the national convention at Albany as early as 1866. At that convention the delegates had counseled local YMCA's to "a stern adherence to a line of service among young men." The leader in securing adoption of this resolution was Robert Ross McBurney, the secretary of the New York YMCA. McBurney continued his campaign for a more specific definition of young men's work at subsequent conventions. In 1868 he vigorously disputed the claims of those associations "who have the idea that they are organized to carry on general Christian work." He called such a program "a great mistake" and insisted that "The chief object is to reach young men."

A strong supporter of McBurney was William Early Dodge, Jr., president of the New York Association and a leading layman in the expansion of the national YMCA movement. It was Dodge who proposed that the YMCA statement of purpose be expanded to include the word "physical"—thereby broadening the purposes of the Young Men's Christian Association to include "the improvement of the spiritual, mental, social, and physical condition of young men." This concept of the YMCA's goals, which rapidly came to be known as the "four-fold program," was quickly adopted in New York. The transition to this program was not to be accomplished so readily in Chicago.

The Chicago Association, with its many commitments in the fields of relief, employment help, mission and Sunday School work, could not suddenly withdraw from these responsibilities. The Association, however, did feel the need of trained professional leadership such as McBurney was giving New York. Thus it was in the direction of staff rather than program that the first move toward specialization came.

Frank M. Rockwell, who had been serving the Association

81

as superintendent of the Mission Department, had left to direct the work of the Chicago Relief and Aid Society following the great Chicago fire. When the Board of Managers sought a replacement for Rockwell, it also broadened the duties of the office to those of a general secretary such as McBurney. As there was no professional *cadre* from which to draw, the Board on October 7, 1872, voted to ask one of its own members, Frank G. Ensign, "to take charge and have general superintendence of all branches of the work of the Association in its financial, religious, literary, and social departments, subject only to the direction of the President and the Board of Managers." Ensign, however, was not able to free himself to accept the position, and the following February the Board of Managers accepted his resignation without his having assumed the full duties of the office.

Ensign was succeeded by W. W. Vanarsdale, a clerk in the freight office of the Michigan and Southern Railroad, who was hired in a much more limited capacity in 1873 "to do any work under the direction of the Executive Committee." Among Vanarsdale's duties was the supervision of the Association's publishing program, which could scarcely keep up with the demand for tracts and religious literature—even with the importation of publications that in one year amounted to five tons of religious tracts and periodicals. In 1874 the tract committee distributed more than 2,500,000 pages of tracts.

The religious tracts were augmented by religious papers issued by the Association. One of the first of these was *Everybody's Paper*, a combination religious and temperance periodical. Next came *Heavenly Tidings*, the digest of religious articles that was sold throughout the United States. Then in 1873 the Association started publishing *The Watchman*, intended as a national periodical of all Young Men's Christian Associations but too evangelistic in its content ever to be officially accepted as such.

Vanarsdale was attracted to the publishing field and was soon spending so much time in supervising these periodicals that the Board of Managers passed a resolution instructing him to discontinue the publication of *The Watchman* or vacate his office as superintendent. He chose *The Watchman* and was allowed to continue its publication as an independent venture (with emergency financial assistance from the Board of Managers) for many years. Later its name was changed to *Young Men's Era*, and finally, before it was discontinued, to *Men*. The Association, however, chose the opportunity presented by Vanarsdale's resignation to dispose of the publishing business because of its high costs and the amount of time required for its supervision.

The Board of Managers again turned to its own ranks in choosing a successor to Vanarsdale. He was A. T. Hemingway, a successful Chicago real-estate dealer who relinquished his private business in order to become "superintendent" of the Chicago Association "at a fixed salary of $1,500 per annum and an additional sum of $300 to be paid him at the end of the year if the funds could be secured by the Board." Soon after taking office, Hemingway was being referred to as "general secretary" rather than "superintendent." On March 5, 1881, the constitution was amended to provide for the employment of a "general secretary" and Hemingway officially assumed the duties of first general secretary of the Young Men's Christian Association of Chicago.

The Chicago Association continued its independent course under Hemingway. Although the new general secretary made several innovations in the Y's program, he insisted that they should not come at the expense of general evangelistic work. "Since we are a Young Men's Christian Association, our great object is to win young men to Christ and building them up in Christian character," Hemingway said in one of his reports—

A. T. Hemingway, first officially designated general secretary of the YMCA of Metropolitan Chicago, put his chief emphasis on religious work.

indicating by his omission of any reference to the other aspects of the Y's program that he considered them subsidiary to the evangelistic work. His first annual report in 1879 was devoted almost entirely to the religious program. He spoke with special pride of the noon prayer meetings, which continued daily as they had for twenty-one years. Hemingway reported that more than 61,000 people had attended these meetings and that written requests for special prayers had been sent in writing from as far away as Europe, India, and Africa. Hemingway was also responsible for reactivating the Yokefellows.

Hemingway, although insisting upon the pre-eminence of the religious activities, did not oppose the development of other interests within the organization. In retrospect it is possible to see that many of the new ideas which later were to trouble Hemingway so greatly were actually introduced in the YMCA of Chicago under his sponsorship. One of these innovations was the expansion of the physical program.

A gymnasium as a part of a YMCA building had been recommended by the national convention in New Orleans nearly twenty years earlier. But so cautious was the approach of the Chicago Association that in 1875 approval by the Board of Managers was necessary before two sets of chessmen could be placed in the library "to be accessible to any who might desire to use them." Within a year after this timid break with tradition, the same Board was appointing a committee to consider the construction of a gymnasium. For two years the committee studied the problem without recommending action. Then in 1878 Hemingway visited the eastern associations and saw how much their gymnasiums were doing in attracting young men to the YMCA. When Dwight Moody added his own endorsement to that of Hemingway's, the Board of Managers went to work with characteristic speed. In April of 1879 a gymnasium was formally opened on the fourth floor of Farwell Hall in a room formerly used for small prayer meetings. According to the weekly *Bulletin*, the gym was furnished with "the following apparatus in it: vaulting bar, parallel bars, chest bars, ladders, swinging rings, striking bag, rowing machine, pulley weights, Indian clubs, dumbbells, single trapeze, peg pole, climbing rope, traveling rings, and climbing pole." The Board hired a supervisor, Otto Miller, at a salary of $7.00 per week. The gym was immediately successful and was used by members and their guests a total of 13,427 times in its first year.

Baths were also constructed in connection with the gymnasium. These proved to be extraordinarily popular—so much so that the bathers could not be dislodged from their tin tubs of warm water (each in an individual booth) within the prescribed time. This Gordian dilemma was finally solved when contractor John E. Scully, later a Chicago alderman, cut out the partitions between the tubs, installed two overhead pipes with improvised shower heads, and provided twin sprays of hot and cold water. The bathers were forced to dart back and forth between the two showers—believed to be the first shower baths in Chicago—and the contrast in water temperatures served the purpose of minimizing the time any but the hardiest could spend under either spray.

The popularity of the gym produced an area of congestion not so easily relieved. In July of 1882, a group of gymnasts petitioned the Board of Managers for better facilities, reminding them in a petition "that young men should be encouraged to have not only sound minds and morals but sound bodies as well." The Board was completely sympathetic and replied in a resolution of its own that everything possible would be done to fix up "a first-class gymnasium in every particular." Within a short time, the athletic room had been remodeled into a two-story gymnasium with a corresponding increase in the number of baths and dressing rooms.

Washroom and lockers at the Madison Street Department (now Central) following the installation of showers.

Boys' work was also introduced in the Chicago Association while Hemingway was general secretary. Previously, the term "young men" had been rather strictly defined as applying only to young adults. But with the development of family life in Chicago and the rapid influx of workers who brought their families with them, there became an increasing need to provide a program of activity for boys. The first committee on boys' work was formed in 1878. It offered only a limited program. "It is our plan to have a distinctively religious work for boys," Secretary Hemingway said. The boys were invited to an afternoon Sunday School and to an evening meeting where "moral and religious instruction" was combined "with music and entertainment." The *Bulletin* for March 22, 1879, reported that "A neat and tasty room in the basement has been fitted up for the boys. Meetings are held every Wednesday evening. All the street boys, bootblacks, newsboys or others without a home in the city are especially invited to join." The boys' program expanded rapidly. In 1887 the *Bulletin* took note of the fact the boys had been granted the use of the gym, adding the admonition that "Boys under sixteen must be out of gym and baths by 7:00 P.M., except Monday."

Hemingway's greatest contribution to the progress of the Chicago Association was probably his achievement in recruiting new leadership. Moody was giving all his time to evangelism. John V. Farwell, Sr. had moved to Lake Forest, where distance made it impossible for him to participate in the day-to-day program as he had in the past. Both these men had dominated—and sustained—the Young Men's Christian Association of Chicago during its formative years. New problems were arising that required new answers. And the men whom Hemingway persuaded to assume a major part of the responsibility relinquished by Moody and Farwell were to take the Chicago Association in a new direction in which the answers for these problems could be found.

Of those whom Hemingway attracted to the Young Men's Christian Association, three were to emerge as dominant figures, not only in the Chicago program but in the YMCA movement throughout the world. These three—who were to set the course for the next thirty years as Farwell and Moody had set it for the first two decades—were James L. Houghteling, Cyrus H. McCormick, Jr., and John V. Farwell, Jr. All were elected to the Board of Managers the same year—1881. The following year the Board elected one of their number—James L. Houghteling, then only twenty-six—as president of the Chicago Association.

Houghteling, an Episcopalian layman, was a member of the Chicago banking firm of Peabody, Houghteling and Company. With twelve young men from his parish Bible class, he organized the Brotherhood of St. Andrew, national lay organization of the Episcopal church. When he assumed the presidency of the Chicago Association, he was told by John Farwell, Sr. that the outlook was not too bright as there was an outstanding debt on current expenses of $600. At the end of his first year as president, Houghteling was to recall later, the Association was $3,000 in debt—"but brimful of cheerfulness and optimism." This optimism spilled over into the Board of Trustees, which in March of 1883 passed a resolution expressing "their approval and appreciation of the good work accomplished by the Board of Managers . . . and especially through the personal effort of the President of that Board, Mr. James Houghteling, in remodeling and refurnishing the buildings, thereby making them attractive and far better adapted to the wants of the Association, and for the energy and perseverance shown in raising funds sufficient for the accomplishment of this work."

Houghteling was not content with modernizing Farwell Hall. He also wanted to modernize the program of the YMCA, both in Chicago and elsewhere. At the 25th International Convention in Milwaukee in 1883, he made a forceful analysis of the causes of the difficulties in which many YMCA's (including that in Chicago) found themselves at the time. He called his address "What the Community Expects of the YMCA and What the YMCA Expects of the Community." He described the associations then in existence as "in one place a Christian exchange for the accommodation of the townspeople; in another place a city missionary society; in another, an association for the propagation of the Gospel by means of tract distribution; in another, a refuge for all kinds of religious cranks; in another, a union church in effect; in another, a temperance society; in another, a Sunday School union; and so on *ad infinitum.*" Rather than so dispersing their interests, he pleaded, let all YMCA's concentrate on "the elevation and salvation of *young men*—specific work for young men and for *them only.*" Such a program, he added, would enable the YMCA to expect full support from its community. The community, in turn, would have a "right to expect that the work be conducted on such a scheme that the associate members, the men you are trying to save, shall include young men of every creed and nationality, every rank and walk of life."

The ideas put forth in this remarkable speech remain timely after nearly three-quarters of a century. "Specific work for young men" was the goal that Houghteling set himself, and he urged that "all other associations wheel into line and by judicious, but decisive pruning, get upon that platform. We are doing it in Chicago and we are meeting with a success which taxes our utmost energies to live up to." He did not gloss over the opposition that might be encountered. "It is far easier to start a

James L. Houghteling, a Chicago banker, was successful in getting the YMCA to concentrate its program on work for young men.

new Association on this platform than to trim down an old one," he told the convention. "We in Chicago have only fairly begun and we have already weathered several teapot tempests. But if you are to succeed you must do it."

The "teapot tempests" to which Houghteling referred were in part the results of differences of opinion between Hemingway and the triumvirate of Houghteling, McCormick, and Farwell, Jr. After the convention, these "teapot tempests" became so frequent that Hemingway presented his resignation as general secretary, although retaining his membership on the Board of Managers. Finding an adequate successor to Hemingway proved an impossible task. A call was twice extended to W. R. Wardell, then state secretary of Ohio, but it was rejected on both occasions. After the second refusal, Hemingway's friends on the Board urged that he be rehired as general secretary and another attempt be made to reconcile the division of opinion over the emphasis of the Association's program. McCormick opposed the

Cyrus H. McCormick, Jr., son of
the inventor of the reaper, became
a leader in the world YMCA
movement and made generous
contributions to work overseas.

move, but as no other suitable candidate could be found, Hemingway was rehired on August 19, 1884, "for the term of one year at a salary of $200 per month," providing at least a temporary solution to the problem.

The Chicago Association was able to carry on through this period of tension with a minimum of disruption because of the expansion of the professional staff that had taken place since Hemingway was first hired. The minutes of the Board of Managers on January 16, 1883, list the following as "employed officers" of the Association:

Gen. Sec. A. T. Hemingway.........$ 200 per month
1st Asst. George T. Howser..........$1,000 per year
2nd Asst. Israel Bergstrom...........$ 600 per year
Financial Secretary G. B. Townsend...$1,350 per year
Supt. of Membership J. S. Burnell.....$ 60 per month
Supt. of Gymnasium O. W. Miller.....$ 700 per year

Howser, who was Hemingway's assistant, acted as general secretary after Hemingway's resignation and provided a necessary continuity of management. The size of the staff was another measure of the increasing specialization in the Y program. It was clearly intended to implement the objectives outlined by Houghteling at Milwaukee. "We propose to cater to every wholesome taste and inclination found in young men," he had told the convention. "For physical wants we wish to supply bath rooms, gymnasiums, medical talks and the like; for social wants, parlors and social games and amusements; for intellectual wants, classes, lectures, etc.; for spiritual wants, the young men's prayer meeting, the Bible Class and, if possible, the daily meeting for praise and prayer."

The gymnasium—that is, the physical aspect of this fourfold program—played an increasingly important role in attracting young men to the Y. By 1887 the daily attendance at the gym was 300 per day, or more than 7,000 per month (it was closed Sundays). The Board of Managers concluded at a meeting that "more members came into the Association through the influence of the gymnasium than from any other source." It was the gymnasium which was responsible for the installation of the first electric lights in the building. So progressive was Houghteling's management that the arc lights which provided the illumination were the first of their kind to be used in Chicago.

As professional athletics had not yet achieved the affluence and respectability that were to come in the twentieth century, only amateurs were permitted to use the gym facilities. In 1887 it was brought to the attention of the Board of Managers that one "Bert Scherer, who as a member of the Association has attained considerable prominence in gymnastic work," had "entered into wrestling contests for stakes of $100 or other amounts." As a result of this lapse into professionalism, the unfortunate Scherer was suspended. (In Pittsburgh, the Association there refused to let evangelist Billy Sunday use its gymnasium because he had once played professional baseball.)

Although these incidents appear trivial by modern standards, there was at least one other in 1887 which was not. An unsuccessful lawyer who had been a Reconstruction official in Florida was found encouraging immoral practices among boys at the gym. The Board of Managers, to its credit, made no attempt to conceal the episode but rather voted publicly to castigate the lawyer for his conduct, expel him from membership, and to publish a circular so that other Associations and organizations might be warned about him.

Houghteling and his colleagues did not neglect "mental" diversions for young men. In 1882 educational classes were inaugurated in Farwell Hall. Within a few years, students could take their choice of courses in "vocal music, penmanship, phonography, physiology, bookkeeping, German, and arithmetic." The music classes were taught by George F. Root, a Chicago music publisher famous as the composer of such great Civil War songs as "Tramp, Tramp, Tramp, the Boys Are Marching" and "The Battle Cry of Freedom." One of the students who enrolled for these classes was Frank O. Lowden, later governor of Illinois, who was supplementing his legal education with training at the YMCA in penmanship and public speaking.

Several debating societies were organized. One of these —The Senate—was established to debate the political issues of the day, but its discussions proved so vigorous that it was disbanded by the Board of Managers for involving the Association in a political controversy. One of the young "Senators" who participated in these debates was a law clerk named William Jennings Bryan, then preparing for the political career that was to make him three times the Democratic nominee for President by studying public speaking at the YMCA and reading law in the office of Senator Lyman Trumbull. Another of the societies was the Lyceum, which although it sought to avoid politics, scheduled a debate in December of 1880 on a topic that has divided Chicagoans ever since. Its title was "Resolved: That the City Ought to Take Charge of the Street Car Lines." The audiences followed these debates with interest and partisanship. So much enthusiasm was expressed that one member wrote the editor of the *Bulletin* in May of 1884 complaining about the "indiscriminate applause." If it was not stopped, he warned, "Farwell Hall audiences soon will have an unenviable reputation for applauding everything—good, bad, and indifferent."

The addition of new program activities and the dropping of others, such as publishing, the special Bridewell and jail committee, and the relief work (transferred to a forerunner of United Charities), were evidence of the ferment of this period. This ferment was one of growth rather than decay, but the changes it produced were often puzzling to the young men who might be approached about becoming members. "A great many young men have wrong ideas concerning the YMCA, its work and the requirements of its members," said the monthly *Bulletin* on May 1, 1885. "Some think that it is a society composed entirely of Young Men who are professing Christians and that its work consists altogether in holding religious meetings, of which each member is required to attend a specified number or else forfeit his membership. . . . For the information of these and others who are misinformed, we would say in the first place that our members are not all Christians but that any young man of good moral character may become a member. The holding of religious meetings is only part of the work, as the Association aims not only at the spiritual but also at the mental, moral, and physical development of its members. The

matter of taking part in the religious meetings is left entirely
to the option of each member."

This candid educational program brought quick results. By
1885 the Chicago Association could count more than 3,000 members. Among them was a young man who signed his name
Fremont Lawson and who was just beginning to make a name
for himself as publisher of a new Chicago newspaper called the
Chicago Daily News. In 1875 he had become a member of the
Marine Hospital Committee and the following year he made his
first donation to the YMCA of Chicago of $25. Marshall Field
was so impressed with the Y's work that he paid for memberships for fifty clerks from his store. And in the weekly *Bulletin*
in 1885 there was a note that among the persons to call during
the past few days was "Samuel Insull of the London, England,
YMCA."

It was obvious that a single building erected for the needs of
a much smaller Association could not provide facilities for 3,000
men and boys plus the visitors who attended the religious services
and lectures in Farwell Hall. The erection of a single building
to accommodate the activities of such a large number of people
did not appear practical. The alternative was to divide up the
work and establish branches in different parts of the city. Such
branches had already been set up in several eastern cities and
had proved successful. And in Chicago many men were being
brought into Association work through specialized railroad
branches located near their place of work.

The railroad program had been started in Chicago in January of 1878 after a committee of railroad executives had asked
the Board of Managers "to promote the cause of Christ among
the railroad men of Chicago." Such work had been launched on
a national scale in 1868 under the direction of Robert Weidensall. Its program was particularly adapted to Chicago—both be-

cause Chicago was already the country's greatest rail center and because the number of transient workers, whom the railroad branches were intended to serve, continued to be especially high in Chicago. The first railroad reading room was opened at Kinzie and Canal Streets in 1879. In less than four months, more than 8,000 men had used the reading room or companion bath facilities. A report of Y work at the Baltimore & Ohio shops in South Chicago for 1879 gives a picture of the way in which these reading rooms were used as bases for further work among the railroad men. The report listed "899 cabooses and engines visited, 5,666 switch and flag houses visited, 242 depots and offices visited, 10,562 tracts distributed, 56 visits made to the sick and injured, 82 visits to families and 597 personal religious talks." Much of this work was supported by the railroads. In 1880 contributions were listed from the Burlington Route, the Chicago and North Western, the Rock Island, the Chicago & Alton, the Pittsburgh, Fort Wayne & Chicago, and the Michigan and Southern. Within the next ten years, other railroad branches were opened at 634 South Canal at Sixteenth Street and at the Rock Island car shops, 4645 South State Street.

In 1886 the Board of Managers began a consideration of branches for the general membership, and Secretary Hemingway was asked to make a report on the operation of these branches in the East. He reported favorably on the idea, and a decision was made to establish a branch on the West Side.

In April of 1887 McCormick called a meeting in his home to consider means of establishing such a West Side branch. The guests were for the most part ministers from the area. After the meeting, a resolution was passed that it was "the sense of the meeting that it is desirable to establish a branch of the Y upon the West Side, and we as Pastors pledge the hearty co-operation of the churches under our charge to the support of such an enterprise." A month later, encouraged by this pledge of co-operation from the area, the Board of Managers approved the purchase of a lot at the intersection of Monroe, Ogden, and Ashland avenues for the erection of a building for the West Side.

Pressure for other branches was coming from outside the Association. While plans for setting up the West Side branch were going forward, Moody organized a Chicago Avenue branch of the Y in his church basement. By September of 1887 the group had enrolled eighty-six members and was petitioning the Board for help in erecting a building. By legacy, the Association also became the owner of a building at 3131-3133 South Cottage Grove Avenue, in which it was hoped a South Side branch could be established. However, the West Side building required

First railroad reading room of the Association at Kinzie and Canal streets.

so much of the energy and attention of the Board that plans for the other branches were deferred.

McCormick, in addition to pushing through the West Side branch, served as chairman of the finance committee. By 1884 the operating debt had reached $6,773, but McCormick was determined that it be wiped out before the year was over. Of this indebtedness, $2,750 was owed to McCormick, $1,100 to Farwell, Jr., and $400 to Houghteling. All three offered to cancel their notes if the other members would raise enough cash to pay off the balance within the year. Reaching the final total was agonizingly slow. It was not until the final night that a telegram arrived from the East with a contribution which put the drive over the prescribed goal. Totaling up the funds, McCormick found that at last the YMCA of Chicago was debt-free—but it had only two cents to spare!

Another great interest of McCormick was bringing the Chicago Association into a closer relationship with the International Committee of the YMCA, then the co-ordinating body for the national YMCA movement. On several occasions, he invited Chicagoans to special dinner parties for Richard Cary Morse, then international secretary, in an effort to break down some of the opposition which had kept Chicago from entering fully into the program advocated by the International Committee. Integrating the Chicago work with that of the International was made somewhat easier when Robert Weidensall was appointed general agent for the YMCA in the West and opened his headquarters in Farwell Hall. Weidensall was well liked by the Chicago group, which not only received him cordially but supported him generously in promoting YMCA work in other cities throughout the Midwest.

Weidensall was a pioneer in recruiting and training young men for careers as general secretaries in the many new asso-

A local chapter of the American Railway Employed Boys' Club organized by the Chicago and North Western Railway Department of the YMCA.

ciations which were being formed. In 1884 he organized a Western Secretarial Institute at Camp Collie near Lake Geneva, Wisconsin, at which YMCA secretaries could meet for a short time each summer for devotional services and an exchange of ideas concerning YMCA work. The opening of the Western Secretarial Institute dramatized for Chicagoans the need for increased professional training for those who were to direct its program. The volunteer committees set up in the early days could no longer give enough time to provide detailed direction for Y activities. Specialization required men with special training, and Hemingway had no such special training. In addition, as Houghteling, McCormick, and Farwell came to realize, he was not wholly in sympathy with the total program they were trying to put into effect.

The conflict over policy with Hemingway that had led

to his resignation in 1883 divided the Board of Managers a second time in 1887. Houghteling, McCormick, and Farwell were against retaining Hemingway. The older members of the Board —who actually represented a majority—were in favor of letting Hemingway continue, but they did not feel they should obstruct the larger plans of the three who opposed him. Hemingway was still pressing for more evangelistic work. In March of 1887 he had arranged for Moody and Farwell, Sr. to make a special plea with the Board for employment of a full-time evangelist. Out of respect for the two men, the Board acceded to the request—though only for a period from May 1, 1887, to January 1, 1888.

Friction continued, and in September Hemingway presented his resignation, saying that "after prayerful exhortation" he had "decided to retire from the office of General Secretary at the expiration of my engagement with you which closes December 31 of this year." When the resignation was voted upon by the Board of Managers, only three votes were counted in the affirmative. But as the remainder of the Board abstained from voting, the effect was to approve acceptance of the resignation.

A month later, Hemingway issued a statement to the *Chicago Herald* giving in detail his reasons for quitting:

"My policy has been to follow Mr. Moody's line of work and that adopted by J. V. Farwell who gave the land on which the building stands," he said. "Their idea was to make evangelistic work prominent, to cause the young men to be active in Christian work. The policy of the New York Association and of the International Committee is not to engage in evangelistic work but to make the Association a sort of club. J. V. Farwell, Jr., president, and J. L. Houghteling, treasurer, both of whom are members of the International Committee, are my most active opponents." Hemingway added that several meetings with John V. Farwell,

John V. Farwell, Jr.
succeeded his father as an
outstanding supporter of the
YMCA. His service was to cover a
period of 63 years—from 1881
until his death in 1944.

Jr. had preceded his resignation. At these meetings, Farwell had explained to Hemingway why it was felt there was a need for a man with greater professional training. Hemingway also quoted Farwell as saying that there were "some very closely connected with you who differ with you in your methods." From this, it may be inferred that the younger members were pressing the Board to hire a general secretary more in sympathy with all the aspects of the four-fold program. Farwell later confirmed the essentials of Hemingway's emotionally charged interview with the *Herald*. Farwell said the primary reason for Hemingway's resignation was that he was not "in full sympathy with the desire of the Board to develop a broader work; . . . his interests were primarily in the direct evangelical efforts of the Association."

Although following divergent paths, Hemingway and his Board of Managers had actually formed a remarkable team. When they finally dissolved their partnership, the Chicago Association was at an all-time high of membership and financial prosperity. When Hemingway had entered upon his duties in 1878, the Chicago Association had less than 800 members; when he resigned, it had a membership of 5,106. The educational program had grown in a few years to an enrollment of more than 1,000 students. The railroad departments had expanded into four locations, each in charge of an efficient secretary. The annual report for 1888 gives a picture of the size of the Y's program during Hemingway's final year:

Gymnasium had in attendance.................	76,453
Bath rooms furnished free baths to.............	78,781
Attendance at 21 outings and field sports........	16,839
Jobs secured through employment office........	4,962
Attendance at lectures, receptions.... (Total)...	223,717
Attendance at religious meetings..... (Total)...	283,163

At the end of thirty years, the YMCA of Chicago could be proud of a remarkable variety of achievement. But it was on the threshold of even greater accomplishments.

CHAPTER 5

Romans 15:30 and 32

FOLLOWING THE resignation of Hemingway, a committee composed of John V. Farwell, Jr., Cyrus H. McCormick, Jr., and Edwin Burritt Smith, a Chicago lawyer who was assuming increasing responsibilities in the Chicago Association, was named to find a successor. They were looking for a man who had professional experience or training, a man who had sufficient administrative ability to direct the affairs of an Association as large as that of Chicago, and a man who was in sympathy with their objective of working specifically among young men toward the goals of the four-fold program.

Richard Cary Morse, general secretary of the International Committee, suggested to McCormick that the Chicagoans approach Loring Wilbur Messer, then general secretary of the YMCA at Cambridge, Massachusetts. Messer was not unknown in Chicago. In 1881, when only twenty-five, he had been named secretary of the YMCA in Peoria, Illinois. During his two years of service there he had taken a leading role in extending Y work throughout the state and in organizing informal training programs for young men interested in making the YMCA a career. In 1883 he left Peoria for Cambridge, where in five years he had built an unorganized group of men into an Association with more than nine hundred members and assets in excess of $50,000.

Like Farwell and Moody, Messer was an Anglo-Saxo-Yankee. Like George Williams of London, he had also been a clerk in a dry-goods store. He had been born in Somersworth, New Hampshire, on March 1, 1856, and educated at Reading, Massachusetts, where his father had moved to take a job with the Boston & Maine railroad. He had been forced to leave school when only fourteen. After four years of working on the railroad, he entered a dry-goods store as a clerk. He soon found the satisfactions of his spare-time activity with the YMCA were much greater than his interest in the vocation of a clerk. When he was twenty-five he resigned from the store to accept the position which had been offered him at Peoria.

In December of 1887 McCormick went East on business and made an appointment with Messer to discuss the Chicago situation. He reported so favorably on Messer after the interview that the Board of Managers voted immediately to instruct him to "secure L. W. Messer as general secretary for one year at a salary of $2,400." Messer was uncertain about accepting the offer and it was necessary for Morse to intervene a second time. In a letter to McCormick, Morse pointed out that Messer was the man Chicago "ought and must have" and suggested two steps which might be "calculated to increase the chances of a favorable response from Messer." They were:

(1) "As to salary, the difference between $2,100 at Cambridge and the $2,400 offered for Chicago might be wisely in-

creased to say $3,000. One of the strong factors used by Boston to secure Douglass from the International force was the offer of a salary of $3,500 which he now receives there.

(2) "As to M's visit to Chicago, I believe it would be also wise to include Mrs. Messer in the invitation."

Both suggestions were acted upon by the Chicago Association. Mr. and Mrs. Messer were soon being entertained at the McCormick home and every possible argument was advanced to persuade Messer that Chicago presented an incomparable opportunity to him. On his side, Messer was wise enough to secure a pledge from McCormick, Farwell, and Houghteling that all three would continue their strong support of the Association's work if he should accept the call. But even with this assurance, he deferred his final decision until after his return to Cambridge.

A few days after Messer's visit to Chicago, a telegram was delivered to Farwell, then serving his fourth consecutive term as president of the Association. It read:

CLEAR CONVICTION OF DUTY LEADS ME TO ACCEPT CHICAGO SECRETARYSHIP. ROMANS 15:30 AND 32.

L. W. MESSER

This telegram is still preserved in the historical records of the Chicago Association. And pasted to it is a clipping of the two Bible verses to which Messer referred:

Now I beseech you, brethren, for the Lord Jesus Christ's sake, and for the love of the Spirit, that ye strive together with me in your prayers to God for me:

That I may come unto you with joy by the will of God, and may with you be refreshed.

105

Loring Wilbur Messer guided the Chicago Association from 1883 to 1923 and was one of the most prominent figures in the city during these years.

This Scriptural reference in Messer's telegram underscored the fact that the Association was in no way moving away from an emphasis on religious values. Rather, it was seeking through the four-fold program to find new avenues by which young men could be brought into contact with a wholesome religious experience.

Messer assumed his post as general secretary of the Chicago Association on April 1, 1888. An idea of his activities during his first month on the job may be gained from his first official report to the Board of Managers:

"My work of the past month," he wrote, "has been largely on the lines suggested to you and approved by the Board at its last meeting; namely, the organization of the Bridgeport Department, preliminary steps of the West Side Department, estimates and plans for the improvement of the Madison Street building, enlistment of ladies in furnishing the parlors, improvement of committee work, familiarizing of all departments, systematizing of the duties of employees, assistance at 48th Street and 55th Street railroad departments, and organization of summer work."

Messer had also started a literary society, increased the attendance at the Y's religious meetings, and visited five of the city's churches, "believing that the general secretary can greatly further the interest of the Association by coming in close contact with the church life of the city." The new secretary also made a keen inspection of the facilities available at the Madison Street building (now so designated to distinguish it from the main auditorium which retained the name of Farwell Hall). "The need of a general overhauling and brightening up [in the building] is apparent," Messer told the Board of Managers. "To make the Association adapted to all classes of young men in our city, its building and facilities must be suited to their needs."

Messer quickly showed a Yankee concern for the business requirements of the Association. He told the Board of Managers that "the financial condition of the Association calls for immediate and united effort on the part of members of this Board that the present deficiency and finances needed during the summer months may be immediately provided for." To expedite the handling of business affairs, Messer recommended the hiring of a young man named Walter T. Hart as office secretary at a salary of $10 per week. That Messer was a good judge of men was never more demonstrated than in this appointment; Hart advanced in the Chicago Association to the post of assistant general secretary and went on to a distinguished career as general secretary of the Winnipeg, Canada, YMCA.

Another need which Messer was quick to recognize was that for a new constitution to provide a proper framework for the rapidly expanding activities of the Chicago Association. In May a committee of Farwell, Smith, and Dr. Horace M. Starkey was named to draft a constitution so that it would be ready for a vote of the membership at the annual meeting in December. Meanwhile, Messer went steadily ahead with the development of a program for work among young men only.

The overhauling of the Madison Street building began almost immediately. Messer asked the Board to reserve the building—above the first floor—for Association purposes. At the time there were twelve other organizations using rooms on the third and fourth floor for meetings and other activities. "This brings to the building a large number of ladies who have no connection with the Association, who frequently use the parlors and other rooms of the Association to suit their convenience and to the annoyance of the members of the Association," Messer told the Board. As a means of opening the way for the restriction of membership to young men, Messer proposed establishment of a women's auxiliary for the women members and canceled the arrangements by which ladies' groups had been using the Madison Street building. The ladies did not take this discrimination lightly. A report to the Board of Managers noted that "a conference of ladies" held at the home of Mrs. McCormick for the purpose of setting up the auxiliary "was not very largely attended." However, the ladies were finally persuaded that they would gain more than they would lose from a prosperous Association and they pledged themselves to help in refurnishing the parlors and reading room of the Madison Street building.

Although the tempo of the work in every field was greatly increased during Messer's first year, the revision of the constitution was unquestionably the greatest accomplishment of this period. The adoption of this new constitution on December 3, 1888, ended the great controversy over purpose. The primary purpose was now clearly stated as that of developing "thoroughly rounded manly character in young men—a trained mind in a sound body with right relations to God and man." This pur-

The third Farwell Hall, home of
the YMCA of Chicago, as it
appeared in 1888.

pose was to be achieved by a diversified program of physical,
social, educational, and religious activity in keeping with the
goals of the Association.

As the Young Men's Christian Association of Chicago was
governed under this constitution for almost half a century, it
is worth examining in some detail.

The new purpose was stated in Article I: "The object of
this Association shall be the improvement of the spiritual, mental,
social, and physical condition of young men." This was a revision of the statement in the earlier constitution which had
stated the purpose as "the spiritual, intellectual, and social improvement of all within its reach, irrespective of age, sex, or con-

dition, but especially of young men," and had made no reference to a physical program.

The membership provisions of the 1888 constitution rigidly limited membership, both active and associate, "to any man over sixteen years of age." Active members, who had the right to vote, were still required to be members of evangelical churches; associate members could include any young man over sixteen and "of good moral character."

These changes were explained in an article in the *Bulletin* for January, 1889, that probably was written by Messer himself. As the years went by, Messer used the *Bulletin* more and more for pouring out his ideas, admonitions, and commendations to the Association. "The change in purpose," he wrote, was based on the fact that "the most successful associations . . . are those concentrating their efforts on the special class for which the work is organized. In the early history of Association work it was natural and necessary in some cases to undertake more general Christian work, but with the development of the various organizations making a specialty of mission, temperance, and charitable work of various kinds, this need in the community is now provided for."

Messer defended the limitation of membership to young men over sixteen as a temporary measure imposed by necessity. Gymnasium facilities were already overtaxed, and other parts of the Y's program at the time (such as reading rooms, library, etc.) were not adapted to the interests of younger boys. Messer made it clear that boys would not be totally excluded but would be given special tickets for activities approved by the committees in charge. "There are cases," he added, "when the presence of a large number of boys is decidedly detrimental to the enjoyment and benefit of young men. Frequent complaints have been made by members of the ill-behavior of boys at entertainments, social gatherings, and in the gymnasium. The new constitution regulates the privileges so that a special work will now be provided, attracting and benefiting the boys whom we desire to hold and train for future usefulness."

The most foresighted change in the new constitution was the provision for the organization of the YMCA of Chicago according to what has since become known as the Metropolitan Plan. Until the adoption of the new constitution, the Board of Managers had been responsible not only for all the Y branches within the city but had been directly charged with responsibility for the Madison Street Department (now Central). With an expansion of branches inevitable because of the growth of Chicago, this dual responsibility carried with it a potential cause of dissension. On the positive side, Messer saw that a more complex organization was needed to supervise the activities of young men in widely separated areas of a city of one million people than had been the case when the Y program had been oriented around an evangelistic program carried on in a single meeting place.

Under the new constitution, the Board of Managers was charged with the "general supervision" of the Association and the authority "to establish and maintain departments,"* and "to organize and discontinue them when it seems to them advisable." Under this provision, the Board had the same relation to the Madison Street Department as to all other departments in the city. Each department, in turn, would administer its work in detail under the direction of a Committee of Management ap-

---

*The use of the word "department" to designate a branch organized under the Metropolitan Plan is distinctive in Chicago. Most other cities with metropolitan associations describe the different YMCA's within their jurisdiction as branches. In Chicago, however, the basic unit is a department; branches are subdivisions of departments within the YMCA of Metropolitan Chicago.

pointed by the Board of Managers of the Chicago Association. The Board of Managers was to consist of twenty-one men, all from evangelical churches. Each was to serve for three years, with one-third of the members retiring each year. In addition to supervising any branches which might be founded, the Board had charge of the receipt and expenditures of all funds, was charged with the responsibility of enlisting and training all salaried officers, and controlled the relationships of the Association with the International Committee and other associations in the YMCA brotherhood. In accordance with the charter, the Board of Trustees retained control over the property.

The Metropolitan Plan was not a Chicago invention, but through the administrative talents of Messer it was exploited in Chicago to the greatest possible degree. It was a plan—both in conception and execution—which met the standards of efficiency and economy that the Chicago business community expected in its own enterprises. Because the leadership in the YMCA as well as the plan itself met these standards, Chicago businessmen were willing to place their confidence in the organization it represented.

The clarity with which Messer saw these advantages of the Metropolitan Plan is revealed in one of his speeches. "The well-developed Metropolitan Association delegates to the general office of the Board such features of business as in their nature admit of centralization, in order that the departments (or branches) may specialize on the conduct of local Association activities," he said. "In adopting such a policy, the Association has followed the course usually pursued by large business organizations. For example, all property interests are managed by the general office, where experts are available for this important work. All insurance against fire, theft, explosions, accidents, etc. are cared for by the general office, also the design and construction of new buildings. Legal aid and advice are also furnished by the general office. To the department or branch management, on the other hand, are committed all remaining features of business which are strictly local in their nature and which, therefore, can best be cared for by strong local management, such as the securing and retaining of members, enlisting of a local contributing constituency, and the management of restaurants, dormitories, schools, and kindred activities."

Messer spent much time on the details of this plan and consulted many experts on management practices before its final details were approved. He felt that its advantages were that it allowed enough freedom for independence on the part of the departments but kept enough centralized control so that the Association as a unit would have a real impact on the over-all life of a city as large as Chicago. It would also prevent the organization of a new department within the territory of another and the resultant division of support and financial resources which might lead to the bankruptcy of both. In operation, Messer described the plan to a questioner as providing for "The maximum of co-operation and the minimum of intervention." Another important aspect of the plan was that any member of any department was automatically a member of the Chicago Association; but no one could become a member of the Association without joining and supporting a specific department or branch.

Before one goal was reached, Messer was proposing another. In his final report for 1888, he noted that the employment department had been brought into the Association office to protect the Y's reputation from those "who by not being thoroughly investigated have brought the Association into ill repute with businessmen"; that the boardinghouses were now being listed in the register only if "properly recommended"; and that Bible training work had been "reorganized entirely." He also succeeded in limiting the Sunday evening worship service, sparsely attended by women, to men only. At the first service after the adoption of this plan, he reported the attendance had increased to 434 men from 325 men and 60 women the previous week.

Among the work yet undone, Messer listed plans for a new building in the central part of the city better suited to the Association's new program, the organization of an Intercollegiate Department, the aggressive pursuit of funds to erect a proposed building on the West Side, and the finding of a successor for E. W. Bliss, the evangelist. "The spiritual work of the Madison Street Department is sufficiently large and important to require the services of at least one man," he said. ". . . The work does not need a preacher as much as an organizer and developer of the material we have at hand."

Messer was to find this spiritual leader in an unusual place— he was playing center field for Cap Anson's White Stockings (now the Cubs). His name was Billy Sunday.

Sunday had been center fielder for four championship White Stocking teams from 1883 to 1887. While in Chicago, he had taken up Christian work after being converted at an open-air revival meeting conducted by the Pacific Garden Mission in a vacant lot at the corner of State and Van Buren. He soon became interested in the YMCA and enrolled in the Y's Bible Training Class. He frequently gave talks before Y groups in cities where he was playing ball. After his first appearance on a platform in Chicago, the next day's paper reported "Centerfielder Billy Sunday made a three-base hit at Farwell Hall last night. There is no other way to express the success of his first appearance as an evangelist in Chicago." One of Sunday's favorite themes was that of "Earnestness in Christian Work." "I love to see a man in earnest in everything he does," he said, "and

W. A. (Billy) Sunday in his baseball uniform while he was a member of the Pittsburgh team.

God has no use for a milk-and-water man. To succeed in business, in a profession, or in athletics, you have got to be in earnest."

In 1888 Billy was sold to the Pittsburgh ball team, but he did not forget his pleasant times with the YMCA. In 1891 he secured his release from Philadelphia (where he had played after leaving Pittsburgh) and returned to take the post of religious director for the YMCA of Chicago at a salary of $83 per month. After his release from Philadelphia, Billy received an offer from Cincinnati to join the Redlegs at a salary of $500 per month. He turned it down. "You promised God to quit playing baseball," his wife told him when the offer was made, and he turned it down without debating the matter any further.

Billy Sunday worked from early in the morning to late at night for the YMCA. Often he walked to work to save money, and almost as often he went without lunch. To save money on new clothes, he dyed his old ones. "We have never had a man on our staff who was more consecrated, more deeply spiritual, and more self-sacrificing," Messer said. "He was especially strong in his personal effort among those who had fallen by the way." Sunday seemed to be everywhere—distributing tracts on street corners, seeking out alcoholics in saloons, getting speakers for the noon prayer meetings, leading prayer meetings himself, and even finding time to serve as chairman of the committee on summer athletics. His salary was raised to $1,200 per year and then to $1,500. But like Moody, Billy Sunday wanted to be an evangelist to all men and not just to young men. In 1894 he left the Chicago Association to join Dr. J. Wilbur Chapman, a famous evangelist of the time, and to begin the career that was to rank his name with those of Charles G. Finney and Dwight L. Moody in American religious history.

Messer was as active as Sunday in pushing both the religious and physical aspects of the Y program. Every report conscientiously recorded the number of "inquiries" and "converts" brought in by the Association's religious meetings, including the noon prayer meeting which had also become a service "for men only." Messer was a great believer in the efficacy of prayer. In November of his first year, he told the Board of Managers of his "strong conviction . . . intensified of late, of the necessity of deeper consecration and more earnest prayer on the part of our officers and members if we would be successful in the accomplishment of the large plans and projects which seem to have opened up before us. I am convinced that a great mistake

Bowling alley at the Bridgeport Department, organized in April of 1888.

is made when we lean simply on human wisdom or effort in the prosecution of such an important work as that committed to our charge in this city. God is able to move the hearts of men to generously respond to our needs." He was indefatigable in traveling among the city's churches with sermons, talks, and even—in 1895 when the Association was in financial difficulties —with an illustrated slide lecture seeking support for the Y's work.

The expansion of the physical and athletic program began within a month after his arrival. He persuaded the Board of Managers to rent an outdoor athletic ground at Division Street and Oakley Avenue "for the sum of $150" and to fix it up "at an expense of $150." A notice in the *Bulletin* invited members to take their choice from among the following sports (to be arranged if enough members were interested): Rambling Club, Walking Team, LaCrosse Club, Cycling, Swimming Party, Lawn Tennis Party, Croquet Party, Rowing Club, Cricket,

Football Team, Baseball Nine, Field Days for General Outdoor Exercise.

For swimming, reduced rates were secured at two indoor swimming pools. The West Side Baseball Park was rented two afternoons a week for baseball. The gym was so extensively patronized that it was necessary to hire an assistant to the superintendent. A characteristically forceful Messer note in the *Bulletin* put all these activities in perspective: "To a great many the idea is conveyed that the gymnasium is a place where young men are trained for acrobats, wrestlers, and prize fighters," he wrote. "This is not true. We desire to impress upon the minds of the public that the gymnasium of our Association is a health department and nothing else." To a newspaper reporter Messer said, "We work on the theory that the uniform development of a man conduces to his spiritual welfare. As his mind is elevated and his body strengthened, he naturally turns to a spiritual life of his own accord. At least, we think so and our influence is in that direction."

The development of the educational program was also accelerated. Although evening classes had been conducted in Farwell Hall since 1882, there was no educational director or trained supervisor. William Rainey Harper, the president of the new University of Chicago and a great advocate of adult education, was among those urging the YMCA to do more in this field. He told a banquet at the Madison Street Department (which the newspapers referred to as the "Central Department of the Y" for the first time) that there were a great many men in different lines of business who had not had an opportunity to finish their education in their youth but might do so if given the proper chance. Harper said that while these men might have too much pride "to go to night schools or anything of that kind" he was quite sure that "with proper urging" they would "gladly avail themselves of the opportunities offered by the Y."

Educational activities grew rapidly with the help of such endorsements. In 1893 Walter Wood was hired as a full-time educational director for the twenty-four evening classes and four University extension courses that were then being offered at the "Association College" in the Central Department. Instructors were drawn for the most part from the faculty at Armour Institute. Three years later, a day business school was opened with two instructors to teach bookkeeping, penmanship, business forms, commercial arithmetic, law, and such related courses as shorthand and typing.

Wood described the purposes of this educational program

Education through humor in the early days of the physical program. The illustration shown here portrayed the fate of the young man who thought it would be easy to lift the one-pound dumbbells 300 times.

F.M. HOWARTH

as five in number: (1) to offer a genuine attraction to the Association membership; (2) to provide for the practical educational training of young men; (3) to provide opportunity for intellectual culture; (4) to encourage helpful social intercourse among young men; and (5) to open an easy and natural way for the exercise of a positive Christian influence on the minds of young men who become students and club men.

A more specialized field of education in which Messer had been interested since his service at Peoria was that of professional training for YMCA workers and secretaries. The broadened program and highly charged atmosphere of activity under Messer made Chicago a magnet for young men interested in qualifying for the professional staff of the YMCA. A natural evolution of all this activity was the founding by Robert Weidensall in 1890 of the Chicago Training Institute as an outgrowth of the original Western Secretarial Institute at Lake Geneva. John W. Hansel was named general secretary of the training school (a title later changed to president), and in 1891 the Chicago school was recognized by the International Committee as one of two official training schools for YMCA secretaries. (The other school—at Northfield, Massachusetts—had been founded by the indomitable Moody.) The Chicago training school (later George Williams College) was not a direct interest of the Chicago Association. But it is doubtful if it would have come into being without the interest and support of members of the Chicago Association and the stimulus provided by the activities it generated.

This galaxy of new ideas and enterprises initiated by Messer during his first months in office awakened additional public interest in the Young Men's Christian Association of Chicago. A reporter for the *Chicago Journal* was instructed to visit the Y and give that paper's readers a report on what he found. "In

YMCA secretaries on Ravenswood Athletic Field, 1898.

the reading room, I found a fine-looking lot of men intent upon the periodical literature which is supplied with a lavish hand," he wrote the next day. "The parlors have lately been refurnished and as I entered, my feet sank in the heavy Brussels carpet (a gift of Mrs. John V. Farwell, Sr.) and I felt like sitting down. . . . The furniture is new and rich, one of the most prominent features being the new piano. . . . The rear wall of the back parlor is covered with an oaken bookcase that is filled with the best of books. 'Twas with a feeling of reluctance that the reporter left the parlors."

But if the reporter was satisfied, Messer was not. Less than a month later, he was urging the Board to put forth "a consecrated effort" to secure "a desirable site for a new Central building and raise the money for its purchase." In this plea, Messer was echoing the sentiments of the Association's former president, E. G. Keith, who had put the need for a new building as "most urgent" back in 1881. Keith, who in 1889 was a member of the Board of Trustees, backed Messer's plea. He called the Central building "a discredit to the Christian people of our city and a drawback to the work." Cyrus McCormick also urged immediate action. He said he was "ashamed of the Chicago building after visiting all the principal Y buildings in the United States. The public expects better things of us." To this, E. S. Albro, another trustee, added, "We can and all will help. Those who cannot bring an ox or a sheep will at least offer a pair of turtledoves or two young pigeons." What the Association received, however, was far more than an ox or sheep—it was an unexpected bequest of $50,000 from the manufacturer and merchant John Crerar in the same will in which Crerar established John Crerar Library of Science and Technology, now located in its own building at the northwest corner of Randolph and Michigan.

MONTHLY BULLETIN

Summer Athletics
and Outdoor Sports....

FOR THE MEMBERS OF THE

Young Men's Christian Association

OF CHICAGO.

ATHLETIC GROUNDS.

A heading from the *Bulletin* announcing a program of outdoor summer athletics.

122

CHAPTER 6

"The Most Stately Temple"

THE BEQUEST OF $50,000 from John Crerar was for the general purposes of the Association and could be used for any purpose approved by the Board of Managers. The sentiment of the Board was quickly and unanimously expressed; it wanted the Crerar gift to be used as the nucleus of a building fund. Once this decision was reached, two friends of Crerar, who remained anonymous, added $25,000 each to his bequest to make the total available $100,000. With this formidable sum in hand, a building committee was appointed of N. S. Bouton, chairman, S. M. Moore, E. G. Keith, A. L. Coe, Cyrus H. McCormick, Jr., John V. Farwell, Jr., Henry M. Hubbard, and James L. Houghteling. They called in as special advisors from outside the Board of Managers three young men who were to become future leaders of Chicago—Byron L. Smith, John J. Mitchell, and Owen F. Aldis. The first two were bankers and the third a specialist in Loop real estate.

As one of its first acts, the committee voted to exchange the property which faced Madison Street for similar frontage at 19 South La Salle, formerly known as the Andrews block. This would permit the erection of a building facing both La Salle and Arcade Court, the narrow street running along the south edge of the property. On this lot, the committee recommended that a building fourteen stories high be erected. The plan was to make the building pay for itself. One floor in front and six in the rear would be used for Association purposes; thirteen stories in front and eight in the rear, including all the best office space, would be available for tenants. The architect for the new building was to be William LeBaron Jenney, who only a few years before had designed and erected in Chicago the world's first skyscraper, the Home Insurance Building.

The cost of the new building and property together were estimated at more than one million dollars. Of this amount, it was expected $400,000 would come from contributions, $175,000 from sale of the Madison Street property, and $600,000 in thirty-year bonds sold to the First National Bank. The bonds were to be secured by a mortgage on the property (then worth $50 a square foot). By December of 1891, $200,000 had been raised; four months later the total was $325,000. The fund as finally completed totaled $408,123.

Most of this money was secured in large sums by the personal solicitation of a team of Messer and Farwell or Messer and McCormick. The routine of Messer during this period was to call at McCormick's office in the morning and go with him to call on McCormick's friends. In the afternoon he would go to the office of Farwell—or occasionally another member of the Board—and call on his friends. The size of the subscriptions indicates the effectiveness of this technique. Of the final sum of $408,123, only $9,123 was contributed in sums of less than $1,000. There were ninety-eight pledges of $1,000 each and thirteen of $5,000 each. When the drive slowed in the financial panic of 1893, Mc-Cormick offered to raise a dollar for every dollar raised by any other member of the Association.

As the rear section of the new building was planned for the same site as a portion of the third Farwell Hall (Madison Street building), it was necessary to wreck the existing structure before starting on the new building. A farewell service was held in Farwell Hall in May of 1892, and from that time until the opening of the new building, the Chicago Association was forced to operate in makeshift quarters.

It was hoped the new building would be completed by November of 1893, but construction was delayed by the 1893 depression and the consequent lack of funds which prevented the finishing of the interiors of the upper floors. Although the building was formally opened on November 11, 1893, the ninth, tenth, eleventh, twelfth, and tower floors were still not completed. So that too much revenue would not be lost through the failure to have the space ready, an outside syndicate was formed among the Board members to supply funds for finishing each of these floors. When the ninth floor was finished and the syndicate reimbursed, another group put up funds for the tenth floor. This procedure was followed until the building was completed finally in 1895.

The lack of plaster on the upper floors could not keep the young Association from celebrating in its new building on New Year's Day of 1894. A reception was held in the newly furnished parlors and library on the third floor and the guests taken on a tour of everything from the engine room and natatorium to the unfinished tower. The hostesses at the reception included the most famous names in Chicago at the time: Mrs. Philip D. Armour, Mrs. Emmons Blaine, Mrs. J. V. Farwell,

Mrs. F. C. Farwell, Mrs. James L. Houghteling, Mrs. Cyrus H. McCormick, Jr., Mrs. A. C. McClurg, Mrs. L. W. Messer, Mrs. William Blair, Mrs. Edward Blair, Mrs. Harlow N. Higinbotham, Mrs. William McCormick, Mrs. Mahlon Ogden, and Miss Elizabeth Isham. Among the visitors were men who could recall the earliest and most obscure days of the Chicago Association—including Samuel Dexter Ward, who had organized the first YMCA of Chicago in 1853, and John V. Farwell, Sr., Benjamin F. Jacobs, and Simeon W. King, all of whom had been charter members of the Chicago Association.

A yellowed clipping from an unidentified newspaper has provided a record of this reception and the impression it made. The reception, said the reporter, was "a very different affair from what would naturally be associated in the public mind with the opening of a YMCA house. There were no lean and sanctimonious young men with white cravats, long faces, and patronizing manners at the door. There were no tedious sermons or deep lectures. Out in La Salle Street, carriages lined up as if for a great society event. A number of sturdy and congenial young men waited just inside the entrance to direct visitors to the reception rooms which were aglow with electric lights and decorated with palms and flowers that gave out a pleasing fragance. . . . Off in the library, Lyon's orchestra played *Two Little Girls in Blue* and other popular airs. The Linden male quartet sang rollicking songs. Back in a large room refreshments were served, where the men drank a white frappé from red cups. It was a very enjoyable and eminently proper occasion."

Following the reception, the guests were able to inspect any of the facilities of "the world's most costly YMCA building" which might interest them. These included the basement bowling alleys; a swimming pool on the first floor; the reading room and general offices on the second floor; reading parlors, recrea-

The Association Building at 19 South La Salle Street. It was dedicated on January 1, 1894. The tower was removed when three floors were added.

One of the parlors in the new Association Building, showing the arched windows which may still be seen from the street.

tion room, writing room, magazine room, and library on the third floor; lockers, baths, dressing rooms, and steam baths on the fourth floor; and the gymnasium on the fifth (with a special room for physical examinations). The gymnasium extended up through the sixth floor; on the second-floor level was a combination indoor running track and gallery for spectators at gymnastic events. A corner of this floor had been equipped as a dark room for the Central Department's photography club. The classrooms, restaurant, and barbershop were on the seventh floor. Above the unfinished floors reserved for offices were classrooms for woodworking and machine tools on the twelfth floor, and handball and tennis courts plus a chemistry laboratory on the thirteenth floor. In the tower there was a small observatory for studying the stars, which in that pre-neon era could still be seen from Chicago's Loop.

The successful completion of the new Central Department building and Association headquarters brought that increased public recognition which is always a concomitant of success. At the first religious services in the new building, many young men had to be turned away because there was not enough room to seat them. *Harper's Weekly*, taking notice of the new Chicago Association Building, commented editorially that "From whatever side we approach the magnificent edifice the Young Men's Christian Association has been rearing, we shall find it the most stately temple to the power and prowess of unsectarian Christianity erected in modern times." It was no cause for surprise, then, that the *Tribune* reporter who attended the first annual meeting in the new building reported that when Messer arose, "the noise which everyone made . . . indicated that he must be an exceedingly popular fellow."

The growth of the Chicago Association was, of course, only an accelerated version of the development of the entire YMCA movement during these years. In a quarter of a century, the YMCA had grown from 64 associations to 1,373; its total membership had increased from 15,000 to a total of 227,000. Only three decades earlier the work had been largely in big cities and had consisted chiefly of religious work of a missionary nature. In 1893 the YMCA counted, in addition to its more than 1,000 general associations, over 400 college groups, 97 railroad branches, and a large number of other specialized departments.

The Central Department of the Chicago Association was the chief benefactor of the new building and the extensive new quarters it provided. Attendance at the gymnasium, reading room, swimming pool, and running track often reached 600 in a single evening. The first executive secretary of the Central Department was Daniel Sloan, who chose as his special assistant an outstanding young graduate of that year's class at Northwestern named James F. Oates. In reporting the addition of the new assistant to the staff, Messer told the Board of Managers that Oates had been president of the college Y association, a prominent athlete, the leader in the recent religious movement at the University, the Class Day orator, and "I believe is the most popular student at that institution." When Sloan retired in 1898, Oates was named his successor. Although Oates served only until 1904, the Central Department flourished under his leadership. His scholarly articles in YMCA publications contributed much to the development of new program ideas and techniques on a national level. He was also an early advocate of a vigorous extension of YMCA work among boys. Among the staff working at Central with Oates was a young secretary named S. Wirt Wiley, later to be a leader in the work of the National Council of YMCA's.

In addition to finishing its new building, the Chicago Association had been busy during 1893 with a program of special services for visitors to the World's Columbian Exposition in Jackson Park. A World's Fair headquarters was set up in the Hotel Curtis, an information bureau established to recommend boardinghouses for young men, an exhibit of YMCA work set up in the Liberal Arts building at the exposition, and regular religious services conducted during the summer. The Fifty-fifth Street Department converted a part of its building to a dormitory for Fair visitors—the first time the YMCA of Chicago could offer dormitory facilities since the burning of the original Farwell Hall.

With the Central Department successfully established in adequate quarters, the Board of Managers and Messer next turned their attention to the extension and development of the branches provided for under the Metropolitan Plan. This work fell into four categories: the general branches (such as that proposed for the West Side), the railroad branches, foreign language departments, and the newly organized (1890) Intercollegiate Department composed of student associations at the various colleges in the Chicago area.

The first ten years' operation under the Metropolitan Plan may fairly be described as a period of experimentation in an effort to work out successful techniques for fostering new departments. There were as many failures as successes. It was quickly discovered that something more than a petition from a group of well-meaning citizens was needed to assure the establishment and continued operation of a YMCA department. Many of the early departments found themselves unrealistically in debt and had to appeal to the Board of Managers for assistance. Some could be rescued; others could not.

The Bridgeport Department had been closed on May 1, 1891, when the Chicago City Railway Company withdrew its

The Fifty-fifth Street Railway Department, where a dormitory was established for visitors to the World's Columbian Exposition in 1893.

annual contribution. The department had been operating in a rented building in a poverty-ridden section of the city and there was no hope of developing other resources within the Bridgeport area. At Pullman, a department which had been opened in December of 1889 became a victim of the disruption caused by the Pullman strike in the summer of 1894 and had to be closed the following year. Nearby, in South Chicago, another department had been established in 1890 after four ministers spoke to the Board of Managers about the need for a YMCA in an area where there were "plenty of young men, noble young men" but also "plenty of saloons not so noble." (It was estimated there were 3,000 young men in the area and 300 saloons—a ratio of one saloon to every ten young men.) This department was dependent upon contributions from the Illinois Steel Company (later to become a division of U. S. Steel) and on limited support from neighborhood businessmen. Although it survived the depression of 1893 and a large fire in the steel mills the same year, it finally had to be discontinued in 1897. Another department which failed was that organized at the Millard Avenue Methodist Church in November of 1894 to serve the area west of Western Avenue and south of Twelfth Street. It was discontinued in December of 1896.

A department was added by annexation in 1897 when the Englewood YMCA—organized eleven years before when the area was not yet a part of Chicago—voted to end its separate existence and affiliate under the Metropolitan Plan. It brought with it a burden of overwhelming weight; its quarters in a converted house were inadequate for its program and the house was sagging under a mortgage for almost half its value. After two years of wrestling with the building problem, the Englewood group voted to disband temporarily—a decision which was reached with the understanding that work in Englewood would be resumed as soon as funds could be procured for new quarters. Many years later this commitment was to be honored.

In 1900 the Board of Managers extended the Metropolitan Plan to Roseland, where 220 men had signed up as members of a new department; this branch also had to be discontinued in 1904 because the community at that time lacked sufficient population and means to support it.

The record of these years before 1900 was by no means only a chronology of failures. In many instances the difficulties were met and overcome. An outstanding example was the West Side Department (now Duncan), for which an organizational meeting had been held in 1887 and a fund drive started in 1889. Unable to get enough support for a building, several of the groups from the West Side petitioned for the immediate estab-

Parlor and gymnasium of the California Avenue Department (now Duncan). The blackboard identifies the physical instructor as W. A. (Billy) Sunday.

lishment of a department in the vicinity of California Avenue and Madison Street in December of 1889 so that an organized program could be set up for the boys in the vicinity. This permission was granted, and in January of 1890 the California Avenue Department was opened in rented quarters at 1225 West Madison. A gymnasium and a hall for religious meetings were located on the ground floor, while the upper two floors were devoted to reading rooms and parlors for receptions and smaller meetings. Much of the impetus for the organization of the California Avenue Department had come from the King's Daughters, an organization of women representing many of the churches on the West Side. After the opening of the department, these women reorganized themselves as the Women's Auxiliary and continued their active interest in helping underprivileged boys from the neighborhood.

Meanwhile, another group from the West Side continued their efforts to organize a "Central Department of the West Side." The original site chosen for such a department was considered undesirable after work was started at California Avenue, and a further complication arose over the question of determining boundaries for the two departments. This dilemma was not resolved until December of 1891, when the Board of Managers voted to rent larger space at Madison and Paulina streets and merge California Avenue with a new West Side Department. Within a year even these new quarters had been outgrown and the West Side Department members were seeking $45,000 to purchase the La Salle Club building at 542 West Monroe, which had originally been the home of Charles N. Holden, a Chicago lumber dealer. (Holden's son, William N. Holden, was to serve as a member of the Board of Trustees for many years and his grandson, Charles R. Holden, as a member of the Board of Managers.) The Holden house was a large mansion of white

La Salle Club building at 542 West Monroe Street, home of the West Side Department after merger with California Avenue.

marble with a special wing that had been added by the La Salle Club. It contained a bowling alley, bathrooms, a lecture hall, and a room suitable for conversion to a gymnasium.

Learning of this opportunity on the West Side, Messer interrupted his fund raising for the Association building to work with a community committee on the West Side in raising the necessary $45,000. Aided by a substantial gift of one-third the total needed ($16,000) from Jacob Beidler, another West Side lumber merchant, Messer and a group of West Side ministers and businessmen secured pledges for the additional money in six weeks. By the fall of 1893 the West Side was offering a program of activities comparable to that at Central. Evening classes were given in bookkeeping, shorthand, vocal music, penmanship, geometry, and algebra, and facilities were provided for university extension courses.

135

One of the most unusual and most generous propositions ever to be put before the Board of Managers resulted in the opening of a new department in Ravenswood (now the Wilson Avenue Department). Robert J. Bennett, a Ravenswood businessman, offered the YMCA the rent-free use of a new building he was constructing at Ravenswood and Wilson avenues if the Board of Managers would organize a branch of the Chicago Association in the area. Bennett, a stern Puritan who was a direct descendant of a Pilgrim family that had settled at Plymouth, had been disturbed by reports there might be Sunday games at public athletic fields in Ravenswood. He wanted the YMCA to provide alternate athletic facilities under proper supervision. His offer was accepted and the new Ravenswood Department dedicated on December 8, 1891. Bennett was joined in his vigorous support of the new YMCA by David Paul Brown, an energetic young man who had attempted to run a private bicycle track and athletic field in Ravenswood some years before. With the support of Bennett and Brown, the department grew rapidly. Its first report recorded a membership of 166, and the secretary reported: "The commodious building is attracting large numbers of young men, the gymnasium being especially attractive; the classes are increasing weekly and all lines of work are being rapidly developed. The Gospel meetings on Sunday afternoons have an average attendance of over fifty."

With departments firmly organized and generously supported on both the North and West sides, a meeting was held in the spring of 1895 to plan a YMCA department in Hyde Park on the South Side. The organization of this branch was to be a model for others to come. It may be inferred that the careful planning in Hyde Park was a reflection of the experience gained from the failures in other parts of the city. Before signing up any members, the Hyde Park founders appointed a committee of twenty to raise $100 each for operating expenses. By June these funds were available, and Albert W. Harris appeared before the Board of Managers to ask for the authorization to organize the Hyde Park Department. When the authority was granted, the Hyde Park Committee of Management leased a fourteen-room house at Fifty-fifth Street and Monroe Avenue (now Kenwood) for thirty-one months at $100 a month—sixteen members of the local committee personally guaranteeing the rent. Almost 300 men were signed up as founding members and the department formally opened with a religious service on October 20, 1895. Its first executive secretary was George C. Blakeslee of Rock Island, but in 1896 the post was taken over by Peter C. Atkinson, who continued to direct the work for twenty years.

A championship track team of the Ravenswood YMCA.

The railroad branches were a special problem because of the rapidly changing nature of the neighborhoods in which they were located. In 1888 Messer had found "the most encouraging work of any railway department at present" in the Forty-eighth Street Department near the shops of the Rock Island railroad. But by 1891 conditions had changed so radically that the problems of providing adequate management became insuperable and the Forty-eighth Street branch was discontinued on May 1 of that year.

A similar situation developed at the Sixteenth Street Railroad Department. This branch, located on Canal near the Sixteenth Street viaduct, was supported by contributions from the Burlington, Wisconsin Central, and Chicago & Alton lines. As industries displaced homes near the center of the city, this location proved to be a poor one. A spokesman for the department told the Board of Managers that it was almost impossible to reach "the floating population among whom the work is done . . . as scarcely any of the men live within a half a mile of the rooms." This department was discontinued February 1, 1891.

Both the Kinzie Street and Garfield Boulevard (Fifty-fifth Street) railroad departments had a more propitious sponsorship. Marvin Hughitt, president of the Chicago and North Western Railway Company, secured from his board of directors in 1891 a pledge of $15,000 for a new building for the Kinzie Street Department if the employees were sufficiently interested to raise an additional $5,000. Three of the directors promised further to purchase the site for the new building and donate it to the Association. Robert Quayle, superintendent of machinery for the railroad, headed up an enthusiastic committee of rail workers who obtained $6,500 in subscriptions from 1,550 men. On October 28, 1897, a new two-story and basement building for the Kinzie Street activities was dedicated and given the name of the

The 1903 basketball team at Roseland (now the 111th Street YMCA).

Chicago and North Western Railway Department of the YMCA of Chicago. The facilities included a reception hall, library, reading room, recreation room, barber shop, basement bowling alley and baths, an auditorium that could seat 250, and even a special area for "bicycle storage." A first floor restaurant was open day and night; a dormitory of twenty beds was provided on the second floor. The executive secretary during this period of growth was William Cook, the senior member among the secretaries in the Chicago Association during these years.

The Garfield Boulevard (Fifty-fifth Street) Railroad Department was generously supported by both the Pennsylvania Railroad and by neighborhood businessmen. A committee from these groups had raised funds for a new building in 1889 and completed it the same year. A Ladies Auxiliary raised the money to provide the furnishings. An extensive program was carried out, including four religious meetings each Sunday (a Swedish Bible Class, a boys' meeting, a prayer meeting, and a general service for young men). In 1899 the name was changed to the Pennsylvania Railroad Department as all the members were from among the company's employees and the Pennsylvania was the only rail line supporting the department.

Although the boys' work at Fifty-fifth Street had to be discontinued in 1891, there still exists a memento of the good it accomplished in a letter from a grateful beneficiary:

DEAR FRIENDS:

Having been called to leave school to go and work for my uncle I send this in as my resignation paper. I do not think I will be able to attend meetings of our Branch for some time anyway.

Thank God for what the Branch of the 55th Street YMCA has done for me in the way of stopping me from swearing, smoking, and going for liquors of all kinds, but thank God I am now leading a Christian life and on a straight road to heaven where, sometime, it shall be my home.

I remain,

Your obedient servant,

———————————

The *Bulletin*, which reprinted the letter, did not give the author's name but did tell its readers that he was only fifteen years old. In 1897 branches were opened at the Polk Street station (discontinued after a short time) and at the Dearborn Street station. Another department was opened at the instigation of the Grand Trunk Railway at the Elsdon junction (now Fifty-first Street and St. Louis Avenue). The railroad offered a site and half the cost of the building if the Chicago Association would provide the other half. This offer was accepted and a new building was soon opened "seven miles out" on the Grand Trunk where railroad officials reported "three hundred men had been spending six to thirty-six hours with no door open to them except that of the saloon."

The predominance of foreign-born workers among Chicago's population created both a problem and an opportunity for the Chicago Association. David Jones and the Yokefellows had pioneered with aid for the Chinese. A special department of YMCA activities for Scandinavian immigrants had been established in the 1880's. And in 1889 a department was organized for Germans in a rented building at Wells and Carl (now Burton Place), described in the *Bulletin* as "in the center of the German population of that part of the city." The German program was attractive to a small but loyal group (whose brass band was in frequent demand for entertainment at other departments) but there was no source of funds for such specialized activity. As Americanization proceeded, the German-born members overcame their language difficulties and in 1896 the German department was disbanded, its members being absorbed into the regular departments.

Another area of expansion during the 1890's was that of student work. In 1888 a group of students at Chicago Medical College had petitioned for the organization of a YMCA, and shortly after the arrival of Messer a student association was formed at the college. In 1891, following a study and report by a special committee, all student work was brought together in an "Intercollegiate Department" and the Chicago Medical College association was brought into this new department. (One of the comments of the committee was that "The students at one of our Theological Seminaries are so impressed with the needs of the medical students in particular, that they say unless we look after them speedily, they will undertake to do so. We think this would be unfortunate, because the medical students

German Department of the YMCA of Chicago at Wells and Carl (now Burton Place). Sign over the door reads "Christlicher Verein Junger Maenner."

would be likely to resent any interference on the part of the 'theologs' as impertinence. . . .") Within a few years after the establishment of the Intercollegiate Department, student YMCA associations were established at Armour Institute, The Chicago College of Dental Surgery, the University of Illinois College of Dentistry, the College of Physicians and Surgeons, Hahnemann Medical College, Northwestern Medical School, the Northwestern Law, Pharmacy and Dental Schools (the two groups were then on separate downtown campuses), Rush Medical College, and the University of Chicago.

As general secretary for the Intercollegiate Department, the Chicago Association in 1897 hired William J. Parker, a young graduate of the University of Minnesota who was willing to accept as one stipulation of his employment that he must raise his own salary! Parker soon made it evident that this requirement—or any other—held no terrors for him. Six months after his arrival, he was able to report that all bills of the Intercollegiate Department (including his own salary) had been paid and that funds for all local budgets were raised. This prosperity was not achieved at the expense of the principal purpose of his work; in one month he arranged for forty-two devotional meetings and twenty Bible sessions. The financial acumen and energy displayed by the new Intercollegiate secretary were quickly recognized as extraordinary. In 1902 Parker was promoted from his post with the Intercollegiate Department to that of business secretary (business manager) for the entire Chicago Association. As a leader in the professional staff of the Association, he was to make a series of impressive contributions to its growth.

The turn of the century in 1900 found the Young Men's Christian Association of Chicago well set on the course it was to follow in the future. John V. Farwell, Jr. had served as president for the ten important years from 1884 to 1894 that resulted in the hiring of Messer and completion of the new Association Building. Farwell was succeeded by Henry M. Hubbard, a Chicago stove manufacturer who served from 1895 to 1900. In 1900 the Association elected James H. Eckels, former comptroller of the United States and president of the Commercial National Bank, as its new president.

Eckels could look at the balance sheet of the YMCA of Chicago as it faced the new century with considerable satisfaction. Membership was at an all-time high—6,463. There were five general branches, four railroad branches, and eighteen student associations. They listed these activities as part of their four-fold program:

Spiritual. A total of 1,513 religious meetings held with attendance of 70,608; 1,064 Bible classes with an attendance of 20,165.

Mental. Fifty-three different classes were offered by 32 instructors drawn from Chicago area colleges and high schools. There were 12 reading rooms open throughout the city and 39 public lectures had been sponsored by the Y.

Social. An average of more than 3,000 young men a day used the rooms of the various YMCA's.

Physical. Six gymnasiums had a total attendance of over 71,000. More than 200,000 baths had been given and more than 51,000 men had used Central's swimming pool. The Ravenswood track team had won the championship of the Central Section Athletic League and its basketball team had defeated that of Yale University in an exhibition game.

The popularity of basketball was evidence of the contribution which the YMCA was making to a recreational program for young people. The game of basketball had been originated at the Springfield, Massachusetts, YMCA College in 1891 by a physical instructor, Dr. James Naismith, in order to meet a need for an indoor sport that would permit group participation and teach team play. Four years later another YMCA physical director—William Morgan of Holyoke, Massachusetts—devised and introduced the game of volleyball.

The value of property owned by the Chicago Association amounted to approximately $2,000,000, and the Association Building reported 98 per cent of its office space was rented. More than a hundred men a day were using dormitories and eating facilities of the railroad departments. Nearly a thousand men each year were being placed in jobs through the Association's employment office.

Evidence of the growing influence of the Association was also to be found in the unexpected bequests it received from outsiders who wished to support its program. In one year the Association received grants totaling $40,000 from five benefactors—not one of whom was known to any member of the Association.

The Y's leaders were also successful in persuading women to increase their support of the YMCA departments through the organization of auxiliaries at Hyde Park, Ravenswood, Roseland, West Side, and the North Western Railway. All these auxiliaries contributed to the furnishing of the buildings and often gave special dinners for members and their guests.

Recognition was also coming from outside Chicago. In 1898 Messer was asked to be one of the principal speakers at the 14th World's Conference of YMCA's in Basle, Switzerland. And in 1901 the educational program of the Chicago Association won the first national award of merit in this field.

The football (soccer) team from Ravenswood (now Wilson Avenue) in 1893. The insignia on the sweaters was typical of the wide variety used before the adoption of the familiar red triangle.

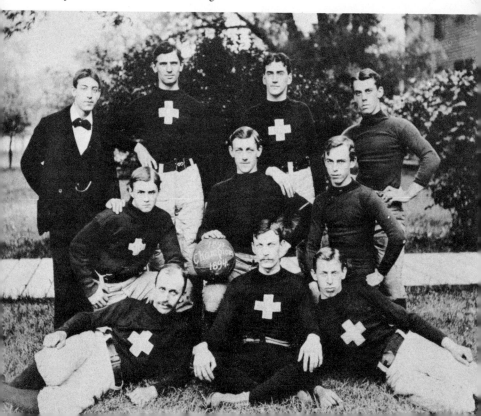

This record of accomplishment did not prevent Messer from jotting down even greater goals for the new century. Among them he listed these:

(1) An endowment for rescue work of the destitute and unemployed to be operated as a mission rather than with membership fees.

(2) A dormitory with living accommodations for Y members only.

(3) A special department for boys from twelve to sixteen. "The latest scientific studies of the religious life indicate that the average age of conversion of male members of our churches is a fraction over sixteen years," he wrote. "This startling fact would indicate the necessity of a concentration of intelligent practical Christian effort upon boys before that age is reached."

Messer added one further conclusion to these notes. "In Chicago we have the opportunity of becoming in the future perhaps the greatest Association center of the world," he wrote.

It was an opportunity that the YMCA of Chicago was not to let pass.

CHAPTER 7

"A Million-Dollar Town"

THE METROPOLITAN Plan of organization speeded the expansion of the YMCA movement in other cities as well as in Chicago. In 1891 the International Convention at Kansas City passed a resolution endorsing the principle of the Metropolitan Plan and making it a matter of policy that only one YMCA organization be recognized in cities "where such Associations already exist." Ten years after this resolution was passed, the YMCA could count ten associations organized under the Metropolitan Plan. These ten metropolitan associations carried on one-seventh of the work of the movement in the United States, owned one-third of all YMCA property, and employed more than two hundred professional workers.

With the parallel development of activities on the national level through railroad associations, student groups, YMCA's serving Negroes, and special branches in the Army and the Navy, a conflict of interest soon began to develop between the large metropolitan associations which sought to preserve the traditional local autonomy they had enjoyed and the International Committee which was naturally seeking closer and more direct contacts with all the branches of the YMCA throughout the United States. Messer, who with McBurney was the most able of the local general secretaries and administrator of one of the most successful local associations, emerged as spokesman for the big city associations. Robert Cary Morse, efficient director of work on the national level and general secretary of the International Committee, defended the prerogatives of that committee as the national co-ordinating body for the YMCA.

For several years a great debate over the delineation of authority between the local metropolitan associations and the International Committee was to echo through all the proceedings of the Young Men's Christian Association of North America. C. S. Bishop, general secretary of the Kansas City YMCA, was to describe it in his biography of Messer as "analagous to the early Jefferson-Hamilton discussions about government. On the one side, Messer was the thorough-going democrat, unschooled but refined, who had risen from plebeian small-town surroundings to outstanding leadership in a big city and had climbed from the bottom to the top in his vocation, defending the principle of local self-government and state rights. On the other side [Morse], was the favored, city-bred patrician, highly educated but inexperienced in local Association work . . . favoring a national form of the successful but highly centralized commercial and industrial type of organization."

In an effort to arrive at a common policy, Messer and Illinois State Secretary I. E. Brown called a conference at the Chicago Beach Hotel in April of 1899. It was attended by six secretaries of large city associations, seven state secretaries, seven International secretaries, and representatives of *Association Men* (published by the International Committee) and of the Secretarial Institute and Training School. This conference forwarded a resolution to Morse asserting the right of each local Association to "exist as an independent unit" and relegating the International and state committees to the role of "independent supervisory agencies." A measure of the emotion surrounding the discussion of this issue may be found in the resolution, which referred to "undesirable and even dangerous tendencies" in the policies of the International Committee. The conferees concluded, however, with the conciliatory statement that they believed the problem could be solved and they added that they were joining "our Association brethren in earnest prayer that by the blessing of God this consummation may be reached."

When the national convention was held in Grand Rapids, Michigan, the following month, a group of resolutions was passed intending to clarify the relations of the local associations and the International and state committees. The resolutions proved subject to so many interpretations that a committee of seven—headed by Cyrus McCormick—was appointed to study the whole question of association relationships and report back to the next convention. The appointment of McCormick, who was also serving on the board of the International Committee, served to emphasize the difficult situation in which Messer found himself. McCormick was a strong supporter of the International Committee's work; in the months that followed, Messer was often in the position of being at odds with the man who was one of his chief supporters in the local field. To the credit of both men, there is nothing in the record to indicate this dispute over principle ever overflowed into personal animosity—or even into disagreements severe enough to impair their efficient work together on behalf of the Chicago Association.

The point at issue was so fundamental to the organization

of the various associations, however, that no amount of good will could keep it from erupting over and over again. In October of 1900 it was necessary to call a meeting of forty-two YMCA leaders in Philadelphia to attempt a new interpretation and definition of the Grand Rapids resolutions. Messer presented the principal paper at this meeting. In his own words, it "called attention to the increasing administrative and authoritative tendencies of the International Committee and set forth how these tendencies might be overcome." The Philadelphia conference produced no agreement; so wide was the gap separating those present that all papers presented were destroyed to keep the friction over this administrative issue from spoiling the Boston Jubilee convention in 1901.

Meanwhile, the Board of Managers of the Chicago Association was seeking to halt the practice of the International Committee in dealing directly with the railroad branches for which the Chicago Board considered itself responsible. In May the Board passed a resolution requesting the International and state committees "to send all blanks intended for reports from departments of the Association through the office of the Board of Managers." This request was at first ignored; after a reminder was sent on July 15, Messer received a reply from Morse in which Morse said he felt it wise to wait for the Boston convention to rule on the matter.

The issue was pointed up further when J. M. Dudley, secretary of the Dearborn Station Railroad Department, refused to conform to the wishes of the Board of Managers and insisted on sending his reports directly to the International Committee. It was finally necessary for the Board to pass a special resolution directing Dudley "to conform to the plan under which his department was an integral part of the Chicago Association" and "to have no communication with the railroad companies supporting his department except through or with the approval of the Board of Managers" and "to send no reports . . . save through the Board."

This question of supervising the railroad branches was more complex in Chicago than elsewhere because of the number of railroads which had their company headquarters in Chicago. The railroad work had been instituted originally on a national scale and the railroads generally preferred a system-wide organization. But the plan of organization which might be best for a department at a small-town division headquarters of the railroad was not necessarily the most beneficial for departments located in the same city as the executive offices. In Chicago, for example, the railroad departments had not been established as part of the national program but rather by local agreements between the Chicago Association and the executive officers and boards of directors of the various railroads with headquarters in the city. Also, Messer foresaw that if an exception to the authority vested in the Association under the Metropolitan Plan was made in the case of the railroad branches, other exceptions might be demanded in the future. This would have subjected the authority of the local associations to constant challenges and have vitiated the principle involved in the Kansas City resolution.

At the Boston convention, Messer secured passage of an additional resolution reaffirming the Grand Rapids statement and authorizing McCormick's committee (which was increased in membership and thereafter known as the "Committee of 21") to continue its study of association relationships. This action did not clarify the line of authority to be followed in the case of the railroad departments in Chicago. As a result, it was not long before the Chicago Association was pressing Morse to acknowledge its authority over the railroad departments organized as part of the YMCA of Chicago.

On October 25 Messer wrote Morse that the International Committee, by continuing to send report blanks directly to the railroad departments when requested by the Board of Managers not to do so, was "directly declining to grant an official request which the Chicago Association wishes to put into immediate effect. If you find it necessary to disregard this request, such action is contrary to the understanding of this Association as to its plans of organization and its relation to the International Committee." Morse replied with an alternate suggestion that the recourse of the Chicago Association lay in a constitutional change and added that he did not think it within his authority to change the procedure on reports. Messer must have replied to this in rather plain language (the letter is missing), for on December 4 Morse suddenly capitulated to the Chicago position:

"The International Committee will have no objection to sending through the office of the Board of Managers of the Chicago Association all blanks for reports to the several departments of the Association, such of course being the desire of each department," Morse wrote. "Possibly a request to that effect from each department addressed to the committee would have been the natural method of bringing about the desired result, but it does not now seem necessary to impose that burden on you or on them, and therefore the committee is sending the enclosed letter to each of your departments." The letter which Morse enclosed instructed each department within the Chicago Association to send all future reports through the Board of Managers.

These direct instructions to all local departments, even in acknowledging the International Committee's withdrawal from its previous position, provoked an official reproach signed by James H. Eckels, then president of the Chicago Association.

Although expressing satisfaction with the new policy of the
International Committee, Eckels characterized its action in sending letters of instruction to each of the departments as "unofficial, ill-advised, unnecessary, and reflecting on the authority
of the Board of Managers of this Association; [and] a menace
to the unity of this Association. The YMCA of Chicago is in
fact so united that its departments concur in objecting to the
action of the International Committee in sending this letter."

The great debate continued throughout 1902. In April a
letter signed by three local secretaries who opposed Messer's
view was circulated throughout the United States. Messer was
so disturbed by this attack that he wrote a fifteen-page letter to
Cyrus McCormick citing thirty-four instances in which he had
been misquoted or considered his position incorrectly inter-
preted. The following month he published his famous pamphlet,
Association Relationships, in which he traced the origins and
history of the dispute and set forth his own position with great
clarity. An unofficial committee was then formed to raise funds
for printing and distributing this pamphlet throughout the
membership of the YMCA movement in North America.

Messer's principal conclusions in *Association Relationships*
were these:

1. The local association is the original and independent unit
in the brotherhood of associations. . . . This principle applies to
railroad, college, army, and navy associations as well as to the city
association.

2. The metropolitan association . . . is an independent association unit. Whether and how long the departments or branches
shall continue to have direct representation in state and international
conventions is for such conventions . . . to determine [but] whether
the . . . branches of the metropolitan association shall have direct

official relationships to the State and International Committee is to be determined, in each case, by the metropolitan association. [A side issue was that of determining convention representation for branches of a metropolitan association.]

3. The relation of the state organization to the local association is purely advisory and not authoritative.

4. The International Committee also represents the local associations. Like the state committees, its relation to the associations is purely advisory and not authoritative.

With another quadrennial convention scheduled for Buffalo in 1904, a subcommittee of six from the Committee of 21 met at the Stratford Hotel in Chicago in 1903 in an attempt to resolve the dispute before it was brought to the convention floor. This committee had on its agenda:

1. Relationship of the International Committee and state committees to the railroad work.

2. Proper position of the metropolitan associations in the YMCA.

3. Proper relationship of the International Committee to training schools and summer conferences. (The committee had assumed control of the Training Institute and Lake Geneva conference over the protests of Messer and other midwest secretaries.)

4. Situation in Decatur, Illinois. (A lax superintendent of a railroad branch had defied attempts of the city association there to end irregularities. The situation was finally remedied through the joint efforts of the city association and the International Committee.)

5. A plan of arbitration.

Both Messer and Morse testified extensively before the subcommittee. Messer insisted that the metropolitan associations should have jurisdiction over railroad and student associations in their area. The International Committee—through Morse—claimed direct control of these branches as part of its policy of "unified work." The proceedings of this subcommittee, too extensive to be quoted in detail, provide an outline of the contrasting philosophies of Messer and Morse with respect to relationships within the national movement. In the testimony, each man was able to cite instances in which the view he advocated had produced beneficial results for the YMCA movement.

The hearings of this subcommittee were used as a basis of discussion by the Committee of 21 which produced both a majority report (signed by thirteen members) and a minority report (signed by eight members) for submission to the Buffalo convention. The majority report substantially favored the position of Morse. Both reports were submitted to the convention by McCormick. The majority report was finally passed, but it had been so modified by conciliatory amendments that Messer found very little cause to object further. Although the convention gave the International Committee priority in organizing railroad branches, for example, an important amendment restricted this activity where local associations were already established to "exceptional cases where for the time being organic relations cannot be established or maintained." Another amendment specified that "nothing in this report shall be construed as in any way interfering with the right of the local association to organize branches of its own in any department."

Messer was also cheered by an editorial in the *Association Seminar* written by L. L. Doggett, later a historian of the national movement. "All parties generally agree that the local association is the independent unit and is limited in no way by outside control," Doggett wrote in interpreting the convention action. "This has certainly been the contention of all deliverances in the past at international conventions and it has been held that the supervisory agents are advisory and not authoritative in their relations to local work."

A much briefer but equally spirited debate between a leader of the Chicago Association and the International Committee was that initiated by Professor Graham Taylor, the head of Chicago Commons, one of the nation's most successful social settlements. Taylor, who occupied the chair of Christian Sociology at the Chicago Theological Seminary, became an enthusiastic and hard-working supporter of the Y's program shortly after his arrival in Chicago. It was his desire to have the YMCA broaden its program and use its organizational energies for an attack on such social evils as the slums and crime rather than restricting its program to work among young men and boys. In 1895 Taylor had presented a major address to the International Convention on "The Relation of the YMCA's to the Social-Economic Questions of the Day." The following week he appeared before the Secretaries Conference to urge a broadened program of social regeneration sponsored by the YMCA movement. Although Messer was in general sympathy with Taylor's objectives, he did not press the issue when the consensus of those present at both conventions seemed to be "if a man's heart is changed, he will change his own conditions." As a result, the national movement continued to press for that specific work "for young men and for them only" that had been advocated by Houghteling.

With the question of the relationships of the Chicago Association and the International Committee temporarily stabilized (even if not permanently resolved), Messer was able to direct his energies once more toward the expansion of the work in Chicago. The result was the appearance within the next few years of a series of additions to the physical plant of the YMCA of Chicago. A Dolton Junction railroad branch supported by the Chicago & Eastern Illinois Railroad was opened June 27, 1905, at a cost of $20,000. Wilson Avenue, aided by a gift of $20,000 from its original benefactor, Robert J. Bennett, raised funds for a new building that was opened on October 9, 1905, and included a dormitory with living quarters for young men. In Hyde Park, after a five-year building campaign, a new $137,-000 structure was dedicated at Madison Avenue (now Dorchester) and Fifty-third Street on December 30, 1906. The Hyde Park Y also included a dormitory. These dormitories were immediately filled to capacity and resulted in an increase in membership in each of the departments. As a result of these two successes, the Board of Trustees invested $42,500 of its endowment fund in a dormitory adjoining the West Side Department. This dormitory was occupied for the first time in

A typical room in a YMCA dormitory, 1908.

November of 1907. The rates at all these dormitories were very modest; a note in the *Bulletin* during 1907 set the rates at 15 cents per night—with an accompanying explanation that they had been raised from 10 cents per night only because of increased costs and wages.

Ever since the Boston Jubilee convention in 1901, the leaders of the Chicago Association had been discussing the approaching fiftieth anniversary of the Young Men's Christian Association of Chicago. Edward P. Bailey, who succeeded Eckels as president in 1903, had sought through discussions with the Board of Managers and with local Committees of Management to plan an observance which would call attention to the YMCA's program and secure the financial means to expand it to new areas of the city. In June of 1907, letters were sent from Bailey to one hundred outstanding Chicago citizens inviting them to serve as members of a general committee to plan the details to this fiftieth anniversary celebration. John V. Farwell, Jr. was appropriately named chairman of the committee.

On January 27, 1908, the committee met for lunch at the Mid-Day Club to hear reports from the various subcommittees on publicity, receptions, banquets, speakers, and finally, on financial objectives. Messer had been urging the raising of a large endowment to safeguard the program of the Association during the recurring periods of economic depression. Those responsible for raising such a fund were not optimistic about their chances of getting a large sum, however; at the luncheon the subcommittee reported that the highest amount they felt feasible as a financial goal was $600,000, of which $500,000 would be for endowment and $100,000 to meet existing debts.

Among those at the speakers' table for the luncheon was John G. Shedd, who had been named president of Marshall Field & Company, following the death of Marshall Field I. While

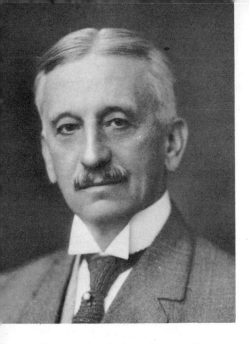

John G. Shedd,
president of
Marshall Field & Company, who
reminded a group of businessmen
that Chicago was
"a million-dollar town."

the report of the subcommittee on financial objectives was being discussed, Shedd abruptly left his seat at the speakers' table and went to the rear of the room where he was seen to confer briefly with Thomas Templeton, former treasurer of Marshall Field & Company. He then walked briskly back to the speakers' table and at the first opening asked for the chairman's attention.

"Gentlemen of the Citizens Committee of 100," he said, "I am one of those who are interested in the Young Men's Christian Association because of what it has done in our city. I am especially interested in the Association's plan for the housing of young men by building dormitories, because it seems to me these dormitories do two things: they furnish much-needed homes for young men, and at the same time they furnish endowment with which to sustain this work. I think this committee should plan immediately to raise a much larger sum of money. I, for one, am willing to give $50,000 [the room was as silent as if it were empty when he named the figure] with which to build one of these dormitories, provided you will proceed immediately to raise a total fund of $600,000. I will give $100,000 provided you will make this total a million dollars." Then turning to the men at the speakers' table who represented businesses of a size comparable to that of which he was the head, Shedd added: "Gentlemen, this is a million-dollar town and there are men seated at this table who are more able to give than I am."

William A. Wieboldt, pioneer Chicago merchant, then rose to say that he would give a site near Division and Ashland to the YMCA if the Association would erect a suitable dormitory at that location.

These offers unleashed a tumult of conversation. It was obvious that a new list of objectives for the anniversary would have to be drawn up to meet the conditions proposed by Shedd. The luncheon guests, who had expected only to ratify the actions of a subcommittee, found themselves instructing that subcommittee to meet again "to give further consideration to the purposes and amount to be sought from the community in recognition of the 50th Anniversary of the Association."

The day following the luncheon Messer received another offer. Julius Rosenwald, president of Sears, Roebuck and Company, told Messer that Sears (the company, not Rosenwald personally) would contribute $100,000 to the anniversary fund if the YMCA would erect and equip a building at Kedzie and Arthington with dormitory facilities for employees at the Sears headquarters nearby. Rosenwald also said Sears would guarantee that the additional $150,000 which the Association would put into such a plant would earn no less than 4 per cent interest for the next ten years.

With these pledges of support, the subcommittee on financial objectives reported back at another luncheon of the Citizens'

"The Stranger"—a cartoon drawn by John T. McCutcheon and published by the *Chicago Tribune* in support of the 50th Anniversary campaign.

Committee on March 27, 1908. The new objectives were:

1. A total fund of $1,000,000.

2. Not less than $600,000 should be raised during 1908.

3. Subscriptions should be payable in not more than three years.

4. The endowment raised was to be invested as soon as practicable in new dormitory buildings.

The subcommittee reported that it already had received an additional group of large contributions. Wieboldt solicited an anonymous gift of $70,000. Mrs. Nettie Fowler McCormick, widow of the first Cyrus, joined with her two sons, Cyrus, Jr. and Harold Fowler, in a gift of $50,000. Joseph N. Field gave $10,000. Mrs. T. B. Blackstone, J. Ogden Armour, and the two John V. Farwells each gave $25,000.

The formal celebration of the anniversary was planned for the two weeks from April 12 to April 27, 1908. Messer was insistent that the spiritual element not be neglected in the observances, and an extensive program of religious services and activities to be carried out in co-operation with the city's churches was planned. During the first Sunday, the departments of the Association held twenty-eight different worship services, and special sermons were preached in many churches.

On April 25 a special physical work exhibition was held in the First Regiment Armory and more than one thousand YMCA members participated in the various events. Among the entertainment of the evening listed by the *Record Herald* the next day were "a band concert, boys' drills, two basketball games, a relay race, gymnastic dancing, men's drills, wrestling

This cartoon in the *Chicago Daily News* also helped to arouse public interest in the YMCA's 50th Anniversary Fund drive.

contests, pyramid building, tumbling, fencing, and an interdepartmental track meet."

The climax of the formal observance was a citizens' banquet at the Congress Hotel on April 27, 1908. Woodrow Wilson, then president of Princeton University, was the principal speaker. Among the 250 men in the audience were seven railroad presidents, ten bank presidents, thirty or forty corporation presidents, two university presidents, and a majority of the leaders of Chicago's business community. "If those 250 men were removed from their spheres of action, Chicago would be at a standstill this morning," the *Tribune* commented in its report of the dinner.

The fund goal which the Association had set for its anniversary year was one which could hardly be met by a few men, no matter how influential. The methods of fund raising suited to a small organization with a limited program were no longer adequate for the city-wide activities of the YMCA of Chicago in its fiftieth year. Because the fund-drive leaders were slow in recognizing this fact and in facing the necessity of taking their appeal to the general public, the quest for the million-dollar endowment fund lagged badly behind schedule. On December 28, when the final report meeting for the year was held, the total subscribed was under $500,000. Shedd made a short statement expressing his disappointment at the failure of the public, and particularly of the wealthy businessmen, to contribute as generously as he felt they should have. But he withheld any final action on his conditional subscription and left the door open for his $50,000 or $100,000 gift if and when the goals of the campaign were reached.

Through all of 1909, loyal Y workers pushed toward their goal. By October the fund had reached $628,311—more than enough for Shedd's first conditional gift. In December of 1909, aided by a gift of $100,000 from Victor F. Lawson, publisher of the *Chicago Daily News*, the fund total was $731,134. Messer and the other leaders in the Association were determined to reach the million-dollar mark. "Right here allow me to say that I most earnestly recommend that the canvass should be continued, even for a period of ten years, if necessary, or until we ultimately have an endowment fund of One Million Dollars," he said in a report to the Board of Managers. "Then and only then will this Association be in a position to do the broader work of which it is capable."

Encouraged by Lawson's gift and urged on by Messer, the Board of Managers voted to undertake a special twelve-day, short-term canvass of the kind that had been successfully used to raise funds for the Cleveland YMCA. The period set for the campaign was from March 30 to April 12, 1910; the goal was set at $350,000—enough to provide for a million-dollar endowment and to wipe out current indebtedness. Harry A. Wheeler, vice-president of the Union Trust Company and a leader in the Association of Commerce and Industry, was named chairman of the campaign. A headquarters was set up in a second-floor office at the southwest corner of State and Monroe where workers could meet and report their contributions each day of the campaign. Outside the campaign headquarters overlooking State Street was a clock fourteen feet in diameter and marked with sums up to $350,000; when the hands on the clock showed midnight, the goal would have been reached.

Each department named a group of fund-raising teams. Division Street had five teams, and the West Side, Wilson Avenue, Central, and Hyde Park ten teams. There was also a "metropolitan committee" of forty men which included such civic leaders as Julius Rosenwald, Cyrus McCormick, Harold McCormick, A. Stamford White (president of the Board of

A crowd on State Street watches the posting of new figures on the big clock that registered the growth of the YMCA's 50th Anniversary Fund, April 3, 1910.

Trade), N. W. Harris (president of the Harris Trust and Savings Company), Curtis N. Kimball, the piano manufacturer, and Judge C. C. Kohlsaat of the United States Circuit Court.

Aided by generous support from the newspapers, the campaign attracted the attention of all Chicago. At 1:30 P.M. each day, when the hands on the big clock were moved to show the latest fund total, a crowd that on several days was large enough to block traffic assembled on State Street to learn the latest figures. One of the greatest days of the campaign was Friday, April 8. The sums brought in by the solicitors, including

165

a contribution of $5,000 from the International Harvester Company, amounted to $21,662. Joseph N. Field increased his gift to $100,000, of which $25,000 was given as a memorial to Marshall Field I. These gifts brought the million-dollar fund to completion. As the hands of the clock moved from $151,218 slowly past the $200,000 mark (in the twelve-day campaign), a crowd of nearly one thousand people jammed State Street to cheer the workers.

Saturday was another big day. Workers brought in pledges totaling $48,617, of which Dr. D. K. Pearsons gave $20,000 and the Illinois Steel Company $10,000. But even with these gifts and an additional $4,000 from John V. Farwell, the drive was still $55,000 short of the $350,000 objective on April 12—the final morning of the campaign. By noon the volunteer solicitors had reduced this deficit to $17,379; in the afternoon the pledges they obtained were enough to wipe out this deficiency and put the $350,000 campaign over the top with more than $1,000 to spare.

The money raised during the anniversary drive was quickly put to work. It freed the Association from debt, furnished funds for both Hyde Park and Wilson Avenue to increase their residence rooms, modernize their swimming pools, and install new bowling alleys, and made possible the erection of the $125,000 building of the West Side Department and the construction of the Division Street Department building. The $300,000 Division Street building was dedicated on December 15, 1910, at the corner of Division and Marshfield. Joseph R. Noel was elected chairman of the first Committee of Management and Ralph W. Cooke, later to serve many years as manager of the YMCA Hotel, was named first executive secretary.

The 50th Anniversary funds also made possible an extensive modernization of the physical facilities at Central, where an energetic new physical director, G. M. Martin, was rapidly developing a new type of physical program. First to be remodeled was the locker room. Out-of-date storage lockers which required large areas of floor space for the storage of stale athletic clothing and equipment were replaced by a more hygienic system of individual storage boxes and dressing rooms. Gym clothing was automatically laundered after every use and stored in a safe place between the owner's visits to the gymnasium. This system reduced the amount of space needed for storing clothes and equipment so radically that enough floor area was gained to provide an auxiliary gymnasium. Another change introduced by Martin was that calling for increased intramural competition among groups of equal skill rather than the development of star teams and athletes. "Everyone . . . will be given an opportunity for informal competition," said a notice in the *Bulletin*, "and the emphasis will be placed upon the social and educational side rather than the expert side of athletics." Music was introduced as an accompaniment to calisthenics. Businessmen were quick to seize this new chance for athletic participation and recreation. Among the young men who registered for the new classes and games were Sewell Avery, later to be chairman of the board of the U. S. Gypsum Company and Montgomery Ward and Company, and Barney Balaban, who was to become head of Paramount Pictures. Some years later, a young Chicago newspaperman named Lowell Thomas was preparing himself for a lifetime of adventure and travel by learning to swim in Central's pool.

All the benefits of the 50th Anniversary campaign were not immediately apparent. The increased services which the YMCA was able to give as a result of the campaign won it many friends among those who did not participate actively. Evidence of this widespread reputation often came in the form of unexpected bequests. One of these—from Thomas Murdoch, one of the founders of the wholesale grocery firm of Reid, Murdoch and Fisher—was for $815,084.42, the largest legacy any YMCA had received at that time. Another bequest from Sarah E. Hawley was for $25,000.

The most extraordinary accomplishment of the 50th Anniversary campaign, however, was in the record of the teams of men who helped achieve the million-dollar goal. More than 400 men acted as solicitors. They secured 6,684 individual pledges. Each man made an average of 100 calls during the final twelve-day campaign. About $100,000 was raised in amounts of $100 or less. Over 3,000 of the pledges were for less than $5.00. It was plain from these figures that the Young Men's Christian Association of Chicago was no longer the responsibility of just a few; its work and its goals now reflected the aspirations of all Chicago.

The 50th Anniversary campaign medallion.

CHAPTER 8

"The Needs of These Boys Are Many"

WITH IMMEDIATE money problems relieved by the establishment of the million-dollar endowment fund, the members of the Chicago Association next turned their energies toward an expansion of their program which would reflect the wide community support enlisted through the 50th Anniversary campaign. The extension of the Association's interests took it into many new areas. Among these were the full development of boys' work and a related camping program, special help for immigrants, the broadening of the Association program to include the Negro community, the addition of new courses and the establishment of formal standards for the educational activities (particularly at Central), and the adaptation of the religious program to the changing social conditions of the twentieth century.

Special activities for boys had been offered by several Chicago departments since the first boys' program at Central in

An Association Product. "Homeless Employed Boy, now a Resident of the North Side Boys' Club, of the Young Men's Christian Association of Chicago. Through the help of the Association he has become a virile Christian boy, restored to the Church, assisted to a good position, and attends the Association Night School." Interest in boys' work was promoted through this picture and accompanying caption in the *Bulletin*.

1878. On the national level, work for boys was frequently on the agenda at conventions but had not been pushed aggressively by the International Committee until around 1900. About the same time, Messer was listing the extension of boys' work as one of his goals for the new century. In 1902 the boys' department at Central had 431 members—the second largest of its kind in North America. Of these 431 boys, commented a writer in the *Bulletin* (probably Oates, who was a leader in extending work among boys), 90 per cent consisted of "the boy from the store, the bank, and the office." The same predominance of employed boys existed at the West Side and Hyde Park departments, which also had boys' programs.

In 1910, following a special conference on boys' work, a long-range plan of making the YMCA more attractive to boys was approved and Fred A. Crosby of the International Committee joined the Chicago Association as Boys' Work Secretary. With the approval of the Board of Managers, membership privileges were extended to boys between the ages of twelve and sixteen.

"The Young Men's Christian Association [is] alive to its opportunity of enlisting the active interest and service of boys in their teens," Messer wrote in the *Bulletin*. "Boys of this age are likely to go somewhere, if they have any go in them. If they do not go right, they must go wrong. The Association makes it as easy as possible to do right, and as hard as possible to do wrong. . . . The Association seeks to supplement the home, the church, and the school in the supreme and strategic work of preoccupying the life of the boy with such activities and forces as to insure his religious inheritance."

One of the major accomplishments of the first year's activities under Crosby was the YMCA sponsorship of the launching of the Boy Scout movement in Chicago. Under the leadership of Crosby and A. Stamford White, chairman of the city boys' work committee for the YMCA, a council of fifty civic organizations was formed for the promotion of Scouting. White was named as president of this first council, and D. W. Pollard was hired as the first Chicago Boy Scout secretary.

The *Bulletin* commented in December of 1910 that once the official organization had been set up, the Y would have done its special work and would "enter the city-wide movement just as any other agency, thus avoiding the accusation that we are trying to dominate the movement. Our whole idea is to see that it is properly organized." Seeing that these first Scout troops and patrols were "properly organized" proved a formidable task. Crosby and other speakers from the YMCA spent many hours in recruiting boys for the Scout troops while other staff members from the various departments established special training classes for those who volunteered to act as Scoutmasters. When the first general assembly of Boy Scouts in the Chicago area

171

was held in February of 1911, more than 2,500 Scouts—1,200 in uniform—paraded down Michigan Avenue and west on Jackson Boulevard to the Board of Trade building for special ceremonies and a speech of recognition by Former President Theodore Roosevelt.

Correlated with this encouragement of the Scout movement was an increased tempo of YMCA activities intended to appeal directly to boys. Boys' membership increased 56 per cent in 1911. The special religious meetings for boys had an attendance of nearly 10,000 during the same year—a jump of 653 per cent over 1910. Under the direction of eight full-time boys' secretaries and four part-time assistants, active programs were instituted in fifteen of the city's twenty public high schools. For the first time, boys from all the city's high schools were brought together at a city-wide conference with the theme of "clean living, clean speech, and clean athletics." Special "councils" were organized at Lakeview, McKinley, Lane, Wendell Phillips, and University (of Chicago) high schools to carry out the theme of the conference.

Boys who were forced to leave school to go to work were not neglected. "Open house" social events for boys were a regular feature at all departments; and evening programs of athletics for the working boys were added to the schedule. The West Side Department, located near the Juvenile Court and Detention Home, followed in the tradition of John V. Farwell, Sr.'s Bridewell meetings by scheduling special religious services and gymnastic competitions for boys confined at the home. Other activities throughout Chicago included a "learn-to-swim" campaign and a summer camp for employed boys at Sears Roebuck; a training class at Hyde Park to stop "the terrible leakage of 70 per cent of our boys who leave Sunday School during their teens," and an experimental program at Wilson Avenue for younger boys

172

from nine to twelve years old. (Among the difficulties encountered in this "experimental" approach and reported by a writer in the *Bulletin* were the growth of the group, which increased so quickly that more supervision was required than could be given, and the friction resulting on occasions when the presence of "kids" was resented by the boys who had reached the mature age of twelve!)

The most highly specialized program for boys was that offered by the North Side Boys' Club after its founding in 1908. The club had been established with the aid of a bequest of $100,000 by Albert Keep in memory of his deceased daughter, Lucy Keep Isham. After a conference with Mrs. Keep, the Board of Managers voted to invest the bequest as an endowment for a boys' club to serve the needy and neglected boys from slum homes on the near North Side. Before the club was established, a commission of twenty-three leading business and professional men in the area was requested to make a survey and recommend a suitable location for the club. This survey required six months to make; when it was finished the Board of Managers voted approval of the commission's proposal to open a boys' club in a building leased for the purpose at 1336 Fullerton Avenue.

When the club was ready, the *Bulletin* dealt candidly with one of the problems that had been studied in the survey. The opening of the North Side Boys' Club, the writer explained, had come "only after a thorough test of the Association's adaptability to meet boys of the rougher and more neglected classes." This self-examination was but one phase of a continuing debate that was to perturb the conscience of the Chicago Association. The principal question of this debate could be simply put: "Did a social agency such as the YMCA dare put the boys from a normal home environment together with boys from a world of street gangs and petty thievery bred by poverty?" It was not any easier a question to answer in 1908 than it is today. To the editor of the *Bulletin*, the slightest chance of gaining a boy demanded a certain amount of risk if the YMCA program was to have any vitality and fulfill its evangelistic objectives. "Association Boys' Work in Chicago as well as in most other points has been for years mainly for the schoolboy, the class from well-to-do homes," the *Bulletin* commented. "The needs of these boys are many and urgent but are not so great as the needs of the immigrant boy, the boy of foreign parentage, and the wage-earning boy, who is often from the former two classes. The Chicago Association seems now to have reached a point where we are realizing more than ever our responsibility toward these great classes of boys who are from the lower social scale." Although this language may sound archaic by modern standards, it reflected a sincere desire to make the Y program equally available to all; and it was at the North Side Boys' Club that this principle was put to the test in the Association's first coordinated effort to influence a neighborhood where the problems of delinquency were complicated by poverty, overcrowding, language difficulties, and even religious differences.

The boys of this area, of course, proved as susceptible to kind treatment and an opportunity for self-betterment as those from any other environment. When a baseball diamond was established at the corner of Oakdale and Seminary under the sponsorship of the Boys' Club, the *Bulletin* reported that it was being used by a group who "if not THE toughest bunch" from the area was "one of the toughest." The *Bulletin* added that while "they did not lose any of their bad reputation the first month," the second month showed a great difference "as the forces of Fair Play and Good Fellowship began to exert their powerful influence." Within a short time, sixteen different clubs had been organized around the North Side Boys' Club, and these smaller groups in turn were formed into patrols and troops of the Boy Scouts under the sponsorship of the YMCA.

The development of the work in this area was so rapid that in 1912 the Board of Managers approved a plan to organize a new department, including work for young men, to serve the district around the North Side Boys' Club. With the aid of an additional $100,000 gift from Mrs. Keep, a North Avenue-Larrabee Boys' Club building was dedicated in June of 1916. Dues were geared to the economic level of the neighborhood and kept very low; earnings from the dormitory in turn were used to support the boys' work of the department.

Many boys' activities were carried on outdoors. This fact, plus the interest in Scouting, led naturally to the development of a camping program. The honor of being the first to organize a

Boys amusing themselves in the North Avenue-Larrabee Boys' Club.

summer camp in Chicago apparently belongs to the Hyde Park YMCA, which conducted its first summer outing in 1899. There were no permanent camp sites at the time; camping trips were conducted to various parks or lakes not too far from Chicago, usually lasting for about ten days. Shortly after its founding, the Sears Roebuck Department began conducting special weekend camps. In 1902 the Central Department held a series of three camp periods at Hamlin Lake, Michigan, with each camp segment being limited to a different age group. (The cost for these Central camps was $12 for a two-week period). In 1905 the Hyde Park and Central departments held their summer camps at Camp Kish-wau-ke-toc at Lake Geneva, using the facilities of the YMCA Institute and Training School. The same year the West Side Department ran a camp at Wolf Lake near Mus-

Off for Camp Channing—in an early motor bus guaranteed to provide plenty of fresh air.

kegon, Michigan, and the following year Wilson Avenue held its first summer camp at nearby Bear Lake. In 1913 the various departments scheduled a total of thirty-one weekend camps. This summer also marked the first time that a city-wide camp was held, the site being near Michillinda, Michigan. The popularity of these summer camps and their rapid growth led in 1914 to the adoption by the Board of Managers of a resolution requesting a boys' camp committee to secure a permanent camp site. However, almost ten more years were to elapse before this plan was translated into reality.

Boys' work was not the only field in which the Chicago Association found it necessary to develop highly specialized techniques of dealing with new social problems. Many of these problems arose from the continued high proportion of foreign-

An early view of Camp Channing, conducted by the Division Street Department. Early camps often had to use makeshift facilities.

Overnight hikes were arranged for boys to provide experience in outdoor living before the establishment of permanent summer camps.

born workers in the city's population. Chicago remained the terminal of the search for opportunity, whether the seeker was merchant, trader, real-estate promoter, or common laborer. Throughout the nineteenth century, the Germans, Irish, and Scandinavians had been arriving by the thousands to take jobs in Chicago industries. Toward the end of the century this stream of immigration diminished, but it was replenished by a fresh tide of immigrants from southern and eastern Europe. This new flood reached its high mark between 1900 and 1910 when some 30,000 Italians, 120,000 Russians and Poles, 24,000 Hungarians and 5,000 Greeks helped swell the population of Chicago to a total well over two million. Of this number, experts estimated that some 40 per cent—783,340—were foreign born and another 25 per cent were children of foreign-born parents.

The Young Men's Christian Association was trying to deal with the problems created by this immigration through all its agencies. The International Committee had stationed YMCA secretaries at twelve ports of embarkation in Europe and nine ports of debarkation in America. Wherever possible, these Y secretaries would attempt to learn the immigrant's destination in America and furnish him with a card of introduction to the Association in the city where he intended to settle. In Chicago, a special reception committee was appointed to meet these newcomers; volunteers made two trips a day to each of the city's six railway stations to help anyone in need of assistance.

The YMCA was not content with these fleeting contacts with Chicago's newest citizens. Messer felt a continuing program should be set up to keep in touch with the immigrants throughout the difficult period of their adjustment and Americanization. His first step was the establishment in 1909 of a "Commission on Young Men and Boys of Foreign Parentage" to make a study of the conditions under which the immigrants were living and to ascertain what their greatest needs might be. Abraham Bowers, a graduate of the University of Chicago, was hired as immigration secretary to direct the studies of the commission and the work among the immigrants. Just as the YMCA had waged war on the overcrowded second-floor dormitories in early Chicago, it now attacked the problem of the disease-ridden slums where these immigrants were forced to live. English lessons were given to speed the process of Americanization. After the language barrier was broken, additional lectures were given on sanitation and the omnipresent slum threat of tuberculosis. The enthusiasm and gratitude of the immigrants who benefited from these lectures were often so great they were impelled to express their gratitude before graduation. Some of their letters convey the degree of their excitement—which often outstripped their English:

GENTLEMEN:

I am Walter Buczynsky. I am very well satisfied with this teacher, who makes us happy in his teaching of the English language, so now goodbye.

WALTER BUCZYNSKY

I like the school very good. I learn how to speak more English. I know how to speak more now. And I think about the shool evry day and the teachers are learning very good. It is heavy to learning for us Englich.

STEPHEN FRANKS

DEAR SIR:

I am now going to your school. I cannot read or write very well, but I am learning fast. All the boys in school hope that the teachers will come all summer for then we could learn to read and write easily. We all try to come every night but sometimes we cont. We thank you for sending the teachers to us and try to do our best so they will stay and help us to be better citizens of America.

Yours truly,
JON KOSTA

By 1911 the YMCA was conducting sixty-three English classes for various nationalities in forty-seven different locations. A special program was inaugurated for Japanese young men. In June of 1911 the Chicago Association hired Misaki Shimadzu, who had been converted to Christianity by American missionaries in Kobe, Japan, as "special secretary" for this work among

We push the trucks under the car

Railroad workers learned English from pictures like this one. This represented a quick way of relating a knowledge of English to their work.

the Japanese. Nor was the Chicago Association's interest limited to the foreign born who came to Chicago. The Central Department supported a missionary in Ceylon, and when Cyrus H. McCormick gave $50,000 toward the erection of YMCA buildings in Europe and the Orient, a matching fund of $50,000 was donated by other members of the YMCA of Chicago for the same purpose.

It was not only immigration from abroad which was changing the character of Chicago's population. Shortly after the turn of the century—and particularly after the start of World War I, when immigration from abroad dried to a trickle—the Negroes in the South began to leave their caste-bound rural society for the greater freedom of opportunity to be found in the North. Attracted by promises of higher wages in the stockyards, packing houses, steel mills, railroad yards, and factories of Chicago, more than 15,000 Negroes arrived in Chicago between 1900 and 1910. These new arrivals brought the Negro population of Chicago to 44,103; in the next decade this figure was more than doubled and the Negro population zoomed to 109,458 in 1920.

Although the Board of Managers had encouraged J. W. Moon to form a YMCA branch for Negro men some fifty years earlier, the Negro community at the time had been too small (and too impoverished) to support such an enterprise. However, on the national level the YMCA was definitely committed to a program of work for the Negro. As early as 1871 the national convention had passed a resolution putting the YMCA on record against discrimination. The resolution said: "The Young Men's Christian Associations are organized to labor for and among young men; they constitute a Union Board of the Church of Christ, charged with the performance of a specific duty; in the prosecution of their work, the Associations, as such, have no politics and know no distinction among men except between those who love Christ and those who love Him not." In practice, the carrying-out of this resolution was one of "equality of opportunity" rather than of integration. But, considering the social conditions of the time and the complete lack of recognition by government or society-at-large of the Negro's special problems, even this program put the YMCA into a position of leadership in efforts to bring to the Negro his full American heritage. By 1900 there were a number of Negro departments in the South, and several Negro Y secretaries were developing the work among members of their own race.

In Chicago, the man who provided the spark—and the means—to extend the YMCA program to Negro neighborhoods was Julius Rosenwald, the unorthodox philanthropist who was president of Sears, Roebuck and Company. Rosenwald had become acquainted with Messer during the 50th Anniversary

Julius Rosenwald regarded the YMCA as the best agency through which he could help the Negro. He also made the first gift toward the erection of Chicago's YMCA Hotel.

campaign when Sears offered funds to erect the Sears Roebuck Department building. During this campaign, Rosenwald and Messer often discussed the need of the Negroes for special help, and it was agreed that as soon as the 50th Anniversary campaign was concluded, the YMCA would undertake such a program. Within a few months after the close of the campaign, the Association asked Dr. Jesse E. Moorland of the International Committee to come to Chicago to help raise funds for a YMCA to serve Negroes on the South Side.

Together with Parker, Messer and Moorland met for lunch with Rosenwald to outline the plans for the fund drive. At this lunch, Rosenwald surprised his three guests with a sweeping offer. He not only suggested he was willing to give $25,000 for a YMCA to serve Negroes in Chicago, but added that he would match this offer in any city in the United States "where an additional $75,000 is raised among white and colored people."

The sweeping magnitude of this offer must have surprised

even the perennially optimistic Messer, for Rosenwald laughed and added:

"Well, I guess you can't do more than one a month, but I hope you can."

Messer then confessed that he was embarrassed that Rosenwald—under the 1888 constitution—could not participate in the management of the YMCA's he was willing to support so richly. To this explanation, Rosenwald gave a frank reply.

"I want nothing to do with the management," he said. "I have been studying the colored people and have come to the conclusion that they need help more than any other group . . . I believe the Young Men's Christian Association is the best medium I know for accomplishing what I would like to see done for the colored man."

Eventually, Rosenwald made good on his matching offer for YMCA's to serve Negroes a total of twenty-eight times with gifts that amounted to $637,000. Another $6,000,000 was contributed throughout the United States by those raising funds to match the terms of his offer.

In Chicago, the Board of Managers had already laid a solid groundwork for expanding into the Negro areas with a survey conducted under the direction of Parker. Evaluating this survey, Parker described the "forces of evil" as extremely well organized and added that "The temptations of young men are terrific." In the area bounded by Twenty-fourth and Thirty-ninth streets, Wabash and Wentworth avenues, Parker's investigators counted 167 saloons. "The questionable places of amusement, the gambling dens and brothels which infest this district . . . the unattractive living accommodations in rooming houses, have much to do with the fatal loneliness which sends men adrift through numerous avenues of vice," Parker commented. He also reported that the churches and other moral agencies in the Negro neighborhoods were without staff or funds to offset the forces generated by overcrowding, poverty, and ignorance.

A second major gift for the new YMCA building came from N. W. Harris, president of the Harris Trust and Savings Bank, who specified that the $10,000 he had given during the twelve-day campaign of 1910 now be applied toward a department building to serve Negroes. When this was done, Harris increased his gift to $25,000. Although cheered by these generous contributions, the Board of Managers knew that the department could not be successful unless it was supported by the community it was intended to serve. Their next step was to launch an organizing drive among the Negroes.

On January 1, 1911, more than five hundred Negro men

Cartoon appearing in the *Chicago Defender* before the start of the campaign for the Wabash Avenue YMCA.

met at Odd Fellows Hall, 3335 South State Street, to launch a movement to raise $100,000 for a YMCA building. After a short talk by Julius Rosenwald, plans were made for a ten-day fund-raising campaign under the over-all direction of Messer and Moorland. With $50,000 already pledged, the Negroes had a goal of $50,000 which was to be raised among their neighbors. Before the meeting was over, several of the men in the audience rose to announce pledges to the fund. The most dramatic of these was that of J. H. Tilghman, janitor for the Chicago Telephone Company, who walked to the platform and handed the chairman $1,000 in cash—his entire savings—as a gift for the building fund. As far as the records show, this was the first substantial gift by a Negro anywhere in America to a YMCA building fund. The zeal of the other workers was on a level with Tilghman's generosity. In only ten days, teams of young men working as volunteers raised a total of $66,932.32—or more than $16,000 above their quota.

Underscoring this new recognition of the Negro was the choice of Booker T. Washington as principal speaker at the Association's fifty-third anniversary dinner the following June. In his address, Washington emphasized that the real importance of the new department lay not so much in what had been done for the Negro but in what the YMCA was permitting the Negro to do for himself. "If you ask me why, with such zeal and energy, they [the Negroes] seized the opportunity of giving their services and their money in planting a Y building and organization in this city, I answer it was because they never had the chance to do it before. They said for the first time in the history of our race, in a great metropolitan city of the North, we have a chance to show the world what we can do in this new movement. So, my friends, they set an example that has made us all proud of the colored man in Chicago. I have always been proud of my

A second cartoon from the *Chicago Defender* after financial goal for Wabash Avenue YMCA had been reached.

race, proud that I am a black man; I wouldn't exchange places with the whitest man on earth. And I was never more proud of my race than since they have done what they did in Chicago. . . . This YMCA building branch for our people will come further, in my opinion, in helping the Negro young man in finding himself, to articulate himself in its civilization, than any other movement that has been started in the city of Chicago. It has for its object not only the saving of the Negro soul, but the saving of the Negro's body. Now there never has been much question about saving his soul, but the trouble comes in regard to his body down on this earth, and the question of his body gives a lot of trouble and you not only propose saving his soul, which is of first importance to him, but you mean to save his body through this organization by helping him to put himself in that relationship to life where he can earn enough money to keep his body saved."

The opportunity for a YMCA department to serve Negroes in Chicago captured the imagination of the nation. In December of 1911, President William Howard Taft spoke to a meeting at Quinn Chapel on the South Side and asked for public support of the new department. The churches and fraternal orders also lent their support. A building plan was approved, and on June 15, 1913, the new Wabash Avenue Department of the YMCA of Chicago was dedicated with Leroy Tucker as its first executive secretary. The five-story building contained a swimming pool, lockers, showers, and a boys' department on the first floor; a reading room, billiard room, gymnasium, dining room and offices on the second floor; and 114 dormitory rooms on the upper three floors.

That the Wabash Avenue Department met a real community need was evident from its immediate success. The Pullman Company contributed $10,000 to the department so that its porters might use the dormitories and have a decent place to stay during their layovers in Chicago. At the end of the first year, the department had 639 members. There was only one year during the first eight when the local Committee of Management was not able to report a surplus of income over expenses. In 1919, when the race riots made it impossible for Negroes to enter the Union Stockyards, they were able to collect their back pay checks from the packing companies at special pay windows set up in the Wabash Avenue YMCA.

The extension of work among boys, the special program for

immigrants, and the opening of the Wabash Avenue YMCA still found Messer dreaming of one more major goal. This dream, which he had nurtured for years, was for a means to help the young men just arriving in Chicago before they were forced by economic conditions or naïvete into an undesirable environment. The problem of the stranger in the city was one that all young men had in common—whether they came from the countries of distant Europe, the cotton fields of the South, or the prairie farms of the Midwest. It was a problem that Messer now decided he was ready to deal with; and the man to whom he turned for help was the same man who had already done so much—Julius Rosenwald.

CHAPTER 9

"The Doorway of City Life"

A PRINCIPAL objective of the 50th Anniversary campaign had been the erection of YMCA dormitories to provide decent living quarters for young men working in Chicago. This dormitory program had proved tremendously successful and the use of YMCA facilities by residents had become an attractive inducement to membership. The dormitories, however, were intended for young men who had already established themselves in the city; they were not organized or located so that they were easily accessible to strangers or transients.

Having established a program for young men after they arrived in Chicago, the YMCA now turned its attention to providing a means of looking after them when they arrived. Many of the young men who came to Chicago were forced by poverty or ignorance of the city into the dreary world of flophouses and cheap hotels; they often became the victims of this shoddy environment before they could find the means to escape from it. Feeling that the YMCA's function was to prevent social evils as much as to cure them, Messer dreamed of a low-cost hotel where young men new to the city could stay until they had a chance to find a job and a permanent place to live. Such a hotel, of course, would have to be open to all young men—in this it would be radically different from the YMCA dormitories which were only for Y members.

The size of the problem was enormous. City officials estimated that 20,000 homeless men were forced to sleep every night in lodginghouses where beds could be had for from 10 to 15 cents per night. It was not hard to imagine what conditions were like in such hovels. But the Association was not ready to proceed until it had the hard facts. Before asking for public support for a low-cost hotel, it wanted to make sure that the investment was justified. Among the questions to which the Board of Managers wanted exact answers were these: What conditions existed in the lodginghouses? Were they a health hazard? How much vice did they spawn? And—most important —how many of the young men in the lodginghouse population could be salvaged as good citizens if they were given a chance to live in clean and wholesome surroundings?

To get these answers, a committee of the Board of Managers formed an investigating team from a group of YMCA volunteers. The members were to disguise themselves as destitute vagrants and gain admission to each of the lodginghouses and cheap hotels to be investigated. As the influx of young men into Chicago was known to be at its highest in the spring, the period chosen for the study was from March 24 to April 5, 1911. Supervising the investigators were Abraham Bowers, immigration secretary, and C. J. Primm, who had been an associate of Professor Willard E. Hotchkiss, supervisor of the Federal census of 1910.

The eighteen students who made up the investigating team

—most of them graduate students from the University of Chicago—outfitted themselves in dilapidated clothing and in groups of two spent two nights each at the lodginghouses and hotels picked for study. Each of the volunteers was burdened down with a sizeable load of equipment—a lantern or candle, a steel tape (for measuring the size of the wire "cells" allotted to each man), thermometers to measure the temperature of the rooms (often overheated and stifling from overcrowding), and paper for notes. In some instances, the men concealed long white sheets under their clothing; when they went to bed they wrapped themselves in these sheets for protection against the vermin which infested all the places they visited. In a few cases, the men carried cameras and flash materials to take pictures. As this was before the invention of the flash bulb, such equipment constituted a bulky and—in the case of the flash powder—a dangerous burden.

Once inside the flophouses and assigned to their rooms, the volunteers would get as much information as possible about the other men assigned to the floor. This information was immediately recorded on special blanks—filled out with the aid of their lantern or candle underneath the blanket so as to avoid detection. When the investigators were discovered at their work they were manhandled, beaten in a few instances, and always thrown roughly into the street.

Despite these very real dangers, as well as those from filth and disease, the investigators persisted. When their reports were in, they furnished all the documentation that anyone could require. In fact, as the *Bulletin* commented discreetly, some of the information belonged "more appropriately in the report of a vice commission" than in a survey of lodginghouses.

Among the more direct observations of the investigators were these:

Ometc Hotel.—The men stank, the floors stank, the closet stank, the beds stank, but the eight big windows remained tightly shut.

Starr Hotel.—The bed was filled with bugs.

Hibbing House Attic [later burned in a fire in which six men lost their lives].—The air was so stuffy and loaded with carbonic gas and vile odors that it put my candle out.

From other investigators identified in the *Bulletin* only by number came these comments:

No. 53.—The general capacity of this house is 600 and there were 495 lodgers this night. There are two bathtubs in this place.

No. 52.—The sign on the wall, "Do not spit on the floor", was not obeyed. There were no cuspidors.

No. 31.—Finding it impossible to sleep amid the stench of whiskey and over-breathed air . . . we went out at 3 A.M. in search of a bed.

Of the lodginghouses and cheap hotels in the downtown area, the report asserted, "there were scarcely half a dozen where a man may go and be reasonably sure of coming out uninfected or uninfested." Among the lodginghouses of the better grade, Bowers said, "there may be fifteen which can be called fair without violating the conscience of a reasonable man. The remainder of the houses are to be classed as bad. . . ."

The report concluded that among the cheap hotels there were two obvious divisions: "One is the place where no questions are asked and which can be used by those who rent the room from twenty-five cents to one dollar for any purpose whatsoever; and the other is the hotel where it is expected that men and women will mingle more or less promiscuously."

Putting together the information obtained by the investi-

Two University of Chicago students dressed as vagrants to participate in the YMCA investigation of the cheap lodginghouses of Chicago.

gators and the figures compiled by the census takers the previous year, the report estimated that of 20,000 lodginghouse dwellers, chiefly congregated in the center of the city, there were about four or five thousand who were "new to the game" every year. Of these newcomers, it was estimated that half stayed in the same environment "simply because once becoming down and out, diseased and marked with the appearance of vagrancy, they have neither opportunity nor, after a few years, any ambition to pull themselves up." The members of the commission were of the opinion that the problem of the young immigrant in the city was not essentially different from that of the young men from the farms who "come to take up city life" and that a program which would help the one would also be of benefit to the other.

Fortified with the vivid portrait of wasted opportunity and unwholesome conditions painted by this survey, Messer called his friend Julius Rosenwald on a Sunday morning shortly after-

The *Bulletin* of May, 1911, reported that "the investigators spent the night in cheap lodging-houses wrapped in sheets. They were not always then immune to attack!"

ward and said he would like to talk with him. No historian could want a more accurate record of that meeting than the one provided by Rosenwald himself.

Messer "outlined a vision of what now stands here as a wonderful realization," Rosenwald said at the dedication of the Hotel in 1916. "He said the YMCA had just completed an investigation of the cheap hotels and lodginghouses by young college students dressed like hoboes, who for ten days and nights mingled and talked with beggars, professional criminals, and confirmed 'bums.'

" 'It was found,' Mr. Messer said, with an eagerness that gripped me, 'that many good, clean, active country youths who had come to this city full of ambition and hope had been converted into loafers by getting their first experience in Chicago in these cheap hotels and lodginghouses, where they had put up temporarily because they had very limited means and were not aware of the vicious nature of their surroundings. The confiding friendliness natural to the country boys only served to make easier their ruin at the hands of the disreputables with whom they were forced into intimate contact through these lodginghouses.'

"What was in Mr. Messer's mind was the question of the advisability of having the YMCA build a hotel where young men, coming to Chicago to make their fortune, could be received at a moderate charge and properly directed for the first weeks of their residence here while they were strangers and were adjusting themselves to new surroundings and finding positions where they could be told how to guard against the dangers which surround them in a large city, as well as instructed in the advantages afforded them here with little or no cost, such as the various forms of YMCA service, the libraries, night schools, social settlements, Art Institute, public parks with their many features, Field Museum, [now Chicago Natural History Museum] Sunday Evening Club, houses of worship, and places of like nature in our wonderful city. Such a hotel was to provide an agency for helping young men to secure positions, after which homes would be found for them in outlying YMCA dormitories nearest their places of employment, or in carefully selected boardinghouses, where they would come under wholesome influences.

"Mr. Messer thought if donations amounting to $500,000 could be secured, the balance of the cost would be safe investment for the YMCA endowment funds, but in view of the then recent campaign for the One Million Dollar Fund, which had been successfully completed, no widespread appeal could be made at that time, and consequently the $500,000 needed must come from a few large donors. His inspiration enabled him to present his appeal in such a convincing manner that I at once became enthusiastic and told him I would be willing to start such a fund, provided the hotel was to be a temporary home, and provided further that the hotel be built in the downtown district, not necessarily in the Loop.

"Knowing that John G. Shedd was especially interested in bettering the condition of young men, I telephoned, before I left Mr. Messer, and asked Mr. Shedd if he would see me that day. He replied he would at one o'clock. So I went over to his home at the appointed time. Although I was not able to present the matter as well as Mr. Messer had presented it to me, Mr. Shedd said then and there he would be willing to be one of ten men each to contribute $50,000. He also agreed to join me in calling upon Cyrus H. McCormick the following day to present the matter to him. This we did. Mr. McCormick also was interested. He told us he would give us his answer the next day. The answer was favorable and we were greatly encouraged.

"The following Thursday, on the occasion of an anniversary dinner of the YMCA, Mr. Messer made the first public announcement of the Hotel project. The next morning this appeared in the newspapers. About eleven o'clock on the day of publication N. W. Harris called me up on the phone from Lake Geneva, said he had read of the proposed hotel, and that he was so well pleased with our partnership in the Chicago colored YMCA building in which we had equal financial interest, he wanted to have a part in this. He volunteered to be one of ten for $50,000.

"A week later James A. Patten invited me to lunch, and he generously said he would be number five on the list to contribute $50,000 toward the Hotel.

"While I presented the matter to a number of others who declined for various reasons, all agreed that the project was most deserving and expressed the hope that it would materialize."

How Messer and Rosenwald made sure that his dream did

materialize has never been better told than by John Nuveen, Jr. in his booklet, *The Road to Fortune.*

"Since all of the original ten who donated $50,000 are now dead, it is possible to relate a few of the interesting incidents regarding the securing of the original subscriptions," Nuveen recalled in a paper prepared for the Chicago Literary Club and later published.

"Mr. Rosenwald mentioned five of the ten men who contributed $50,000 each towards the initial $500,000 goal. The spirit of the enterprise was apparently contagious. John G. Shedd interested his associate, Joseph N. Field, who became one of the ten even though he was, at the time, a resident of London. Early in the campaign Shedd and McCormick, considering possible donors, came to the name of William Wrigley, Jr. He had the reputation of being rather short when solicited on matters of this kind, but Shedd agreed to make the approach if McCormick would accompany him, and accordingly McCormick phoned for an appointment. From a director who was in Wrigley's office at the time of the phone call, it was learned that after Wrigley hung up the receiver he turned and said, 'That was Mr. McCormick asking for an appointment for Mr. Shedd and himself and I know what they want. They want me to give $50,000 towards the proposed Young Men's Christian Association Hotel. He made an appointment to come here at eight o'clock tomorrow morning. If they get here at eight o'clock I will give them the money. If they are late they won't get a nickel.' McCormick and Shedd fortunately arrived a few minutes ahead of time, were ushered in and started approaching the matter with the usual pleasantries, only to be interrupted by Wrigley who stated that he knew why they were there and that he would give them the $50,000. The whole matter took only a couple of minutes, but it was not until several years afterwards that Shedd and Mc-

Cormick found out how handsomely they were rewarded that morning for promptness.

"Not all of the gifts, however, were so easily secured, and the job of interesting donors was not always a pleasant one. Rosenwald originally approached J. Ogden Armour to become one of the ten but the interview was not a happy one. Whether Rosenwald used an unfortunate approach, or Armour was in an irritable mood, we will never know. He stated that he could not afford to give the money and this Rosenwald pooh-poohed by stating that to the president of Armour & Company $50,000 was only a figure on the books. They continued until Armour became so thoroughly aroused that, after ushering Mr. Rosenwald out of his office, he sat down and telephoned Cyrus McCormick, his best friend among the Young Men's Christian Association trustees, to complain of the intrusion. Now Mr. McCormick, so I am told, possessed an unusual ability to pour oil on troubled waters, and when he received Armour's first excited words of protest on the phone, he replied by saying that he would come right over. By the time he arrived, Armour had cooled down somewhat and McCormick, so I am told, approached him somewhat as follows: 'I understand what you wanted to say to me was that if you are to be approached in regard to a gift for the YMCA, you want me to come personally and not send someone else. I wish to apologize for not having come to you in the first place. Of course, I am sure that you want to be one of the ten men to underwrite this hotel and I want to have the privilege of reporting that myself.' Armour, although completely taken aback, was a good sport and nodded his head, thus adding his name to the list. The names of Mrs. Gustavus F. Swift, the widow of the great packer, and family, and Victor Lawson, the publisher of the *Chicago Daily News*, completed the ten.

"But the contributions did not end at that point. Charles R. Crane and Richard T. Crane, Jr. became interested and gave $25,000 each, as did also LaVerne Noyes.

"It is most exceptional for one who is raising money to have a prospective donor call up on the long distance telephone to announce his gift, as did N. W. Harris, but his was not the only voluntary gift. Such publicity as was given to this project in the papers inspired Benjamin J. Rosenthal, Joseph H. DeFrees, and Robert H. Fleming to send in substantial gifts unsolicited. In addition to Mrs. Swift, four other women, Mrs. T. B. Blackstone, Mrs. Charles A. Chapin, Mrs. Nettie Fowler McCormick, and Mrs. George M. Pullman, widows of former business and civic leaders of the city, also contributed substantially. Edward B. Butler, B. A. Eckhart, John V. Farwell, Arthur B. Jones, and Samuel Insull completed the list of contributors. Before the books were closed the contributions amounted to $657,010, and, as the enthusiasm and contributions for the Hotel mounted, the original plans for a 1,000-room building were expanded to provide 1,800 rooms."

Ground was purchased for the Hotel just south of the Loop at 826 South Wabash and construction pushed at the fastest possible pace. On Sunday, May 21, 1916, the new YMCA Hotel —nineteen stories high, with 1,821 bedrooms, and erected at a cost of $1,350,000—was dedicated.

"Good character," said John G. Shedd at the dedication, "is necessary to business success and it is only possible to develop it in a good, wholesome, moral environment. There is a tremendous waste in the lives and moral tone of young men who drift into wrong companionship and immoral surroundings, because they are not properly welcomed and guided as they enter the doorway of city life. This, then, is the work here. This Hotel will provide these surroundings at a price all can pay."

The YMCA Hotel, 822 South Wabash Avenue, as it appeared when it was dedicated on Sunday, May 21, 1916.

There were 140 men who registered at the Hotel the first night. They paid rates of from thirty to fifty cents a room. Several factors made possible these low rates. All the rooms were small—only large enough for a small bed, chair, and table. None had running water. All the guests used large washrooms centrally located on each of the floors, and towels were supplied at the washrooms. There were no conventional hotel services. No room had a telephone. There were no bellboys; each guest was expected to carry his own luggage and find his room by use of a guidebook and directions posted in the hall. Economies in housekeeping were achieved by clearing all the rooms between the hours of 9:00 A.M. and 4:00 P.M. Every morning at nine o'clock a loud bell was a signal for the guests to leave their rooms while the residence floors were being cleaned and the beds made up; at four o'clock in the afternoon another bell indicated that the men could return to their rooms.

Chicago's YMCA Hotel was distinguished in one respect from the low-cost Mills Hotels in New York city by the fact it was not intended any guest should stay for more than a few weeks. The YMCA Hotel, said a prospectus, was "a temporary residence, where, without membership fee, men could be comfortably and economically housed in a wholesome environment until such time as they could find employment or are ready to locate permanently."

In its first seven months of operation, the YMCA Hotel provided rooms for 61,888 men, who stayed an average of only three and one-half days. Of this number, about 5,000 were in actual poverty, unable to pay more than the thirty to fifty cents required daily (and thus confirming the estimate of the survey as to the number of men forced into cheap hotels by economic necessity). Over 1,600 of the Hotel's guests applied for help, of these 810 were granted loans. These loans were under the direction of an extraordinarily wise judge of human character, W. E. Routson, head of the Hotel's Personal Service Department. Over a period of twenty years, Routson was to lend a total of $141,629.90 to some 50,000 men—most of them strangers with whom he had only the opportunity for a short interview. Yet such was his acumen in distributing this aid, that the rate of repayment was a remarkable 92½ per cent—which, as John Nuveen, Jr. was to comment, is a much better average than most people can achieve with friends they have known a lifetime.

The Hotel was fortunate in having good management from the first. Ralph W. Cooke, the manager, stayed with the Hotel many years and developed an extensive program of entertainment, recreation, and educational and religious meetings for the strangers who formed a preponderant proportion of the guests. Because the YMCA Hotel was open to all young men, the Y was faced with the recurring problem of deciding how much of its effort should be directed toward keeping young men of good character away from deleterious influences and how much the Hotel should be considered an agency for redeeming those who might without strict supervision prove a demoralizing influence on the other guests. Upon the recommendation of Cooke, a policy was established which excluded only the worst elements. The Social Service secretary of the Hotel was permitted to decide after a private interview with questionable cases whether the hope of improving an applicant was greater than the risk that he might lead someone else into trouble.

During its first years of service, the YMCA Hotel was exclusively for men. Its cafeteria was restricted to male customers and all its services were directed toward men. As the years passed, this policy underwent a series of modifications and changes were made in the physical equipment of the Hotel so that it could be used by both men and women as well as families traveling together. Its primary purpose, however, remained that of serving young men in many ways which set it apart from a commercial hotel. Under the leadership of William P. Sidley and Harry J. Dunbaugh, chairmen of the Hotel's Board of Directors for many years, the Hotel established itself as a unique kind of philanthropic enterprise—"not for profit and yet self-supporting," in Dunbaugh's words. Thousands of men were given help in finding jobs or given counsel. Runaway boys were cared for and returned to their homes. As one writer was to put it in an article published in 1920, "The religious work at the YMCA Hotel, wholly aside from the lobby meetings Sunday mornings and evenings, and the nightly vesper services, is subtle, is persistent, and above all things is so practical that it has given hundreds if not thousands of young fellows a new grip on themselves and a start forward on the highroad of clean living or

Waiting in line to register at the YMCA Hotel during the first month it was open. Scenes like this proved the Hotel filled a real need in Chicago.

financial success." Cooke was to describe another element of the Hotel's service as "constructive philanthropy—not charity." In his view, the Hotel often was able to help more through proper guidance than through any amount of economic assistance.

Messer regarded the YMCA Hotel as probably the outstanding single achievement of the Chicago Association. The night before the Hotel was opened, he gave himself the experience of spending a night in one of the rooms. After the Hotel was in use, he would stop in frequently to talk with Cooke and to watch the young men coming in to register who had just arrived on the night trains. One of these young men was to identify himself in later years as Ed Sullivan, newspaper columnist and one of the most famous personalities in television. Then only fifteen (and registering under the name of Frank Keegan so his father could not find him to make him return home), Sullivan worked in the Illinois Central freight yards and slept at the YMCA Hotel, where he paid twenty-five cents a day for his room. His story could have been—and was—repeated by thousands of others.

As Messer watched the young men register at the Hotel or wait for their interview with Cooke, he often was reminded of the sentences he had used in appealing for support to build the Hotel:

"The greatest sight in the world is a man," he had said. "The saddest sight in the world is a wreck of a man. The noblest work in the world is the building of a man."

With the completion of the YMCA Hotel, Loring Wilbur Messer and the laymen who had built the Young Men's Christian Association of Chicago were certain that the Hotel would be a permanent beacon at "the doorway of city life" to help in the "building of a man."

CHAPTER **10**

"Greater Than Its Yesterdays"

IN THE years following the great debate between the metropolitan associations and the International Committee over association relationships, the metropolitan groups expanded their program and influence at an accelerated pace. By 1912 the statistically minded Messer was noting that the ten big-city associations in the United States enrolled "14 per cent of the entire membership; 15 per cent of the volunteer committeemen; 14 per cent of the employed officers; 18 per cent of the total property valuation, and 41-6/10 per cent of the total endowment funds." Of these associations, the YMCA of Chicago was first in endowment, second in number of employed officers, second in property valuation, third in point of membership and fourth in number of volunteer workers.

The year 1913 had marked the twenty-fifth anniversary of Messer's appointment as general secretary. In recognition of the services he had rendered, the Board of Managers voted to grant him a six-months' leave of absence with pay in order that he and Mrs. Messer might take a trip around the world. The minutes of Secretary Charles T. B. Goodspeed, which record this generous gesture, describe the trip as being "for that amount of time" which is "reasonably required for a trip to the Orient or such other parts of the world as he may wish to visit for the study of Association matters and for the rest and recreation which he needs and so well deserves." But although the Board of Managers could generously provide Messer with an opportunity to visit other lands, they could not restrict him to any program of "rest and recreation." His travel letters, still preserved in the vaults of the Association Building, reveal he was as busy on YMCA matters in the far corners of Asia as he had been during the twelve-day campaign on the corner of State and Monroe. His letters are filled with pleas for the support of foreign mission work. Many of his observations are buttressed with detailed statistical tables of the funds required to complete building campaigns in such foreign cities as Colombo (Ceylon) —one of the thirteen foreign associations where the YMCA of Chicago supported a secretary—Hong Kong, Madras, Delhi, and other cities of India. Messer was much in demand as a speaker on the foreign work of the YMCA after his return. In 1914, he was named chairman of a commission to study the relation of foreign work to the rest of the YMCA movement; out of this commission's study came recommendations that led to a broadening and modernizing of the approach to the foreign field.

Refreshed and stimulated by his experiences abroad, Messer promptly embarked upon a drive to increase the membership and participation in committee work of the Chicago departments. These efforts were climaxed by a two-week membership drive in 1915 which added 5,485 new members to the roster. By the end of 1915 the Association reported a total membership of 23,747 men and 5,990 boys enrolled in seven city departments, six railroad departments, three community departments, one Boys' Club, the YMCA Hotel, and twelve student departments. Of these members, more than 3,000 were actively serving on volunteer committees.

The community departments had been started in the Belmont Avenue area, Austin, and South Chicago. These departments were a means of serving communities where a YMCA building and the full program it made possible were not yet practicable goals. Using a small, rented headquarters, community departments conducted Bible study groups, religious meetings, classes in English, gave instruction in citizenship, personal and community hygiene, and disseminated safety information to factory and industrial workers. With a minimum of expenditure, the YMCA was thus able to extend its influence and, through the employment of one or two professional staff members, to support the work of the churches, Sunday Schools, and other constructive forces already established.

Meanwhile, the physical expansion made possible by the 50th Anniversary campaign was continuing. A West Side building was opened and dedicated on April 16, 1912. The same year three additional stories were constructed on top the Association Building at 19 South La Salle. The new Sears Roebuck Department was opened on January 1, 1912, with six hundred men and boys enrolled under the direction of Sears' first executive secretary, Herman A. Stotz, who had formerly been a volunteer leader in the gymnasium at Central. At Sears, the Association experienced its first difficulty in filling a dormitory; but a newspaper advertising campaign—the first of its kind ever undertaken by the Association—soon filled the dormitory to capacity.

Although not a part of the Chicago Association, the Chicago Institute and Training School was benefiting from the growth of the YMCA movement in the city and throughout the Midwest. A $500,000 building campaign in the Midwest states (in which committees from the Board of Managers and local Committees of Management took an active part) produced funds for a new college building at Fifty-third and Drexel that was dedicated in 1915. As George Williams College, the school has continued to give professional training for YMCA secretaries to the present day.

During this period of tremendous growth, Messer was frequently reiterating what he considered to be the central goal and purpose of the entire YMCA movement. ". . . The worldwide purpose of the Association [is] to continue its efforts to associate young men who profess to be disciples of Jesus Christ and to extend His Kingdom among young men," he wrote in 1907. "With this basis, the Association has a well-defined field of effort. . . . Its method must be so direct as to make clear this fundamental purpose. If the commercial instinct preoccupies the time and thought of Association leaders; if the chief emphasis is placed on the sale of privileges for temporary gain; if men are enlisted as paid or volunteer leaders solely because of their efficiency as specialists in their respective departments, will not the associate members and the community at large have reason to believe that the Association is well content with material, physical, mental, or social results?

"In the earlier life of the Association its leadership was composed of men who were filled with a burning zeal to bring their fellows to a personal knowledge of Jesus Christ as Lord and Master," Messer continued. "Is there not now a need of a revival of fundamental religion among secretaries, committeemen, and our so-called active members? . . . Emphasis will then be placed upon the prayer life, the personal conversation of individuals with individuals, the holding of more meetings with a distinctly evangelistic purpose, the expectation of definite results, the enrollment of more men in Bible study who seek to qualify themselves for intelligent Christian service, and on Christian nurture through membership and service in the church of God."

Several times in the next few years, the *Bulletin* was to complain that the religious work was one of the weak points of the Association program. Messer, in his annual reports, referred to the "barrenness of spiritual results" and the small number of conversions and church memberships reported. However, by 1910 Messer was able to report that the "direct spiritual forces of the Chicago Association" included twenty-seven Bible classes for men and boys and twenty-five devotional or evangelistic services each week. Special evangelistic meetings were held and a missionary fund of $4,000 was raised for special work in Hong Kong.

Although Messer continued to emphasize the final religious objective of the YMCA, a process of evolution soon found the Y devoting more and more of its time to those things which the churches could not do and putting the emphasis in its spiritual work on directing young men toward an active affiliation with a church of their choice. In this way, both the church and the YMCA were able to concentrate on the work each was best equipped to do without a conflict in programs.

An analysis of the expenditures of the Chicago Association reveals this trend. The cost of social activities leaped from $875.20 in 1900 to $8,613.50 in 1909—an increase of almost 1,000 per cent. Physical activity expenditures zoomed from $2,678.67 in 1900 to $26,624.85 in 1909. The costs of the educational program more than doubled during the same period, increasing from $9,467.55 to $22,647.98.

Messer regarded these increased expenditures in other than

religious fields as a shifting of the YMCA toward "prevention rather than rescue, construction rather than reconstruction, formation rather than reformation." Most significant of all, he felt, was the Association's "redefinition of its object in terms of the development of Christian character or well-rounded Christian personality" rather than religious conversion.

In no way did this change of emphasis mean an abandonment of religious responsibility by the YMCA. The YMCA of Chicago still acknowledged that it was its responsibility to direct young men toward a church where they might find a full religious life. To make this work effective, a special study was carried out, and in June of 1911 Harry T. Williams was called to the position of Interchurch secretary. He was charged with the responsibility of developing and correlating the various religious interests of the YMCA with those of the churches. The same year, the YMCA assumed responsibility for the local direction of the nation-wide Men and Religion campaign. With Williams acting as Chicago chairman for the Men and Religion drive, a special "recognition day" was held in all the city's churches on June 25, 1911. The purpose of this campaign, as explained in the *Bulletin*, was "to carry out the plan and program of the Men and Religion forward movement, including social service, boys' work, evangelism, missions, and Bible study, laying special emphasis on the effort to increase the male membership of the local church and secure greater efficiency in Christian service in and through the church; in the matter of plan we purpose to work through the regular agencies, laying special emphasis on personal work by men, with men, for men."

A special need for such personal counseling was not far away. In 1914 war erupted in Europe and the possibility of American involvement hung like a billowing thunderhead on the horizon of any plans for (or by) American young men. As

The Y. M. C. A. is to the boys "over there" and in camp.

This cartoon from the *Chicago Evening Post* was typical of many which appeared in Chicago newspapers to support the YMCA War Fund Campaign.

early as 1916, when American troops were sent to the Mexican border, five secretaries from the Chicago Association went with them to carry on work among the troops in the tradition established by Moody during the Civil War. When the United States entered the war in Europe in April of 1917, Messer was among one hundred YMCA leaders who met at Garden City, Long Island, to formulate a program of special work among the troops. This meeting led to the establishment of the National War Work Council, of which Messer was a member of the executive committee.

While many YMCA secretaries went to the front with the troops, the Chicago Association rendered all the services possible to soldiers training near Chicago or passing through the city on troop trains. Men in uniform were granted the use of Y facilities without charge, and discharged veterans were voted a three-months free membership. During the months of the war, volunteers met every troop train with postcards, stamps, pencils, drinking cups, games, bandages, telegraph blanks, fruit, and newspapers. The Association also supplied Army rest rooms and lounges at railroad stations with phonographs, records, books, magazines, newspapers, pamphlets, Bibles, games, and writing materials. More than 200 volunteers vigilantly patrolled the streets, locating soldiers who were lost or who were bewildered by the city and seeking some form of diversion during their leave. More than 11,000 such soldiers and sailors were directed to the Y's dormitories. Sleeping capacity in all departments was increased by providing a special cot service in the gymnasiums and auditoriums; this permitted more than 2,500 men to spend the night in a YMCA who might otherwise have had to sleep on a bench in the park or in a cheap flophouse. Every Sunday YMCA workers traveled to Fort Sheridan and the Great Lakes Naval Training Station north of Chicago to teach Bible classes.

A free automobile service from the YMCA departments to all the rail stations and outlying depots was provided by Y members. This help did not cease with the Armistice. Following the war, the YMCA of Chicago gave 10,438 free memberships to returned soldiers, found jobs for 3,378, referred 4,747 to churches, and found a place to live for 1,415. Special rehabilitation assistance was given to 600 wounded men when they were discharged from the Public Health Hospital at Forty-seventh and Drexel.

Following the war, the Chicago Association withdrew quickly from the National War Work Council, which Messer believed was tending to perpetuate the type of authority to which he had objected so vigorously some twenty years before. An even more urgent reason for his withdrawal was his desire to direct all his energies toward a further expansion of the activities and facilities of the Chicago Association. It was not long before he and Parker were directing a new series of studies to determine just what form this expansion should take.

An Army YMCA building at Fort Sheridan, Illinois.

An Army YMCA truck used in serving soldiers and sailors in the area around Chicago during World War I.

Although Messer was the leader, spokesman, and chief fund raiser for the Chicago Association for many years, another important factor in the Association's growth was the business acumen and management talents of Parker, the business secretary. Together, these two men formed a brilliant team. While Messer was dramatizing new goals and leading the way to their accomplishment, Parker was building a reservoir of public confidence by purposefully and carefully seeing that the money entrusted to the Association was made to do the work for which it was given. For example, in executing the building program made possible by the 50th Anniversary endowment, Parker held in reserve sufficient money to provide for depreciation and the replacement of equipment. By his foresight, he made it possible to use all new funds for new projects and avoided the diversion of later contributions to paying for emergency repairs or operating deficits. This meant that each new dollar raised represented an opportunity for growth.

Following World War I, the Chicago Association had reached a point where it had to make provision for additional equipment and facilities. Parker, in an article in the *Bulletin* in 1919, reported that the YMCA buildings were "bursting with men and boys," the dormitories all had waiting lists, the educational classes were crowded "beyond reasonable limits," and the physical directors were "at their wits' end" in attempting to make their equipment meet the demands upon it. The YMCA Hotel was turning away as many as five hundred young men in a day, although some rooms were always kept for boys who might be strangers in the city. (Manager Ralph W. Cooke reported that for two months there had not been a day when there were not more requests for rooms than the Hotel had been able to fill.) In all departments, Parker said, whether general, railroad, community, student, or the new industrial department, activities

The *Bulletin* followed YMCA members to training camp and to the front.

THE OFFICIAL·BULLETIN.

IN TRAINING CAMP, PORT ROYAL, S.C.
U.S. MARINE·CORPS.

From the
NORTH AVENUE·LARRABEE ST
Y.M.C.A.

were under way "beyond anything the Association has ever undertaken in the past."

Despite this capacity effort, he noted, approximately 85 per cent of the city's population remained outside the range of the Y's present buildings. "By conducting extension work or community work in shops, playgrounds, public schools, and at other places, the Association is attempting to bring at least a little of its service to the great unoccupied fields of the city," he wrote. "It seems very clear, however, that the Association cannot hope for large growth except by the erection of many new buildings. We have gone as far as we can with the present equipment."

Characteristically, the Messer-Parker team made no public appeal for funds until they were able to offer a program as specific as that of the 50th Anniversary campaign. It was not enough for them to know that additional facilities were needed. They also wanted to know (1) where they were the most needed, (2) what kind of facilities would best meet the needs of each community, (3) whether the community could support a department of the YMCA, and (4) whether the present YMCA program justified appealing for more funds.

Their first step in seeking answers to these questions was to divide the city into thirty-three districts on the basis of population homogeneity, cultural communities, neighborhood barriers (such as railroad tracks and the river) and other factors. In each of these districts complete data was collected and evaluated on the population (both as to its number and racial and ethnological composition), hotels, commercial recreation, businesses and industries, social settlements, parks, playgrounds, beaches, lodges and clubs already functioning, schools, churches, and future possibilities and needs. On the basis of this data, an estimate was made of the kind of YMCA service needed in each district. The data as to the needs was then matched with infor-

217

mation from YMCA's in smaller cities with a population comparable in size to that of each district to determine what kind of a program such an area might be able to support.

The survey produced the following conclusions:

1. In the seven districts out of the thirty-three where YMCA programs were functioning, the Y was a success as judged by:

    a. Services rendered.—All buildings were operating at their physical capacity.

    b. Local leadership.—Each was run by a local Committee of Management.

    c. Financial support.—All departments were averaging $10,000 per year in contributions from the neighborhoods.

    d. Test of time.—Development had been steady, uninterrupted even by the "turmoil of war."

2. That a system of buildings would provide the following advantages:

    a. Comprehensive planning, both as to the Y program and relations to churches and other welfare institutions.

    b. Uniformity of practice and availability of YMCA to members moving to different sections of city.

    c. Specialization.—Department programs could be adapted to needs of community.

    d. City-wide personnel program for professional staff. (Messer was interested in a personnel department to deal with problems, salary schedules, efficiency standards, and working conditions of salaried employees.)

    e. Competition would stimulate each unit.

    f. Impressiveness.—"In a great city filled with great businesses," the prospectus commented, "people like to be connected with great enterprises."

The goals approved by the Board of Managers after a study of the survey constituted a "great enterprise" sufficient to impress even the boldest Chicagoan. The Board set as its objective the addition to present buildings of facilities costing $4,000,000; the erection of twenty-seven new buildings at a cost of $11,065,000; and the establishment of six special departments (another Y hotel on the West Side, more Boys' Clubs, etc.) at a cost of $3,200,000. These figures totalled $18,320,000. Undismayed, the Board added to this figure an "allowance for shrinkage in collection, promotion expenses, and errors in estimates" that brought the grand total objective to $19,000,000.

The taking of the survey, compilation of figures, and evaluation of data had taken two years. As the plan was subjected to renewed scrutiny, certain features were eliminated (such as a hotel for boys) but the over-all objective remained intact. In 1922 a Greater Expansion Committee was appointed to carry out the directive from the Board of Managers. The chairman of the committee was John V. Farwell, Jr., one of the men who had brought Messer to Chicago thirty-four years earlier. Another member was Cyrus H. McCormick, who with Farwell and Houghteling had promised Messer their continuing support many years before. (Houghteling had died in 1910.) Other members were T. E. Donnelley, E. J. Buffington, James B. Forgan, William V. Kelley, John G. Shedd, and W. F. Hypes, who had assumed office as president of the Association in 1916.

But even as the Board of Managers was making its verdict on the expansion program known, Messer was receiving another kind of verdict from his doctors. In the fall of 1922 he had become ill at his summer home at Owl's Head, near Rockland, Maine. Returning to Chicago, he heard the specialists at Presbyterian Hospital diagnose the ailment as cancer of the face. There was no hope of a cure.

Weakened by his illness and suffering great pain, Messer was now forced to give up his post as general secretary of the Chicago Association after thirty-five years of leadership. In January, 1923, he was formally retired—but not before he had included these paragraphs in his final report to the Association:

"We surely recognize that we are citizens of no mean city. The assets of Chicago are greater than its liabilities. The goodness here is greater than the evil. . . . The Association has been, is now and ever must be, a great leader in the fight for civic and personal righteousness, looking forward to the time when there will be universal obedience to law, loyalty to the home, to the church, and to every constructive institution.

"On this sure and firm foundation, the Young Men's Christian Association of Chicago has for more than six decades been steadily constructing a symmetrical, enduring superstructure or organization which has increasingly received the good will, confidence, and co-operation of Chicago's best citizens. . . . Today, the best asset of the Association is its good name. The tomorrows of the Association must be greater than its yesterdays. Bounding forward to new tasks, pulsating with young and vigorous life, this Association will surely encompass the city until every young man and boy of whatever nationality, religion, or occupation, whether he be poor or rich, learned or ignorant, may find easily available the equipment, program and fellowship necessary for the building of symmetrical manhood and of useful, dependable citizenship. . . .

"Speaking from the experience of one who for forty-one years has considered it his highest privilege and joy to serve such a noble cause, and whose heart thrills at the remembrance of what he has been enabled to see in the transformed lives of the great multitude of men and boys, I throw out to you, one and

Jottings from Messer's notebook reveal his deep religious faith.

all, the challenge to dedicate the best that is in you, for life, to this matchless service for the growing youth of our city and of the world in order that they may follow in the steps of our Lord and Master 'Who advanced in wisdom and in stature and in favor with God and man' . . ."

Following his retirement, Messer took a short vacation in Atlantic City. Returning to Chicago again, he wrote in his pocket notebook these verses:

If it be possible, let this cup pass from me: nevertheless, not my will but Thine be done.

And my God shall supply all your needs according to his riches in Jesus Christ.

The Lord is my shepherd, I shall not want.

Consoled by the resources of his own faith, Loring Wilbur Messer entered the hospital for the last time, waiting patiently for death that finally relieved him from his pain on July 15, 1923.

The funeral services were held at the Hyde Park Methodist Church under the direction of two old friends—the Reverend Charles W. Gilkey and Fletcher S. Brockman. But perhaps the most eloquent eulogy was that of his friend, Julius Rosenwald, who said: "It is indeed a benediction to have been permitted the privilege of the friendship of this rare man."

CHAPTER 11

"To Promote the Physical, Mental and Spiritual Welfare"

FOR MORE than two decades, Messer had been sharing the responsibilities of leadership in the Association with William J. Parker, and it was to Parker that the Board of Managers eventually turned as its choice to be the new general secretary of the Chicago Association. The fact that Parker was so widely known minimized the dislocations which might otherwise have resulted from the loss of such a strong and admired leader as Messer. Parker was, of course, highly respected for his business judgment. In addition, his vision and strong convictions enabled him to get the best efforts from the volunteer workers associated with him—a skill essential to any successful leader in a voluntary agency like the Young Men's Christian Association. Parker also had the confidence of the Board of Managers, with whom he had dealt through many years, so that the Board gave vigorous support to plans for pushing ahead toward the ambitious goals outlined in the Greater Chicago Expansion Plan.

Hyde Park was the first department to get its expansion drive under way. Through two intensive campaigns in 1921 and in 1923, it had raised $464,543 for an addition known as the East Building. Dedicated in 1923 at a cost of $673,398, the extension wing provided for additional dormitory rooms, a swimming pool, gymnasium, billiard room, assembly hall, and a game room for boys.

The year 1923 also saw the honoring of an old pledge to the citizens of Englewood. This area, which lay south of Fifty-fifth Street and west of State, had a population in 1920 of more than 200,000. Both to the YMCA and to the people of Englewood, there seemed justification for a major effort to re-establish the department closed in 1899. A community program without equipment had been started in the area in 1919. Four years later, an Englewood citizens' committee under the leadership of William B. Wanzer, William F. Friedeman, and William F. Tegtmeier inaugurated a building fund campaign in which it obtained more than 3,000 individual gifts totaling $380,596. An unusual measure of support was given the drive by the Englewood Kiwanis Club, which contributed $10,000 as a club and then augmented this with $56,000 in additional pledges from individual members. Another active leader in the campaign was Theodore P. Day, who had been executive secretary of the first Englewood Department and who returned from his home in Marblehead, Massachusetts, to help redeem the promise that had been made a quarter of a century earlier. With funds in hand, ground was broken for the new Englewood (now Southtown) Department building on November 8, 1924. When the department was dedicated on April 11, 1926, it counted 558 charter members.

On the West Side, in the community of Austin, an equally impressive fund drive was in progress. The YMCA had been

William J. Parker
served as business manager and
general secretary for many years;
his high standards of management
created a sense of confidence
which encouraged the public
to contribute to the YMCA.

represented in Austin since 1913, when a community boys' work
program was organized by Fred A. Crosby and a group of
Austinites who met in the old Oaks clubhouse at Lake Street
and Waller Avenue. World War I had disrupted their efforts to
construct a building. Then, in 1919, A. H. Clement and others
opened new discussions pointing toward a home for the Austin
YMCA. By 1922 a fund drive had been fully organized under
the direction of Clement, Judge C. S. Cutting, P. D. Castel,
A. Frank Durley, and George J. Dehn. Within a few months
volunteer solicitors succeeded in raising $298,798. Subsequent
campaigns in 1923 and 1925 brought this fund up to $415,880.
On February 28, 1926, the new Austin Department building
was dedicated. (As Clement received the keys to the building
from John Nuveen of the Board of Trustees, he remarked,
"These keys open the door to the love of Austin.") There could
be no doubt about Austin's enthusiastic reception of the new
Y building; on opening day a smashing throng of more than five

thousand pushed through the building in less than three hours.

Far across the city from Austin, another fund drive was being organized in an area where the YMCA had convincingly demonstrated its ability to adapt its programs to the needs of a particular community within the city. South Chicago at this time was about as different from other communities with Y programs as it could be. Hyde Park and Austin were located in sections with middle-class homes and very little industry; South Chicago lived completely in the shadow (and smoke) of the steel mills. Austin and Hyde Park were populated for the most part by native Americans and white-collar workers; South Chicago then was predominantly a section of immigrants who made their living toiling at the heavy tasks of the mills. Wages in South Chicago at the time were low; living conditions were only a thin margin above the subsistence level.

The first attempt to establish a YMCA in South Chicago had been made in 1890 but had ended in defeat six years later. In 1909-1910, Abraham Bowers carried the Y banner back to South Chicago with Americanization classes for immigrants. Two years later a group of community leaders asked the YMCA to augment this program with a schedule of activities for young boys. The Y was quick to agree to this proposal, and in a short time was sponsoring outdoor athletic activities in Trumbull Park. During the war years and shortly thereafter, a special industrial program primarily for Wisconsin Steel Works employees of the International Harvester Company was established in the area; the staff of the Y taught English classes, industrial safety, and other subjects which eased the process of integration for foreign-born workers. Many of these activities were carried on in the mills themselves, the steel companies paying ten cents per month per employee to support the work. This program was disrupted by the steel strike after the war, but the men who wanted to see a YMCA in South Chicago refused to retreat a second time. They were in South Chicago to stay.

Andrew Wallace and the other supporters of the young YMCA knew that a building was urgently needed as a focus for Y activities. But they were equally aware that because of the nature of the population, a building could not be erected without a major contribution from the United States Steel Corporation, South Chicago's largest employer. During a period of five years, various proposals were forwarded to Judge Elbert Gary, chairman of the board of U. S. Steel, in New York; but Gary would make no commitment. Finally, in 1923, an appointment was made through Gary's personal secretary, Fred Sites (whose parents had been missionaries in China and who himself had been active in the Shanghai YMCA) for a committee of Chicagoans to call on Gary and present the problem to him in person.

The committee consisted of Cyrus H. McCormick, William J. Parker, J. A. Hiller, Chicago industrial secretary, and Simon Lundquist and Warren W. Smith from South Chicago. McCormick was the spokesman for the group; after describing the need for the Y, he asked Gary to contribute half a million dollars through the corporation. Gary was still reluctant. "You fellows are too much sold on this proposition," he told his visitors. He insisted they give him some names of U. S. Steel executives who might also be willing to endorse the need for a Y building in South Chicago. (All such men had been screened from the committee so that their jobs would not be compromised.) From the names provided, Gary chose that of P. A. Newton, as a result of whose recommendation Gary agreed to give $300,000 toward a new building if the community would guarantee to raise an equal amount. (Later he raised this to $375,000.) The businessmen and industrial executives in the area, led by E. J. Buffington, head of U. S. Steel's Chicago operations, were quick to respond to this challenge. An intensive solicitation of small industries and business establishments quickly produced gifts that brought the total funds available to $700,229.

Meanwhile, the professional staff of the South Chicago Department had been engaged in a remarkably foresighted program of building good community relations. In addition to the classes in the mills, a special gardening program was established for the workers' families. Large lots were staked out, plowed, and turned over to the workers to raise their own vegetables in the manner of the Victory Gardens of World Wars I and II. Other special garden projects for children were arranged through the schools.

Baseball leagues for boys were organized on a basis probably unique in the history of the great American game. The winning team was not the one which scored the most runs, necessarily, but the one which had the most points based on a mathematical formula that included such factors as Dependability, Sportsmanship, and General Conduct. The instructions to the official scorers reflect the chaos which often existed before the games were reorganized. In determining the winning team, the Y's scorer was instructed to give 40 per cent for Dependability (being on time and playing the entire game without getting mad and quitting); 25 per cent for Sportsmanship (this included the players' attitude toward the umpire, who in the past had frequently been chased from the field); 15 per cent for General Conduct (absence of profanity and not smoking during the game), and 20 per cent for the number of runs scored. This program was so successful that the Y staff was asked informally to organize boys' leagues for the Roman Catholic churches in the community on the same basis. South Chicago, in fact, appears to have been a pioneer among Chicago departments in broadening the basis for religious participation by all faiths in the YMCA program. At the laying of the cornerstone for the new building in 1925, the final prayer was given by Dr. G. George Fox, the rabbi of South Shore Temple. And shortly after the new structure was dedicated on November 7, 1926, the Santa Maria Council of the Knights of Columbus marched in a body to join in the ceremonies and reception celebrating the completion of the new building. To many, it appeared that in coming by the hardest route, South Chicago had also come the longest way.

Another South Side community was also stirring with plans. Civic leaders in the communities of Roseland, Pullman, and West Pullman met with J. Ward Nelson of the Chicago Association to formulate plans for reviving the Roseland Department of the YMCA—abandoned in 1904. An appropriation of $258,-044 was made from the new building fund and an additional $267,098 of endowment funds invested in residence facilities to make it possible for YMCA services to be restored to these communities. On December 19, 1926, a new building was dedicated at 4 East 111th Street which represented a total investment of $654,270. Local campaigners under the leadership of R. V. Brown, Charles H. Brandt, and N. W. Wiersema, chairman of the first Committee of Management, raised $145,387 to finish the building fund for the new department, which took as its name the 111th Street YMCA. Serving on the original board with Wiersema were two other lay workers, Orrin A. Eames and G. F. Roberts, who were to serve more than twenty years without interruption in helping build the 111th Street Department.

Earlier in the same month that the 111th Street YMCA was dedicated, a building similar in design and plan had been opened at Kildare and Irving Park Boulevard as the home of the Irving Park YMCA. At the dedication, John V. Farwell, president of the Board of Trustees, revealed that the site had been purchased even before a building campaign had been agreed upon. That the trustees' confidence was not misplaced was dramatically demonstrated when Charles O. Loucks and the local Committee of Management, aided by about two hundred volunteers, brought in $198,956 toward the $647,043 cost of the building within a few months. An equally impressive accomplishment of the fledgling Irving Park Department was its first membership campaign; a committee under the direction of Ralph H. Beesley and executive secretary E. R. Bolin signed up 2,081 members within ten days after the opening of the department.

At Congress and Wood streets, west of the Loop, another new building was under construction for students at the West Side professional schools, where Dr. Truman W. Brophy, president emeritus of the Chicago College of Dental Surgery, had made an initial gift of a building site valued at $50,000 toward the creation of a $500,000 building fund. The new building, erected at a cost of $941,355, included 348 residence rooms, a gymnasium, handball courts, and several clubrooms in addition to a cafeteria, students' lounge, and other facilities. At the time of its dedication in 1927, the West Side Professional Schools Department represented the finest building for student YMCA work in the world. It continued to serve the students at the West Side professional schools until 1952, when it had to be demolished because it stood in the path of the Congress Street Expressway.

On the North Side, a campaign for a department at 3333 North Marshfield Avenue (to be known as the Lincoln-Belmont YMCA) had gone over its goal, and construction plans were being drawn for a new building. The first chairman of the Committee of Management of the Lincoln-Belmont Department was Elmer F. Wieboldt, whose father, William A. Wieboldt, had continued his vigorous support of the Y's program with a gift of $100,000 to the Lincoln-Belmont Department.

The Lincoln-Belmont Department, dedicated on October 7, 1928, and housed in a building erected at a cost of $816,720, was the ninth department to be established of those proposed in the original expansion plan. Although there remained twenty-two districts of the city in which the Y had not yet been able to establish a program, the expansion plan had produced on the positive side an increase of more than seven and a half million dollars in YMCA facilities in Chicago in a period of less than seven years.

The opening of five new department buildings in 1926 made the year one of the most remarkable in the history of the international YMCA movement. Never, in any other city, had there been such a remarkable expansion of YMCA facilities within such a short time. The opening of these new facilities for the youth of Chicago was also the climax of the administration of William F. Hypes, the general sales manager of the Marshall Field & Company wholesale division, who had served as president of the Association for ten years—longer than any other man. During those ten years, the assets of the Association had nearly doubled. The departmental building schedule had been accelerated, and camping had been transferred from a makeshift basis to a planned program carried on at eight permanent camp sites. When Hypes declined to stand for re-election, he was succeeded by William P. Francis, a Chicago industrialist, who was to serve during five years that were to embrace some of the most prosperous—and most financially difficult—years in the Association's history.

The 1920's also saw the development of a more liberal policy with respect to the type of program offered at the YMCA's and the establishment of a modern program of public relations and promotional activities. In 1924, the Wilson Avenue Department held what was believed to be the first dance sponsored by a department of the YMCA of Chicago. It was planned as a group activity, with nurses from a nearby hospital and girls from a women's residence being invited to come as a group and meet the boys from the residence at Wilson Avenue. The dance was a success and continued to be held as a group affair for several years.

The Chicago Association was quick to exploit the new medium of radio. In January of 1924, the physical section of Central began a series of early morning health broadcasts over station KYW between 6:30 and 7:00 A.M. As a result of these broadcasts, Central received more than 54,000 letters and dis-

Paul Leonhardt broadcast setting-up exercises for the Central YMCA in 1924.

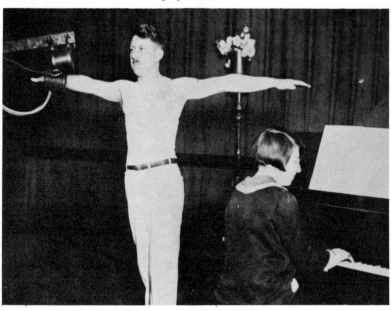

tributed in excess of 64,000 exercise charts. One businessman wrote that the exercises were "reducing my weight and, incidentally, my early morning peeve." A young girl wrote that ". . . when Mama starts to take her daily dozen, the birds begin to sing, the dog barks, and even the gas range vibrates." The Y also conducted a morning devotional service over WLS and a Friday Forum and program of setting-up exercises over WMAQ. When Queen Marie of Rumania visited Chicago, the Hyde Park Department of the YMCA was included on her itinerary. "I only wish we had such a building in our country," the Queen remarked wistfully to her host, President Francis.

As it had done in earlier years, the YMCA of Chicago continued to elicit the support of outstanding personalities from the city's business community. A tremendous impetus to the city-wide development of the Association was the interest taken in the West Side Department by a single man—Joseph S. Duncan, president of the Addressograph Company. Duncan's offices and plant were on the West Side at Peoria and Van Buren. Often, on his way to work, he would see the children of the slums playing in the streets and gutters. Wishing in some way to help these boys, he began a systematic inquiry into the means available for helping them. At the West Side Department of the YMCA, he decided he had found his answer. Although the equipment was inadequate for the number of boys the Y was trying to help in the limited quarters available, Duncan was impressed by the interest and knowledge of the adult volunteers and staff workers who were supervising the boys' program. One of the goals toward which the members were struggling, he learned, was a low-cost summer camp to serve the boys from the West Side. As an experiment, he purchased a plot of land on Fish Lake, fifty miles northwest of Chicago, and gave it to the West Side Department to establish such a camp. Camp

Joseph S. Duncan ranks
as one of the outstanding laymen
in the history of the Chicago
Association. The Duncan YMCA
is named in his honor.

Duncan, as it was to be known, was the first permanent camp site of the Chicago Association.

Duncan did more than contribute funds. A. C. Williams —who was to serve forty-one years at the department, most of them as executive secretary—recalled later that Duncan took a personal interest in the camp program carried on in the make-shift facilities. Impressed with the techniques and results of the YMCA approach and satisfied with his first investment, Duncan increased his contribution to the camp from $3,000 to $11,000 and later provided permanent buildings and other equipment for the camp. Back in Chicago during the winter months, he was making additional plans to help the boys of the West Side. In 1926 he purchased the plot of land adjoining the West Side Department and the following year gave $250,000 so that a new dormitory and boys' work building could be constructed there. The addition of these new rooms brought the total available at the West Side Department to 363—second only to the

YMCA Hotel. But most important to Duncan was the fact that the residences made more revenue possible for a continuing expansion of work among underprivileged boys. Duncan also continued his personal support of the department, which by 1932 had reached a total of more than half a million dollars. In recognition of Duncan's many financial and personal contributions to the YMCA of Chicago, the Board of Managers in 1932 officially changed the name of the West Side Department to that of the Joseph S. Duncan YMCA.

Duncan's first gift for a camp spurred the Board of Managers to make provisions for other permanent camp sites. Previously, camping activities had been almost entirely on an im-

"A True Story of Bona Fide Boys Who Whistle and Smile While Doing Family Dishes" is how the editor of the *Bulletin* titled these pictures of boys demonstrating skills they had learned at a YMCA summer camp.

A young camper
gets "close to nature."

provised basis in whatever location could be obtained. In 1918
the various camp programs had been supplemented by the sending of one hundred boys to Door County, Wisconsin, to help
pick the cherry crop, earn some spending money, and save the
cherries which might otherwise have been lost because of the
manpower shortage due to the war. Among the boys taking
part in this excursion was one named Carl A. Schroeder, later
to be postmaster of the city of Chicago and an active YMCA
layman. During the summer of 1920, arrangements were made
for one thousand working boys to spend at least one weekend
at Sand Dunes camp near Miller, Indiana. Short camping expe-
ditions were also arranged by the individual departments.

Following Duncan's gift for a camp site on Fish Lake (later

renamed Duncan Lake) near Volo, Illinois, the Board of Managers and Board of Trustees authorized the purchase of 246 acres of land on Hastings Lake in Lake County, Illinois, to establish a second camp. Both Camp Duncan and Camp Hastings were put into operation in the summer of 1923.

The *Bulletin* provided a schedule of a typical day at Camp Duncan that first summer:

A.M.

6:30 Reveille
6:40 Assembly, line-up for setup and dip
7:10 Assembly, flag raising and personal inspection
7:20 Mess call—breakfast
7:45 Camp duties—sanitation, KP, clean up
8:45 Assembly, morning chapel, tent inspection
9:15 Instruction period—nature study, first aid, life-saving, camp construction, handicraft
10:15 Morning game period, boating, fishing
10:45 Swimming instruction for beginners
11:00 Swimming period
12:00 Mess call—dinner

P.M.

12:30 Rest period, store open
1:30 Athletic schedule, competition, hikes, games
4:00 Swimming period
5:30 Supper
6:00 Games, boating, athletics, store open
8:00 Campfire and stunts
9:15 Devotions
9:30 Taps

The element of chance was also to have a part in providing a third camp site. Far to the north on the eastern side of Lake

Michigan near Ludington, a Michigan farmer was talking to Ralph W. Cooke, who was vacationing nearby and who had offered to help the farmer put up his hay crop. "I am getting old," the farmer told his new friend from Chicago. "I would like this place used for the Lord's work. He gave it to me and now it should go back to the Lord." It was quite a statement for the sixty-four-year-old farmer who since 1880 had spent his life grubbing stumps, making a little farm, and providing for the needs of his hermitlike existence. But Martin Johnson, the farmer who was speaking, was no stereotype of a rough-hewn woodsman who needed only a log cabin, a pot of coffee, some salt pork and beans. He was an artist as well as a farmer and homesteader. On his farm were acres of orchards and gardens, a mile and a half of cultivated and planted lakeside, and a workshop and studio. To Ralph Cooke, it seemed a place that boys would enjoy as much as Martin Johnson.

Martin Johnson (with beard) poses with Gren O. Pierrel and Ralph W. Cooke, executive secretaries of the Association, President W. F. Hypes, General Secretary W. J. Parker, and C. T. B. Goodspeed.

"Why not make a boys' camp of it?" Cooke asked, as he pitched up another forkful of hay.

"I would like that," Johnson replied. "How can it be done?" (Later, Johnson himself was to write of this moment and say, "Then I knew what I had been working for.")

Within a few months, Johnson had transferred the title of the sixty-seven acres of land he had torn from the wilderness to the YMCA. In return, he received a modest annuity of $540 a year which represented a normal return on the $9,000 at which he had evaluated his farm. The Board of Trustees had wanted to set a value of $12,000, but Johnson insisted on the lower figure which, he said, would provide him with all that he needed. He also surprised the Board by including in the deed not only the land but his workshop, studio, and all he possessed, including his livestock.

In 1925 Camp Martin Johnson was opened with W. E. Clevenger as camp director and Johnson's nephew and namesake as caretaker of the property. To Johnson the opening of the camp represented the fulfillment of his life. "I have finished my work," he told his friend, Ralph Cooke, "and now it is time for me to die." Cooke and others, however, persuaded him to remain in his home on the property; for seven years he was unofficial counselor and nature guide to all the boys who came to Camp Martin Johnson. When death finally came to Martin Johnson in the spring of 1931, he was buried among the evergreens and birches near his home. Today, a boulder and a tablet at Camp Martin Johnson mark the grave of the man who gave everything he had, as he put it, "to be used by and for boys."

The acquisition of other camp sites followed quickly between 1923 and 1925. Camp Wabash, owned and operated by the Wabash Avenue Department, was established on a lake fourteen miles from Benton Harbor, Michigan. Dr. G. D. Searle

Boys at Camp Pinewood, operated by the 111th Street YMCA, enjoy a watermelon feast. Tents served as cabins when this picture was taken in 1930.

made a generous contribution which permitted the Wilson Avenue Department to establish Camp Northwoods on a piece of land in the Lac du Flambeau Indian reservation. Here, and at nearby Camp Nawakwa, boys could get an undiluted taste of forest living. In the evenings they sat around a campfire with Chippewa Indians and listened to stories of tribal legends or watched the Chippewas do their traditional dances. At Camp Pinewood on Echo Lake near Twin Lake, Michigan, two summer camps were operated—one for younger boys and another for older age groups. Originally Camp Pinewood was operated by Central, but as the center of the city became increasingly industrial and fewer boys were within Central's area, the camp was transferred to Wilson Avenue, which in 1929 closed its operation at Camp Northwoods. In 1927, Mr. and Mrs. Claude C. Niles of River Forest donated to Camp Pinewood the buildings for the first outdoor summer schools in the United States. During the years that Central occupied the camp, both the Junior and Senior High Schools of Central held summer classes there. Camp Channing was also established during this period. Originally operated by the Division Street Department in leased grounds at the junction of the Des Plaines and Kankakee rivers, the camp was transferred to its permanent home near Pullman, Michigan, in 1925, where it continued to be directed by the Division Street Department.

Much of the building program in Chicago had been made possible by a bequest from Victor F. Lawson, publisher of the *Chicago Daily News*, who died in August of 1925. Lawson had no official connection with the YMCA in later years, as it was his policy not to be identified with an organization lest his interest in the group compromise his editorial integrity. However, through his friend, John V. Farwell, Jr., Lawson continued to

Kitchen duty at Camp Channing found a group of boys enjoying music from an early model home-made radio.

be interested in the YMCA and had been one of the donors of $100,000 to the 50th Anniversary fund. He was to be even more generous in his bequests after his death. In his will he provided that the Chicago Association should receive $100,000 plus one-fourth of his residuary estate. A recent computation placed the total value of this bequest at $3,590,571—the largest single benefaction in the history of the YMCA of Metropolitan Chicago.

To honor the man who had made it possible for the YMCA to extend its services to so much of Chicago, the Board of Managers and the Board of Trustees voted to erect "a monumental building in honor of Victor F. Lawson." Farwell pointed out that despite Lawson's influence on the city and American journalism, the publisher had been of a retiring nature and had permitted no formal recognition of his place in the city's life during his years of service. Because Lawson's home had been at 1500 Lake Shore Drive, Farwell said a decision had been reached to erect a Y building "on the near North Side, where Mr. Lawson spent so much of his life." A survey of the near North Side area had disclosed there were 25,000 unmarried persons living in rooming houses in the area bounded by the Chicago River on the south and Lincoln Park on the north. The great majority of these were men, some of them students attending the professional schools at the downtown campus of Northwestern University.

The Lawson YMCA building was more elaborate than any that had been constructed in Chicago. As it was intended that it appeal to young men with white-collar jobs or young professional men, its furnishings were more elaborate than those of the regular department dormitory rooms or the YMCA Hotel. The cost of the building, which could accommodate more than eight hundred men in its nineteen floors of residences, was set at $2,823,248.

Victor F. Lawson, publisher of the *Chicago Daily News*, contributed to the YMCA during his lifetime and upon his death bequeathed it the largest contribution of its history.

New to Chicago was the color treatment planned for the exterior of the Lawson building. A "flowing color design," as its architect described it, was to be achieved by the use of vari-colored stones and bricks in its construction. On the ground floor, the exterior was to be of an oriental black and brown granite; from the second to the fourth floors, a very light tan New England sandstone was to be used. Beginning at the fourth floor, which marked the beginning of the residence section, tan bricks of increasingly lighter shades were to be used until a buff color was reached on the uppermost stories. These delicate nuances of color lacked the hardihood to withstand the soot and grime of Chicago at the time, however, and it was not long before it was necessary to abandon this plan for such a fine differentiation of colors in the outer walls of the structure. Inside the building were a Gothic chapel, two gymnasiums, seven clubrooms, a swimming pool, and auditorium. A roof garden was also provided. Lawson's brother and his wife, Mr. and Mrs.

Iver Lawson, augmented the publisher's munificent bequest with the gift of a Lawson Memorial Library of 5,000 volumes—more than the entire library of the Chicago Association in its early days.

On the south side of the Loop, the YMCA Hotel was continuing to prove the need for its services. Harry J. Dunbaugh, chairman of the Committee of Management, reported that in one month young men had registered from every state in the United States and from twenty-two foreign countries. The rate of occupancy in the Hotel from 1916 to 1924 was consistently high, usually averaging from 85 per cent to more than 100 per cent (when some rooms were occupied by more than one tenant in the course of a day). Often it was necessary to turn away more than a hundred young men per day because of a lack of space. To meet this increasing need, the Board of Trustees voted to erect a 900-room addition to the Hotel and this was constructed at a cost of $1,567,745. Work on this addition—which followed the low-cost plan of the original Hotel—was completed in 1927; with this new space the Chicago YMCA Hotel became the second largest hotel in the world, having a total of 2,700 rooms.

The growth of physical properties in the 1920's did not divert the members of the Chicago Association from their primary concern with principles and ideals. It was during this period of great physical expansion that the YMCA—both on the local and national levels—was charting a new course to meet the needs of the twentieth century. In addition, the YMCA nationally was strengthened by the emergence of a proper administrative structure.

Messer's proposed reforms had been voted down in 1904, but dissatisfaction with policies of the International Committee had continued. In 1912 the YMCA's of Canada severed their

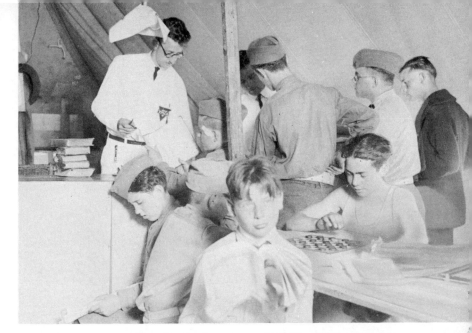

YMCA Service Tent at Camp Roosevelt, a summer ROTC camp conducted by the Chicago Board of Education at Fort Sheridan, Illinois, in 1926.

relations with the committee and formed the National Council of YMCA's of Canada. The same year, delegates to a convention in Atlantic City were discussing "Perils and Weaknesses in the Work of the International Committee." The situation was temporarily improved in 1913 when the International Convention adopted a resolution forbidding the International Committee to establish policies "affecting the associations generally" without convention approval. In 1915 another move reassuring to the local associations was the appointment of John R. Mott as general secretary of the International Committee. Mott had the confidence of the local secretaries and had not made any commitments to those in the earlier disputes.

Good will could not overcome the friction created by an awkward organization. In 1922 a study—financed by the Rockefeller family—was made of the administrative organization of the YMCA. Mark Jones, who made the survey, came to the conclusion that ". . . because the work of the International Committee has reached such proportions in recent years, the present administrative methods are unequal to the task of keeping the organization under control. . . Long handicapped by a complex and illogical relationship to its constituency, the Committee is now facing acute internal problems of its own."

A constitutional convention to establish a more adequate administrative structure was the obvious answer to this problem. After preliminary discussions had been held, a constitutional convention was called to meet in Cleveland in October of 1923. After five days of discussion, the convention recommended a constitution which in some ways was a compromise but which in its essentials recognized the principle of local autonomy for which Messer had argued. The old International Committee was replaced by a new National Council composed of approximately four hundred delegate members, of whom two-thirds were to be laymen. A General Board was established to act as the executive agency for the National Council, but the constitution specifically provided for local autonomy, for control of all general agencies by the local associations meeting in convention and for local control of eligibility requirements for membership from the local associations on the National Council. One observer at the convention was quoted as saying that with the establishment of the National Council, the YMCA's of the United States ceased "being a crowd" and became a unified movement, with control firmly in the hands of the local associations and policies established only by their chosen representatives in authorized conventions.

Of even more urgency than the change in administrative relationships was the necessity of re-stating the fundamental pur-

poses of the Young Men's Christian Association in terms that
would be loyal to traditional ideals and at the same time intel-
ligible and helpful to men living in a highly industrialized, im-
personal, and complex society. In 1915 the Employed Officers
Association of the YMCA had dropped all doctrinal qualifications from their statement of purpose and re-stated their aim
as one "To win men and boys to allegiance to Jesus Christ as
Lord and Saviour and to enlist and train them in service for the
extension of His Kingdom."

The year before his death, Messer was also urging a new
look at YMCA purposes and had devoted an entire issue of the
Bulletin to the subject. The YMCA "must of necessity reopen
the discussion of the evangelical or active membership basis,"
he wrote. He reminded members that since 1869, when the
principle was first adopted, there had been many reasons for
opposing a change. However, he added, that while members
should be sure there are "good and sufficient reasons for dis-
turbing a foundation principle which has been the bedrock of
our Association structure," he urged them "to have no fear of
facing frankly any suggested changes."

In a major statement of policy on this question, the national
convention at Washington in 1925 broadened the definition of
what it considered evangelical churches. (In general, it permitted
anyone to qualify for active membership in the YMCA who
belonged to a church affiliated with the Federal Council of
Churches of Christ in America, predecessor of the National
Council of Churches of Christ in the U.S.A.)

Five years later, a national commission on "Message and
Purpose" was appointed with Ernest Best as chairman. In 1931
the national convention adopted as the official statement of the
purpose of the YMCA the following statement proposed by Best
and the commission:

The Young Men's Christian Association we regard as being, in its essential genius, a world-wide fellowship of men and boys united by a common loyalty to Jesus Christ for the purpose of building Christian personality and a Christian society.

After the statement was approved, Best said he considered it to be the end of the Portland basis (evangelical test) in the YMCA. *The Christian Century* editorialized approvingly that the YMCA had been "reborn." Implementing this general statement of policy was another action of the 1933 convention which permitted each local association to determine the qualifications of its active (voting) members and boards of control, provided only that such member be "in accord with the purposes, ideals, and spirit of the YMCA." This action permitted dropping the last vestige of doctrinal limitations on membership in the YMCA.

The Chicago Association moved rapidly in the direction outlined by the National Council and conventions. On November 10, 1932, a new set of by-laws replaced the constitution which had governed the Chicago Association (with minor amendments) since 1888. The new by-laws established a special form of representative government for the Chicago Association, whose growth had been such that it was no longer possible for all the active members to participate directly in the transaction of business. To afford equal and democratic representation, the by-laws provided for the creation of "voting members" who were to be "not less than 200 or more than 612 in number." Only voting members could hold elective office or be members of the Board of Managers. These voting members were to be chosen by a three-fourths vote of those present at a regular meeting of the Board of Managers. Complete flexibility was allowed with respect to other classes of membership, which the by-laws permitted the Board of Managers to establish in any way it found desirable.

But perhaps the most important break with tradition in the new by-laws was the liberalization of the religious qualifications —spelled out in a clause in 1888 that had forbidden any changes. The new by-laws specified only that "at least 80 per cent of voting members should be members of Protestant evangelical churches." In 1955 this was modified further in an amendment to the by-laws liberalizing the qualifications on voting members to a provision that "at least 80 per cent of the voting members shall be members of Christian churches; but not more than 25 per cent shall be members of any one denomination."

The 1932 by-laws had limited a statement of purpose to one of "establishing free libraries and reading rooms for benevolent and religious purposes"—language taken directly from the charter. In 1939 this was augmented by an official statement of purpose that still reflects the philosophy motivating the members of the departments of the Young Men's Christian Association of Metropolitan Chicago in its centennial year:

The basic objective of the Young Men's Christian Association of Chicago is to aid in the development of Christian standards of living, conduct, and life purpose in its members and constituency.

In the attainment of this goal, the Association seeks to promote the physical, mental, and spiritual welfare of persons, to emphasize reverence for God, responsibility for the common good, respect for personality, and the application of the Golden Rule in human relationships.

CHAPTER 12

"We Laugh at Our Scars"

THE YEAR 1929 found the Young Men's Christian Association of Chicago sharing the general prosperity of the rest of the United States. Program activities were at an all-time high. Expansion was proceeding so rapidly that Frank A. Hathaway, then state secretary for Illinois, was hired in December of 1928 as associate general secretary (a new position) to aid Parker with the multiplying volume of work. The Association was setting new records in almost every area. At the end of the year, the annual report showed:

A total attendance at group events of 2,550,298.

A total attendance at program events of 3,709,279.

Facilities of the YMCA were used 6,077,454 times.

A total of $315,353 contributed by 7,620 people to the current expense fund; membership dues amounted to $398,949. The operating budget was $6,240,720.

The average number of occupants in the Y's seventeen residences was 5,514—a figure remarkably close to the estimate made of the number of young men who might be helped by the Y when the lodginghouse survey was taken.

A total of 3,876 boys attended summer camps of the YMCA.

The collapse of the stock market and the resulting depression changed this picture abruptly in the fall of 1929. Income from dormitory rentals, membership fees, and contributions fell off just when the need for the YMCA program was the greatest. Fortunately, the Chicago Association was better prepared to meet this crisis than many of the business institutions of the city. When George B. McKibbin assumed office as president of the Association, he found it necessary to attend only one meeting of the business committee of the Board of Managers. At that meeting he was told by John S. Broeksmit, a banker who was chairman of the committee, and Hugo Anderson, another banker serving on it, that the YMCA of Chicago "was being run so much better than most of the businesses they knew anything about" that there was nothing more the president could do. McKibbin accepted them at their word; because of the confidence of the Board of Managers in the management abilities of Parker, business decisions on the financial problems facing the YMCA of Chicago were left to him and the business committee.

No organization, of course, was exempt from the economic pressures from which the entire United States was suffering. Many plans of the Association were canceled or delayed. There was no YMCA department in Chicago, however, which had to close its doors because of the depression. In every instance, Parker and the Board of Managers and Board of Trustees had required departments with buildings constructed from endowment funds to establish depreciation reserves in cash to provide

Frank A. Hathaway succeeded William J. Parker as general secretary and sponsored new programs for developing leadership in the local communities served by the YMCA.

for equipment replacement and to maintain their programs during periods of falling income. When deficits began to accumulate despite heroic efforts to keep budgets in balance (in 1930, Hyde Park had a surplus of $9.42 and the West Side Department $12.30), these depreciation reserves provided the money to pay the interest on loans made to meet operating costs and obligations incurred in the construction of new buildings.

Economies were inevitable, although every reduction in expenditures was carefully evaluated so that the least possible damage would be done to the Y's central purpose of helping young men and boys through this difficult period of American history. The chief burden of the economies fell on the YMCA staff. Early in 1930, their wages were cut 10 per cent. Another 5 to 10 per cent cut was imposed later in the same year. Additional reductions in pay in subsequent periods finally brought salaries to a level 20 to 50 per cent below what they had been before the depression. At some of the departments with residence facilities, staff members and their families moved into dormitory rooms; they received as salary only their board and room plus a small allowance "if earned"—that is, if the department budget was not in the red. The schedule for these cash payments at South Chicago, where such a plan was put into effect, provided for payment of $50 per month to the executive secretary (of which $10 went into the retirement fund, leaving a net of $40 per month). Engineers, many of whom were university graduates who could not find jobs in business, received $15 a month plus board and room; janitors received $5.00 per month. Southtown had a similar plan. At all departments, many staff positions had to be eliminated; the employees who remained at reduced salaries found themselves with double or triple their ordinary work load.

The railroad departments were in a particularly vulnerable position. Much of their support had come from the railroad companies, which now found themselves forced to make drastic reductions in expenditures in their own fight for survival. In addition, more modern railroad equipment had reduced the number of division points necessary for servicing trains; as a consequence of this, the total number of railroad departments (or "transportation departments" as they had been renamed by the 1920 convention) had been steadily decreasing. Two Chicago departments, the Pennsylvania and the Dearborn Station, had been discontinued in 1924. In 1929 only three railroad departments remained—the Grand Trunk, the Chicago and North Western, and the Chicago & Eastern Illinois. The Grand Trunk was closed in 1929, the North Western in 1931, and the Chicago & Eastern Illinois in 1932. Thus came to an end a specialized program which had been part of the Chicago Association activity since the founding of the Kinzie Street Department in 1878.

Two other specialized branches which had ended their affiliation with the Chicago Association were the Chinese Department (which had become the independent Chinese Institute in 1924) and the Japanese Department. The Y had had an especially effective program for Japanese since 1911. Program records extant from 1913, for example, show a regular attendance of over one hundred at meetings. In 1925 a bulletin of the Japanese Department listed such activities as Sunday services and Bible discussion classes, a literary society and library, the publication of a guidebook in Japanese, and a special telephone directory for Japanese members. The department also owned its own small dormitory building—worth $30,000—at 745 East Thirty-sixth Street. On February 1, 1929, because of a desire to concentrate entirely on a religious program, the Japanese Department voted to end its affiliation with the Y and establish itself as the Japanese Christian Institute. However, this attempt to go it alone was not successful and in 1937 the Institute failed.

The Wabash Avenue Department, located in one of the poorer areas of the city, was particularly hard-hit by the depression. Although astute management enabled it to show a surplus of $3.69 in 1930, it lost more than two hundred members the following year. By September of 1931, 85 out of 114 beds in the residence were vacant. Even in the face of these financial difficulties, the Committee of Management appointed a group to work out a program of relief such as had been extended by the department after World War I. This subcommittee was charged with finding food and clothing for school children and arranging loans for young men to pay their room rent and buy food. By going beyond the specific program of the Y and providing general relief assistance long before such matters had become the accepted province of government or more specialized agencies, the YMCA was again able to demonstrate its adaptability to special needs.

Throughout Chicago, the chief concern of the Y during

the depression was one of helping young men who had lost their jobs. Former members who were temporarily unemployed were given free membership privileges, including the use of the gymnasiums and swimming pools. Special daytime educational, inspirational, and recreation programs for the unemployed were arranged by many departments. The Board of Managers authorized additional money for the fund from which the YMCA Hotel had been making loans for young men to pay their hotel bills in order that they might be kept out of "unwholesome lodgings and . . . keep some of their self respect." This was done with the expectation, as the veteran secretary C.T.B. Goodspeed wrote in the minutes of the Board of Managers, that "only a very small fraction of the money loaned under these conditions could ever be expected to be returned." Room rates at all the dormitories were reduced. Meals to those without jobs were offered at a 40 per cent discount. In 1933 President George B. McKibbin reported that 1,200 former members had qualified for the free memberships, 1,000 had been given free room rent for various periods of time, and nearly 500 had been accommodated in the dormitories on a deferred payment plan. Many young men had been helped in their search for work by a city-wide council that exchanged information about job openings and made it available to Y members. At the Central YMCA schools more than a thousand students were receiving financial aid from the Association. During the summer, several hundred boys whose parents could no longer afford camp fees were enrolled in the camps without charge.

The reduction in income from the residences (which were only partially filled, had cut their rates, or were carrying their tenants on almost a relief basis) was the biggest single problem faced by the Association. This reduction in income from buildings in which the endowment funds were invested resulted not only in increasing deficits and interest costs but in a continually diminishing source of support for program activities. It was at this moment that the depression-ridden city of Chicago announced plans to celebrate the one hundredth anniversary of its incorporation with the 1933 Century of Progress Exposition. Such an exposition was bound to attract a throng of visitors far greater than the city's hotels could care for. A similar situation had arisen in 1926 when the Y's dormitories were filled with visitors to the World Eucharistic Congress of the Roman Catholic Church. As the Y departments had shown their ability to care for visitors on that occasion, the officers and Board of Managers of the Association decided to offer these empty dormitory facilities for the use of visitors to the Century of Progress.

Accommodations (at no increase in rates) were reserved for Fair visitors at all residences and the YMCA Hotel. The Lawson, Sears Roebuck, South Chicago, Lincoln-Belmont, 111th Street, and West Side Professional Schools departments made special arrangements to accommodate women and family groups. With these arrangements completed, an extensive promotion campaign was inaugurated under the direction of G. M. Martin, who had been transferred from his position as executive secretary at Austin for this purpose. Advertisements were placed in many country-town newspapers; almost half a million descriptive folders were mailed out to church and Y members, and other pamphlets were distributed through gasoline service stations on major highways leading to Chicago. In addition, every Y secretary in the United States was sent a letter explaining the services available at Chicago YMCA's and offering to assist anyone from his city, whether or not they were members of the YMCA.

A Board of Managers committee headed by Vernon R. Loucks and a professional staff under W. S. Miller, later executive secretary at Irving Park, made careful plans for receiving

Visiting boys arrive by taxi at the YMCA before beginning their tour of the Century of Progress in 1933.

visitors. Information bureaus, set up throughout the city, rendered services of a variety that defied any effort to tabulate them. This aid was not confined to helping visitors locate accommodations. Tourists with limited funds were aided in planning their visit so that they might see as much as possible and stay within their allotted budget of funds. A special division of the information bureau provided deaf-mutes with individually prepared, written instructions so that they could find their way about. On one occasion, the bureau obtained a marriage license for a couple and arranged for them to be married by a minister of their denomination. Mail service for visitors was a major project. Much of this mail was addressed only in care of the "Chicago YMCA"; to be sure that visitors received their letters, the ever-changing guest lists from the various departments had to be checked against the voluminous influx of mail.

Those in distress or without funds were also aided. Most of these were boys from fourteen to eighteen who had been lured to Chicago by the promise of excitement at the exposition. All such boys were referred to the personal service department of the YMCA Hotel, where temporary work was arranged for them. Despite the great demand for accommodations, a group of three hundred hotel rooms was taken off the general market and reserved for hardship cases at only fifty cents per night.

Positive action was also taken to prevent the arrival of such boys without adequate supervision. All-expense tours were arranged and community leaders were encouraged to bring groups of boys (no more than ten boys for each group leader) to Chicago for the Century of Progress. Special books of tickets were printed which permitted these boys to pay for their trip on the installment plan and thus enjoy an experience which otherwise they would not have been able to afford. Other groups also responded to the Y's offer. During the American Legion convention, more than 2,000 Legionnaires were housed in YMCA residences. At another time during the summer, the Y was host to 2,400 newsboys from Pittsburgh.

During the first year of the Century of Progress, 141,432 transient guests were served by the sixteen departments which had dormitory facilities. The peak night came during August, when the Y provided beds for 8,008 visitors—1,100 more than rated capacity. Gyms and clubrooms were used for sleeping quarters; in a few cases, when all the cots were taken, guests brought their own bedding and slept on the floor. Taxi service was provided to the departments at a cost of only a dime for nearby buildings and fifteen cents for outlying buildings.

The result of all this activity—described by the committee as one of providing a "sympathetic and human service to solve the bewildering array of problems which confronted visitors to the fair"—was both to win the Chicago Association many new friends and to ameliorate its economic problems. The program had not been carried out haphazardly. Early in the summer, President McKibbin arranged to have inspectors live in each of the departments and make sure that the guests were being adequately cared for. In addition, a second letter was sent to general secretaries in other cities asking for the reaction of visitors who had returned home. The result of this letter, said a report on the summer's activity, "was an astonishing mass expression of praise and approval." But perhaps equally important to the struggling Association was the extra revenue that it would not otherwise have realized from the full use of the residences. Without raising rates in a single instance, the residences and the Hotel reported additional income estimated by auditors at $661,-000, of which nearly a third came from the increased use of the Hotel.

Assistance from other sources also helped overcome the burden of the depression. In 1932 Joseph S. Duncan gave $150,-000 to the West Side Department, which enabled it to pay its building debt to the general office and maintain the Association's cash reserve. Cyrus McCormick, still a bulwark of the Association, entered into an agreement with the YMCA to give the sum of $50,000 every year for a period of five years. And finally, in 1934, the YMCA in Chicago became a participating agency in the Community Fund.

The affiliation with the Community Fund had been under consideration for several years. After the favorable recommendation of a committee headed by President McKibbin, the Board of Managers voted on May 17, 1934, to participate in the annual Community Fund drive. At the end of the 1934 campaign, the Community Fund turned over to the YMCA the sum of $81,090, of which $32,503 was a refund of gifts turned over to the fund by the YMCA; the balance of $48,587 represented additional funds made available through participation in the Community Fund.

This additional help, plus improving economic conditions generally, enabled Parker to report in 1935 that the position of the Association had changed from an accumulated deficit of $317,000 for current expenses in December, 1932, to a surplus of $6,318 on December 31, 1934. Following his third term of office in 1934, McKibbin declared himself not a candidate for re-election. He said he was making his decision because of a conviction that it was in the best interests of the Association for the presidency to be rotated rather than to have the office occupied for many years by a single man—a precedent which was to be followed by his successors. The 1934 surplus was a meager one for a budget of more than six million dollars, but it justified both the faith and judgment of the businessmen on the Board of Managers and Board of Trustees as they—and Parker—sought to deal with the problems of the depression era. "The entire Association has been put to its wits' end," Parker told his audience in an annual report. "Our problem has been threefold. First, to operate the Association without financial loss; second, to preserve the vigor and enthusiasm of the organization; and third, to protect programs from disintegration." After detailing the steps that had been taken to meet these problems, he permitted himself one of his rare departures from the simple, matter-of-fact language he preferred. "Perhaps this was a hard year," he said, "but our heads are up and we laugh at our scars. Our fiber has been toughened like that of a twisted tree on a wind-swept mountain. . . . Nothing has happened which can daunt a courageous soul. . . . Youth needs us; men trust us; God blesses us—what more could we ask?"

It was not surprising, in view of Parker's fortitude, to find

the YMCA plodding steadily ahead with expansion plans even
while it was battling to prevent its existence from being put in
jeopardy. Extension of the Y program to one of the neediest
areas in the city became possible in 1931 when a building at
Maxwell and Miller streets, formerly used as a neighborhood
dispensary by Michael Reese Hospital, was given to the YMCA
by the hospital and Mrs. Emanuel Mandel, widow of one of the
founders of Mandel Brothers. The building was quickly remodeled at a cost of $25,000 and dedicated as the Maxwell Street
Department of the Chicago Association. From its opening day
it was overcrowded with underprivileged Negro and white
children from the neighborhood. Parker, watching the children
at play in a strange, new world of planned and supervised games
under the direction of Maxwell Street's first executive secretary,
H. S. Prince, said, "I am as proud of that little building as I am
of the Lawson."

The Maxwell Street YMCA represented a break with tradition in several respects. Although women had not yet been
admitted to Y membership or the by-laws changed to permit
wider religious representation, members of all faiths and both
sexes became members of the Committee of Management at
Maxwell Street under the chairmanship of G. H. Cross. In commenting on the department, Parker said, "You may be uncertain
whether it is a Y or not. The entire enterprise is a contrast in
almost every visible respect to the Lawson building. But this
contrast is only in externals. Its purpose is the same as the Lawson
building, namely, to help people toward happy, useful living."

Three community programs were started in 1931 in various
areas of the South Side. One was in the South Shore area, with
Andrew J. Reed as executive secretary, another in Beverly Hills,
and the third (known as the Ridge Department) for work
among boys in the Morgan Park, Blue Island, and Harvey areas.

The terms set by the Board of Managers when Glenn D. Adams was transferred from 111th Street to the new Ridge Department indicate the Spartan nature required of a Y secretary during this period. The Board agreed to pay "his full salary for three months, a decreasing share for three more months" and after that he was "to find his own money"—not an easy assignment in 1931.

The new department in Beverly Hills was established following a meeting of fifteen men from the area in the Alumni Hall of Morgan Park Military Academy on September 28, 1931. With E. F. Porter as chairman, the men pledged themselves to work for the establishment of a regular department, beginning with the establishment of Hi-Y clubs and boys' work programs in the schools. In the beginning, these activities were considered a part of the Ridge Department, but in 1934 Beverly became a separate branch with Adams as half-time executive secretary. The attempt to organize a Ridge Department was abandoned shortly afterward. Although Adams was able to get the program in Beverly started and rent office space in a store at Monterey and Homewood avenues, he was forced to take another job when (in the words of the department's history) "the consequent lessening of available funds" found the Y unable to pay even his small part-time salary. He promised to return as soon as feasible, however, and in 1936 came back to the Beverly Department to serve as its executive secretary until after the close of World War II.

An innovation in the organization of the South Shore, Beverly, and Maxwell Street departments was the creation of "governing members" who shared the responsibility for the operation of the department with the local Committee of Management. The purpose of the governing-member plan was to make the administration of the local departments more democratic and representative; in effect, it applied to the local level the same principles that had led to the establishment of "voting members" for the city-wide Association. With the delegation of local authority to the governing members, the Committee of Management was replaced by a Board of Directors elected by, and from among, the governing members. These governing members were not solicited for funds but fixed the amount of their contributions at a high enough level to sustain the work of the department. As Parker explained the governing-member idea: "Instead of being asked to contribute to a fund which the Y will spend, people are invited to become the Y and to accept responsibility for its management and operation. The contributing constituency and the managing constituency become identical. There are no contributors—all are responsible partners." The first of the established departments to adopt the governing-member plan was Southtown, where J. F. McFarland was executive secretary. In later years, as members of the Association's expansion staff, Henry L. Sistrunk, assistant general secretary related to Community Departments and Expansion, and Mc-Farland were to play leading roles in extending the governing-member plan to other departments of the YMCA of Metropolitan Chicago.

On the North Side, Earl M. Dinger was appointed assistant general secretary for the Rogers Park district in 1932, and a committee was organized the following year with Dr. L. A. Rumsey as chairman for the purpose of establishing a department in that area. Initial progress was very slow; contributions the first year were only $166 and in the second year only $60.25. However, by 1936 a full-time secretary, G. Vern Remy, was assigned to the district, office space was rented in a bank building at 7001 North Clark Street, and eighteen clubs organized under YMCA auspices. The following year the Rogers Park

Department (later renamed High Ridge) could count more than five hundred boys and girls as members. In 1938, larger headquarters space was obtained at 6968 North Clark and an "outpost" organized in Northtown.

Outposts such as that in Northtown represented an effort to expand the YMCA program beyond the limits possible with existing physical facilities. These outposts were usually established at some distance from a department in an area where it was not feasible to undertake an organizing or building campaign. By 1938 eight departments were operating thirteen such outposts. No membership fees were assessed or program charges made at these outposts. Partial financial support came from the Community Fund, and the services of recreation leaders from the WPA Federal aid program were utilized to provide adequate supervision. During 1938 these outposts enrolled 2,500 boys and girls who otherwise would not have had a YMCA program accessible to them.

Having guided the Chicago Association through the depression years and the post-depression adjustments, Parker expressed a desire in 1938 to retire and relinquish the post of general secretary to a younger man. He had already tested his successor with characteristic thoroughness and it was without any hesitancy that the Board of Managers accepted his recommendation to name Frank A. Hathaway, then associate general secretary, as the new general secretary. The announcement of Parker's retirement at the annual meeting in 1939 was made without any special tributes which might have been expected on such an occasion. Still averse to sentimentality, Parker had insisted that there be no testimonials. All he wanted, he told George McKibbin, was to "be permitted to leave town tomorrow morning on an extended vacation, unheralded and unsung."

The Association itself was, of course, the best testimonial to his abilities. When Parker joined the general office staff in 1897, there were only four successfully established general departments —Central, Ravenswood (now Wilson Avenue), West Side (now Duncan), and Hyde Park; in 1938, President John S. Broeksmit could report on the activities of twenty-three different departments and ten summer camps in turning over the office of president to his successor, Newton C. Farr. In addition, the Association Building at 19 South La Salle Street was free of a mortgage for the first time since it had been erected in 1893. Parker had been associated with the Chicago Association for forty of the eighty-one years of its existence; in that time he had made enduring contributions to its growth and administrative organization. In fact, it was not until Parker assumed office as general secretary that the centralized business control envisioned under the original Metropolitan Plan had actually been fully exploited and put into practice. Under the direct supervision of James C. Vynalik, the comptroller and assistant general secretary who had been in the auditing section of the Association since he was a boy of fourteen, a new central accounting system was established. A centralized architectural and engineering service under Eugene B. White and a central purchasing department headed by Abijah Jarman were also established. During Parker's sixteen-year tenure as general secretary—a period which had included the depression years—the assets of the Association had more than doubled, increasing from $7,804,269 in 1923 to $16,131,987 in 1939.

The retirement of Parker, who with Messer had dominated the professional leadership of the YMCA in Chicago throughout half a century, was not accompanied by any serious disruption within the organization. The transfer of duties to Hathaway had been made gradually and without any interruption of continuity of policy. But the mere removal of a strong personality such as Parker and the personal tradition he represented was bound to produce a need for adjustments within the organization.

Both Messer and Parker, for example, had tended to retain close administrative control over the various departments. Hathaway saw that while this principle might have been employed successfully when the Association had a limited number of branches, it was not well adapted to an organization expanding as rapidly as the YMCA of Chicago. Hathaway set as one of his first goals a fuller delegation of authority to the departments. This involved putting the primary emphasis of the general office on functions related to supervision and co-ordination. The departments were to assume primary responsibility for operations. The development of new leadership necessary to make such a program work had to take place on two levels: (1) among the lay workers and volunteers who might suggest new programs related to their community's aspirations and needs, and (2) on the professional level where Hathaway hoped to change the position of the executive secretaries from that of being staff assistants (as Parker had regarded them) to one of being considered commanders in the field with the full authority and responsibility of such a position.

As a means of accomplishing his purpose, Hathaway modified the procedure for appointing executive secretaries. Without changing the principle that the professional staff was responsible to the general secretary, Hathaway reached an agreement with the local departments that new secretaries would be appointed only after "conference and agreement" with the local Committee of Management or Board of Directors.

Consultation over appointments was only a first step. Hathaway's next move was to expand the medium of the general secretary's "cabinet"—a group composed of executive secretaries from the various branches and department heads in the general office. There had been regular meetings of this cabinet since it was established in 1913. Hathaway, however, changed the emphasis from that of an informal, advisory group to a planning body with the power and responsibility to make recommendations for the administration of the Chicago Association. Committees were established and given specific instructions as to their scope of authority. New ideas and practices were discussed and tested on the local level through a series of seminars; these group discussions resulted in an increasing participation in policy making by local leadership on both the lay worker and the professional staff level. The effect of the change was reflected in the number of members serving on committees, which increased sharply from about 1,400 in 1938 to more than 2,500 in 1945.

The outbreak of World War II forced postponement of many of Hathaway's plans, including the raising of a $2,000,000 capital fund to provide facilities in eight large areas of the city that were still without YMCA services. The year 1940 did, however, see the opening of two new camps—Camp MacLean and the Palos Hills camp. Camp MacLean was established on a 220-acre tract at Rockland Lake near Burlington, Wisconsin, with a gift eventually totaling $110,000 from Mr. and Mrs. M. Haddon MacLean in memory of their son, John Bartlett MacLean. The Palos Hills camp was an eighty-acre site near the Palos Park Forest Preserve, where it was intended that the various departments should build department lodges for weekend outings and other activities. During the first year, three departments built cabins on the property for short-term and overnight camps. Sears Roebuck completed a cabin in August, Englewood dedicated a Railsplitter's lodge in September, and the Beverly Department—although still without its own building—constructed a lodge for activities which was finished in November. The 111th Street Department finished its lodge shortly afterwards. Later, Hyde Park also constructed a lodge there.

The broadening scope of the Y program in the pre-war years inevitably led to a reopening of discussions concerning the admission of women as members of the YMCA. Nationally, the first Tri-Hi-Y Club for girls under YMCA sponsorship had been formed as early as 1923 in Holyoke, Massachusetts. Throughout the 1920's an increasing number of local associations —particularly in communities where there was no YWCA— established informal programs of clubs, classes, and other activities for women as a group and as participants in co-educational or family groups. In 1931 the National Council of the YMCA was asked to remove "any stated or implied discrimination between the sexes and to make possible identical status,

Calisthenics for women at the North Avenue-Larrabee Department in 1933.

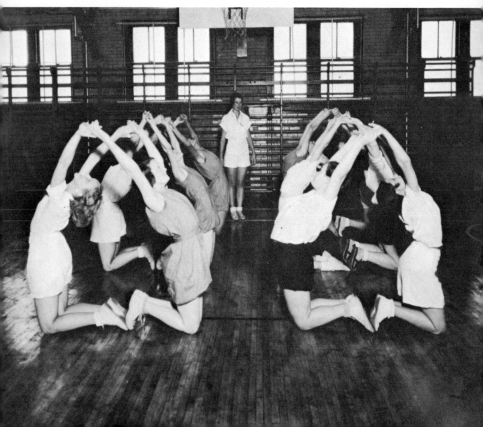

as affecting recognition rights and responsibilities for both sexes in the affairs of the National Council." Two years later the Council took the action which permitted local associations to control the qualifications of their own membership, thereby indirectly permitting them to admit women. In 1934, when women and girl members were first reported, there were 57,458 women and girls in 275 associations.

In Chicago there were a number of pressures accumulating which led the YMCA into more extensive work among women and girls. The movement for the emancipation of women from Victorian customs (which reached a frenetic pitch during the 1920's) was reflected in a desire on the part of the wives and daughters of Y members to participate in activities in the handsome new Y buildings constructed as a result of the expansion plan. Walter Wood, formerly an executive secretary in Chicago, had established a successful women's and girls' program in Philadelphia and many of the lay members, as well as Gren O. Pierrel, then program secretary, were urging a similar program be tried in Chicago.

At first, it was thought that such a program might be conducted in conjunction with the YWCA, which as early as 1928 had rented the west swimming pool and a section of the Hyde Park Department building to carry on a separate program for women and girls. Extensive negotiations were conducted with the YWCA about initiating another women's and girls' program at South Chicago, but when no satisfactory agreement could be reached, South Chicago obtained the approval of the Board of Managers to start an independent women's and girls' program. Lyman T. Crossman, then executive secretary at South Chicago, delegated much of the responsibility for this program to his young program director, Lloyd L. McClow, who had conducted women's and girls' work while serving with the YMCA in

Norfolk, Nebraska, and Bartlesville, Oklahoma, before coming to Chicago. Encouraged by the general program office and local Committees of Management, other departments quickly established schedules of activities for women and girls. By 1930, women's work was established on an experimental basis at Englewood (now Southtown), North Avenue-Larrabee, Lincoln-Belmont, and Division Street (which, however, dropped its women's program the following year). In addition to organized classes in the swimming pools and gymnasiums, there were special mothers' clubs, women's auxiliary committees, and such family activities as drama clubs, young people's federation, Bible classes, leadership training, evening classes, forums, student councils, orchestras, choruses, social dancing groups, bowling leagues, and lobby parties. A conspicuous exception to this trend was the Lawson YMCA; because the McCormick YWCA was

Women's sewing class at Englewood (now Southtown) in 1934.

Following their admission to membership, girls competed in city-wide tournaments of their own. Here a broadjumper makes a leap with pigtails flying.

located only a few blocks away, the Board of Managers directed that no women's work be carried on at Lawson.

In 1932 former president William Francis, chairman of the program committee, reported women's and girls' activities had been conducted by eleven departments. More than ninety different groups had been organized with a total enrollment of about 3,000. In addition to these separate activities for women and girls, there were sixty-six other groups where activities were planned for co-ed or family groups.

The speedy acceptance of these new programs resulted in action by the Board of Managers in 1933 admitting women to full membership. One year later the Board underscored the successful role played by women in the year's activities with a resolution directing that "women's work be recognized as an integral part of the Chicago YMCA program; and that this work be authorized only in departments which organize the program under the conditions and standards approved by the program

271

committee." With the YMCA of Chicago firmly committed to a policy of developing such a program, Wilhelmina Aveling was named first program secretary for women and girls. In 1935 further recognition of the need to serve women led to the setting aside for women of three floors of the YMCA Hotel.

The final step in the integration of women into the YMCA of Chicago came in 1945 when President James F. Oates, Jr. recommended that the by-laws, which provided that only "men twenty-one years of age and over" were eligible to be voting members, be amended so that "any person twenty-one years of age or over" should be so qualified. This action, which granted women an equal voice in the administration of the YMCA of Metropolitan Chicago carried by a vote that was not quite unanimous: 345 to 2. Women members were not only back—as they had been prior to the 1888 constitution—but they had returned as twentieth-century equals of the men.

CHAPTER 13

"To Take Education Out of the Classroom"

EVEN BEFORE the officers and members of the Board of Managers had finished dealing with the problems created by the depression, they found themselves being pressed to make a re-examination of Association policies with respect to formal education. The schools sponsored by the Y, particularly at Central, had grown so enormously that some provision had to be made for their future if they were to maintain their standards.

From the beginning, the educational program of the Y in Chicago had been continually adapted to meet the needs of a changing city. Before 1900 much of the educational program had been directed toward commercial and technical courses that would enable young men to improve their business skills and earning power. Elementary classes were conducted for apprentices and for wage-earning boys whose parents were too poor to keep them in school. The apprentice school conducted by Central, although short-lived, was believed to have been the first of its kind in the country. Its pioneering courses were so enthusiastically received that its techniques were immediately incorporated into the broad program of vocational education that has continued to be an important part of the public high school program of the city of Chicago. The *Chicago Tribune*, in commenting at the time upon these early courses at Central, described the instruction as "the best to be had."

With the spread of compulsory education, the passage of child-labor laws, and the introduction of vocational courses into the public schools curriculum, the need for this type of trade education diminished. Emphasis was then placed on Americanization and English classes for the immigrants who made up such a large part of Chicago's labor force. In turn, these classes played less of a role as the public schools offered evening classes where the foreign born could study the subjects necessary to qualify for citizenship. Whatever the area—whether it was religious evangelism, education, initiating the Boy Scout movement in Chicago, or handling general relief problems through the Wabash Avenue YMCA—the Chicago Association tried to adapt its program to the most urgent need of the moment. When that need was met by a more appropriate agency or the government, the YMCA preferred to withdraw and concentrate its activities on the work it was best equipped to do in its special field.

This special field, whether in education or in any other activity, was considered by the Y to be that of building Christian character. "The educational processes of the Association are based on the principle that true education must include the development of character," Messer had written in the *Bulletin*. James F. Oates, while serving as secretary at Central, had set the theme for the educational program as one of "education in the highest and broadest sense of the term. . . . Ours is no work of education merely because we conduct evening classes," he said. "The Association is an all-around educational institution for young men to draw out the latent powers of their physical, mental, social, and religious natures."

Because of the accessibility of the Central Department in the business district, the wide range of its programs, the availability of good instructors, and the facilities for classroom space in the Association Building, the educational program at Central developed more rapidly than that of any other department. Educational expenditures at Central, less than $5,000 per year in the 1890's, increased to more than $25,000 per year in 1905. The costs of this program continued to grow throughout the next fifteen years, experiencing a phenomenal jump when the budget zoomed from $43,000 in 1918 to $115,000 in 1920. In 1920 there were 2,941 students enrolled in evening classes at Central and another 636 in day courses.

A student at the Central YMCA secretarial school makes a correction in the letter she is typing. Business training, still being offered at Central, has been a traditional part of its educational program.

This sudden growth after the war was an indirect result of the formation of the United YMCA Schools, a federation formed by YMCA educational administrators for the original purpose of standardizing curricula and texts and otherwise improving the level of YMCA education. This new organization was designated as administrator of a War Scholarship Fund, established with more than $6,000,000 left in the treasury of the National War Work Council when the armistice brought an end to World War I. These funds were to be distributed to the various Association colleges on the basis of contributions made from their area to the Council. Messer opposed this proposal, saying that the money should be returned to the local associations to be spent according to the wishes of the original donors. Because of Messer's opposition to the fund, it was not until 1920 that the Chicago Association agreed to accept these funds to be used for scholarships alone. Then, due to the large sums raised by the lay committees in Chicago for war work, these scholarships produced a sudden flood of cash—and students. At Central alone, the scholarship fund resulted in an increased income of $45,000 during the first year of participation.

The staff and facilities necessary to administer such a large educational plant led to a tendency to institutionalize the educational program at Central. Although all the men and boys who paid the nominal tuition ($10 per course was a maximum and $2.00 to $5.00 the more usual range) automatically became members of the Central Department, the educational leaders were pushing toward a recognition which would permit them the independent status of a formally accredited school. The name of the school, which in 1913 had been changed to the Central Department YMCA Institute, was revised again in 1919 to Central YMCA Schools. The purpose of this change, said a 1919 report, was ". . . to convey more definitely the fact that standard schoolwork was offered." It was the view of the school's director that "it has now been quite generally recognized that the function of the Association is not merely to offer supplemental education courses but to offer well-standardized schools of instruction." This view, of course, was in conflict with the philosophy of Messer and Oates, but as the school remained a part of Central's program, the Association continued to encourage its expansion. During these years, according to an estimate by Roger Dunn in his study, "The Central YMCA Schools of Chicago," a minimum of thirty thousand Chicagoans received at least part of their elementary, high school, or business education in the Central Y schools. Among these were Theodore V. Houser, later to be chairman of the board of Sears, Roebuck and Company and president of the YMCA of Metropolitan Chicago; John Holmes, chairman of the board of Swift and Company; Harold Stuart, president of Halsey, Stuart Company, Inc.; and Dr. Herman Bundesen, for many years president of the Board of Health of the city of Chicago.

In 1921 formal recognition came to the schools when the evening high school (which had been founded in 1902) was made an accredited member of the North Central Association of Colleges and Secondary Schools. It was the first evening high school in the Midwest to win such recognition. The same year, the educational authorities secured a charter for a School of Commerce on the college level with the power to grant degrees. Courses were also established in liberal arts; this in turn led to the founding of a junior college offering a general education. This evening junior college won an accredited rating from the North Central Association of Colleges and Secondary Schools in 1924. Like the high school, it was the only one of its kind in the area with such a rating and this fact led to a further increase in enrollment.

Albert F. Gillman, Jr., teaches a chemistry class at Central YMCA high school as his father did. One out of every six day high school students at Central is foreign born.

The rapid growth of the schools and the lack of financial resources because of the low tuition caused the administrators of the educational program constant difficulties. There was never enough classroom space; in fact, it was said that some classes could not have been held if all the students had ever been present at the same time. Many applicants had to be turned away. Dunn, in his study, says, "The success of the schools through this period in meeting their operating costs was no small achievement, but it was accomplished only by overcrowding classrooms, by inadequate equipment and library, low salaries, and utilization of space morning, afternoon, and evening for some forty-eight weeks of the year."

The schools continued to grow throughout the 1920's. Paradoxically, this growth was enhanced—and the problems multiplied—by the depression. Financial difficulties kept many

278

young men at home who might otherwise have gone away to school, and they sought such education as they could afford at the Central YMCA Schools. A day college, opened in 1931, was immediately crowded with students. The total enrollment of all the schools during this period was more than four thousand, a figure almost equal to the student body at that time of such a full-time educational institution as the University of Chicago.

In an effort to appraise the problems faced by the school, the Board of Managers asked Floyd W. Reeves and A. J. Brumbaugh, then professors in the department of education at the University of Chicago, to make a survey of the educational work at Central. Their findings were generally favorable. They reported that the school program was unusually efficient and well-managed for one of its kind, that its faculty was superior to that of most junior colleges, but that, although it was using its facilities more efficiently than any comparable school they had inspected, it was very much overcrowded. Both Reeves and Brumbaugh expressed the hope that the junior college would develop into a four-year college, although they found the library facilities only adequate for two years of college work. "It appears clear that for many years to come neither the public school system nor the colleges and universities in Chicago can provide adequate facilities at the senior college level for students of the adult type served by this college," the report observed. On the administrative side, the survey recommended a 10 per cent increase in salaries and the establishment of the Y schools as an independent department of the Chicago Association with its own board of directors to whom the chief school administrator would be responsible.

The financial condition of the Y at the time made it impossible to approve the expansion to a four-year college. Neither did the Board of Managers immediately accept the recommendation that the schools be made a separate unit, even though this had been done with Y schools in other cities and both the faculty and students had petitioned to have the Central YMCA Schools granted similar status. Opposition to such a move came principally from the Central Department, which was apprehensive that costs of the program might increase unduly and that co-education might be introduced in the schools at a time when Central's own program was still restricted to men.

The frictions produced by this awkward administrative relationship were spotlighted further in 1933 when the school authorities and faculty—with an investment of 10 per cent of their salaries—formed a secret Central College Development Corporation with the hope of buying the college from the Central Department or, if this failed, of founding a new school independent of the Association. Discovery of this plan brought about the direct intervention of the Board of Managers. The Board demoted the administrators who had participated in the development of the separatist movement and at the same time moved energetically to alleviate the worst of the conditions which had given rise to it. The space available to the college was doubled and authorization granted in 1933 for the establishment of a four-year college.

One of the most constructive measures taken by the Board of Managers was that of bringing in T. H. Nelson as temporary director of the schools and assistant general secretary of the Chicago Association. Nelson had been senior secretary of the United YMCA schools for several years and had twenty-one years' experience in Association educational work. Both the Board of Managers and the educational authorities found it much easier to get things done with Nelson as co-ordinator than had been the case before. Within a year the college was separately incorporated as the Central YMCA College of Chicago (also called the Central YMCA College Corporation). It was also granted the status of a separate department of the Association with its own Board of Directors. The college occupied the new space granted to it, the equipment was enlarged and put into good condition, the curriculum was improved, the faculty strengthened, and student service bettered. In 1935 the college had an enrollment of 3,719 students, and the following year it was made a fully accredited member of the North Central Association of Colleges and Secondary Schools as a four-year college with power to grant degrees. With these objectives accomplished, T. H. Nelson stepped aside in 1936 and was succeeded as president by Dr. Edward J. Sparling, who had been dean of men at Hiram College, Ohio, and had a background of YMCA work at Stanford University and in New York. At the same time, the college entered into a new relationship with the other departments. *Chicago Men*, as the YMCA bulletin was now called, described the school as representing "the formal education program of each of the twenty-two departments." It added that members of the faculty were conducting conferences of young people and parents in the various departments and that instructors in the sciences were giving talks in their specialties as part of the department programs, which remained on an informal, unaccredited basis.

Despite a continuing problem of financial support (and an equally durable difference of opinion over the proper method of allocating rental and other charges to the college), the schools continued to grow. In September of 1941 the Board of Directors of the college raised Sparling's salary to $7,500 a year "in view of the excellent progress of the college" during his five years in office. However, the college was already beset with new problems arising from World War II. Enrollment was down 25 per cent in the Day School of Commerce and by small percentages in the Day School of Arts and Sciences and the Evening School of Commerce. School authorities attributed the decrease to the draft and to defense work, reporting that "many students are taking defense work in preference to going to school."

The Japanese attack on Pearl Harbor and the resulting declarations of war found the Chicago Association and the YMCA nationally with a program already under way for servicemen. Even before Pearl Harbor, the Association had welcomed servicemen with free membership privileges. "It is the present policy of the Association to make its facilities available to men in uniform without charge, as members, and to co-operate with the government and the approved agencies of the government in every possible way," Hathaway said in his annual report. As a result of government recommendations, many activities were planned for individuals and small groups to provide a break from the mass routines of the armed forces. YMCA's in Chicago and across the country joined with five other similar agencies—the YWCA, National Catholic Community Service, Jewish Welfare Board, Salvation Army, and Travelers Aid—to set up the United Service Organization (USO) to serve the "religious, spiritual, welfare, and educational needs of the men and women in the armed forces of the United States, and in general, to contribute to the maintenance of morale in American communities." The president of the USO in Chicago was Jeffrey R. Short, who was also serving from 1940 to 1942 as president of the YMCA of Chicago.

From 1939 to 1943 the YMCA Hotel was used by the Army Air Corps for the housing, feeding and recreation of soldiers enrolled in its mechanics training course in Chicago. At one time almost eight hundred of these soldiers were being cared for in the Hotel in a special program developed under the direction of

Servicemen splash in the Central YMCA pool during World War II.

Daniel A. Schaefer, later assistant general secretary related to business operations, who had been designated as liaison representative with the Air Corps.

To support the war program, the Y had to intensify its efforts in building membership and in providing staff replacements for those who were in service. During 1942 more than 4,500 members—22 per cent of the male membership—joined the service of their country, and some 40 per cent of the 165 secretaries of the Association left for war duty. This sudden attrition imposed additional burdens on both the lay members and professional staff. In 1944 the veteran executive secretary

John L. Nelson, who was then serving at Lawson, also took over the direction of the Central Department; in addition, he assumed the chairmanship of several city-wide staff committees. Lawson expanded its activities with the opening of a YMCA trade school to train defense workers. The role of women, as it had been during the Civil War, was an important one. In 1940 the YMCA of Chicago had reported a total membership of 37,722, of which approximately 20,000 were men, 11,500 boys under eighteen and 5,000 women and girls. By 1943 the number of men had dropped to about 18,000 and the number of women and girls had increased to 7,500, a shift in membership which permitted the Association to hold its total loss due to the war to a very small figure.

During the entire period of World War II, more than 10,000 Y members in Chicago served in the armed forces. Many other men in uniform came to Chicago and during their stay were able to benefit from the facilities and services of the YMCA. In a single year, for example, more than 100,000 men used the facilities of the Y in the city without charge. The tremendous number of soldiers, sailors, and airmen wanting to use the low-cost weekend cot service at the departments made it necessary for the Board of Managers to consider special subsidies for Wabash and Central, which were particularly heavily taxed. In 1945 Central Department alone housed more than 9,000 men with its cot service.

Through the women's and girls' sections of the Y, a Girls' Service Organization was established under the direction of Wilhelmina Aveling, program secretary for women and girls. This GSO enrolled girls from eighteen to thirty to assist with activities for servicemen. With the purpose of providing "something more than dance partners," the GSO planned evenings of recreation, discussion, entertainment, and parties—as well as dances. In a single year, the girls in the GSO provided the formidable total of two tons of cookies for GI's.

Another outgrowth of the war was the expansion of activities for high school boys and girls to combat the spreading blight of juvenile delinquency. Such a program had already been started in some departments in the 1930's, when the changing nature of the city had made it necessary to develop techniques for dealing with boys' gangs in deteriorating neighborhoods. Some of these approaches met a quick response. At Sears Roebuck Department, free movies were offered and boys were invited to bring their gangs with them. Fourteen boys' gangs enrolled as groups, and Wednesday night was designated as "gang

The gymnasium and auditorium of the Central YMCA were converted to a dormitory during World War II. The fee for one night was 25 cents.

night." On these nights, the Sears clubrooms and athletic facilities were given over to meetings of the "Panthers," "Lion Tamers," "Biscuit Shooters," "Polk Street A.C.'s" and other clubs with odd and original names. Another department enrolled some 125 gangs with a membership of more than 1,500 in a departmental basketball league. Most of these boys were later to become leading citizens of their communities; many of them maintained through the Y the nucleus of their old organization that had been successfully directed away from rowdiness and possible eventual crime into a constructive recreational program, permitting them to reclaim their place in the community.

As it had in World War I, the YMCA also developed a special program to help prisoners of war and their next of kin. Supplementing the work of the Red Cross, which provided the PW's with food and clothing, the Y sent overseas extensive

Members of the Girls' Service Organization entertain a group of sailors in one of the parlors at the Central YMCA.

supplies of athletic and recreational equipment. In Chicago, under the direction of Mrs. Harriet Hester, next-of-kin groups were organized in nineteen departments in 1944 and nearly three thousand families were provided with instructions on sending packages and mail to PW's. Through regular meetings, these next-of-kin groups exchanged information about conditions in the PW camps and were able to minimize the danger of unsubstantiated rumors which might otherwise have caused needless worry or led to their being made victims of petty rackets.

One effect of the war was to mute observances marking the one-hundredth anniversary of the world YMCA movement in June of 1944. Since June 6, 1844, when George Williams met with eleven other earnest young men to "form a society for improving the spiritual condition of young men engaged in the drapery and other trades," the YMCA movement had grown steadily; in 1944 it embraced more than 5,000,000 members in sixty-eight countries. Of this number, a million and a quarter were members of YMCA's in the United States. The Chicago Association, with a membership of 24,973 men, 12,809 boys under eighteen, 4,350 women, 4,394 girls, or a total of more than 46,000, was the largest in the world. Of these members, slightly more than 13,000 had joined during the course of a world centennial membership drive that—even in the face of war conditions—had brought the membership roster to an all-time high. To serve these members, the Chicago Association maintained, even in wartime, a staff of 1,800 employees.

In preparing for the world centennial, the Board of Managers and President H. Fred Wuehrmann expressed a desire that not only should the observances be appropriate to wartime but that they should be "less concerned about glorifying the past than about planning a greater second century." Carroll H. Sudler, Jr. was named chairman of the World's Centennial Committee which carried out this theme with a pageant of YMCA history at the annual meeting and a "service of rededication" at Orchestra Hall on Sunday evening, June 4, 1944. The same day was designated Church Observance Day. The cordial relations which had been sustained between the YMCA and the city's clergy were reflected in a letter which was sent to 1,300 churches by a joint committee of the Church Federation of Greater Chicago and the YMCA, asking the churches to mark the centennial of the YMCA movement with special devotional services. Other devotional meetings were held in many of the departments, and centennial exhibits were put on display throughout the city.

As the YMCA of Chicago moved into the second century of the world YMCA movement, the man chosen to be its new president was a second-generation representative of the Chicago tradition. He was James F. Oates, Jr., son of the former executive secretary at Central and a lawyer who was to be named chairman of the board of The Peoples Gas Light and Coke Company and subsequently chairman of the Equitable Life Assurance Society of the U. S. Three significant steps forward were taken during Oates's administration: women were admitted to full membership rights, the principle of nondiscrimination was firmly endorsed by the Association, and the question of the Y's role in relation to formal education was resolved. Another link with the past was forged the same year. Cyrus H. McCormick, Jr. had died in 1936 and John V. Farwell, Jr. in 1944. To replace John V. Farwell on the Board of Trustees, the Board of Managers named his nephew, Albert D. Farwell, the third generation of the Farwell family to serve the Chicago Association.

The first problem to be faced by Oates was that of making the adjustment from a wartime program to one of providing special services for returning veterans. All veterans were granted three months free membership privileges and were encouraged to use the YMCA's as headquarters during the period of their adjustment to civilian life. Veterans were given preference in the assignment of residence rooms, and at most residences, older men were asked to find other accommodations so that as many veterans as possible could live at the YMCA. An information bureau was opened which in five months provided counsel to more than ten thousand veterans. For those with legal problems who did not wish to accept free help from Legal Aid, the Y arranged for assistance from the Chicago Bar Association at a nominal fee. As it had in other instances, the YMCA was thus able to aid those who were in need of help but not at a level to be subject of charity.

There were also tasks to be done in other parts of the world. The Chicago Association, through its World Service committee headed by Samuel L. Hypes and assisted from the

Many veterans from Gardiner General Hospital used the physical equipment at the Hyde Park YMCA to speed their rehabilitation during World War II.

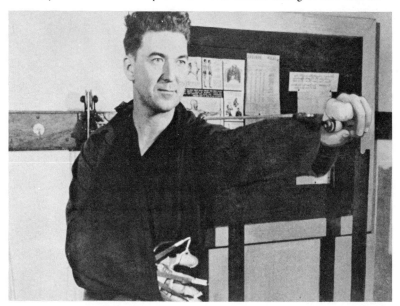

professional staff by John L. Nelson, pledged itself to raise $247,-
000 as its share of an $8,650,000 fund for the restoration of
YMCA work in countries where buildings had been destroyed
during the war or the staff and members dispersed.

At the local level, the activities for veterans had to be integrated with an expanded program for younger boys and girls
which had increased 25 per cent during the time the older
members were away at war. These adjustments were made in
most instances without friction. However, the adjustment of
the problems faced by Central YMCA College was not to be
so easy. During the final year of the war, disagreements had
continued to arise, and the new president, James F. Oates, Jr.,
found himself presented with two points of view that had become virtually irreconcilable.

One attempt to deal with the problem had been made in
1943 after Dr. Sparling, in an annual report, had described the
faculty as "seriously underpaid" and had asked for an increase
and improvement in the physical plant of the college. In an effort
to determine what could be done to eliminate the continuing
condition of crisis under which the college and its predecessor
institutions had been operating since the early 1920's, the Board
of Directors of the college ordered a study made under the direction of George A. Works, emeritus dean of students at the
University of Chicago and nationally recognized educational
authority.

In his study, Dean Works was asked to answer two questions:

1. Was the service given by the Central YMCA College
   needed?
2. Should the YMCA of Chicago attempt to run an accredited college?

Works took a pessimistic view and flatly recommended that

the YMCA withdraw from the field of formal education. This conclusion, he said, was based on the sharply drawn "difference of opinion between the officials of the Association and those of the college on the question of whether or not the objectives of a formally organized, accredited institution of higher education are consistent with the fundamental purposes of the YMCA." Unfortunately, the Y could not abandon the college as there was no other institution or source of support to care for the needs of the students. Further consultations were held with Brumbaugh, who had made the earlier survey, and who took a more sanguine view of the dilemma than Works. Brumbaugh acknowledged that Works was right in saying "the main difference between the college and the YMCA was a religious viewpoint on which fundamentals could not be reconciled." But because there was such a demand for the college's services, Brumbaugh asked that it be continued to provide education for "the student who could not afford to obtain it elsewhere." He was hopeful, he said, that the college could be continued as a department of the YMCA with such adjustments as were necessary "to bring about a compatible administrative relationship."

This recommendation was made in the face of a national trend which found many YMCA colleges moving in the direction of independence from the parent YMCA's which had founded them. Some—such as Jefferson College in St. Louis—had closed their doors when the local YMCA found the burden of running a formal college to be too great. In 1940 there had been ten colleges in metropolitan YMCA's throughout North America. During the next ten years, as these colleges sought to comply with accrediting standards or to solve conflicts over dual administrative loyalties, they moved steadily toward greater autonomy. This evolution took several forms. In some cities the college remained nominally a part of the YMCA but had complete authority for its own program and financing; in other cities there was a formal separation but the members of the Board of the YMCA continued to serve as members of the board of trustees of the college. In every case, this separation was accomplished peacefully after it was discovered that the purposes, personnel practices, program, and problems of tenure and retirement of a YMCA and an institution of higher learning were almost impossible to reconcile under a single administration.

The separation in Chicago was not to be peaceful. In April of 1945, the accumulated tensions of twenty years exploded and Dr. Sparling resigned as president of the college. A large part of the faculty and student body submitted their resignations a short time afterward.

In his letter of resignation, Sparling charged that "During the last year, the college board took action seeking to limit academic freedom, and members of the board, individually, tried to influence me to bring about a change in the entrance policy, limiting certain minority groups. . . . The faculty, the college staff, and I have stood together for academic freedom and equal educational opportunities for everyone, regardless of race, color, or creed. . . . In that time, it has been increasingly evident that the YMCA was not interested in furthering formal education and the kind of liberal institution in which the college faculty and administration believed." At the same time, Sparling revealed that some weeks earlier he had already initiated action (because of conflicts over policy) to establish a separate college under his leadership to be known as the Thomas Jefferson College. The name was subsequently changed to Roosevelt College and is now Roosevelt University.

William P. Wiseman, chairman of the Board of Directors of the Y college, challenged Sparling's assertions. "There is not now and never has been, any restriction upon student enrollment," he said. "The college welcomes any scholastically qualified student, without regard to race, creed, or color. These are facts of clear record." (The percentage of Negroes in the student body, for example, had increased from 4 per cent in 1939-1940 to 26 per cent in 1944-1945). Wiseman said that academic freedom had not been involved in the dispute but rather the fact that Sparling had discharged a dean on the faculty without consulting the Board and had committed the school to monetary obligations without consulting the Board of Directors.

To meet the emergency caused by Sparling's resignation, Oates named Walter D. Gilliland as acting president. In addition, Oates announced that a committee of impartial educational authorities from universities in the area was being called in to make a study of the situation and make public its findings. Dean Works, who had made the earlier survey, was named chairman of the committee. Serving with him were Henry T. Heald, then president of the Illinois Institute of Technology and later chancellor of New York University and president of the Ford Foundation; Raymond B. Allen, executive dean of the Chicago College of the University of Illinois and later president of the University of California at Los Angeles; S. A. Hamrin, professor of education at Northwestern University, and Emery T. Filbey, vice-president emeritus of the University of Chicago.

The committee published its report on May 15, 1945. After analyzing the causes of the split in the college (in which it found no evidence of limitations on academic freedom), the committee made the following recommendations:

1. The Association should withdraw as promptly as it can from education above high school.

2. The Association should limit its program of adult education at the post-high school level to late afternoon and evening classes of an informal nature without credit.

Art class (1947) in "Learning for Living" program at Central YMCA.

3. The educators recommended against any merger of Central YMCA College and Roosevelt College.

4. The high school should be continued because, "unlike the college, it is meeting a need for which no other agency is making adequate provision."

As a result of these recommendations, the Central Department agreed to take over again the high school, secretarial school, and informal educational classes. An agreement was made with the University of Chicago to move its downtown University College into space formerly occupied by the Central YMCA College on the eighth, ninth, and tenth floors of the Association Building. In addition, E. H. McDermott was named chairman of a special committee on informal education at Central and a new approach to Central's educational function in this area was evolved.

The history of the informal educational program at Central since the dissolution of the college indicates that the concentration upon formal education had in effect been keeping the YMCA from doing the job it was much better equipped to do. The informal educational program, a "laboratory of democracy," as director Malcolm S. Knowles described it, was designed "to take education out of the classroom and plant it right in the middle of life itself—to offer practical down-to-earth courses dealing with subjects and problems we definitely know people are interested in." The subjects in these aptly titled "Learning for Living" courses ranged from Vocabulary Building and The Psychology of Social Relations to Discovering and Using Your Aptitudes and The Art of Being a Father. The first year more than seven hundred students enrolled in these informal classes. Ten years later, there were more than nine thousand students enrolled in some eighty courses, including a Real Estate Institute that filled a unique need for both sellers and buyers. Central's high school runs an accelerated course fifty weeks a year for everyone from young boys and bobby-soxers to chorus girls, graying housewives, and other adults. On its curriculum there still remain classes in Americanization and citizenship, an indication that as long as the need exists, the Y will be at work helping make better citizens through its educational program.

CHAPTER **14**

"I Don't Care for Monuments"

THE END of World War II found the Chicago Association impatient to extend its services to new neighborhoods. Material shortages and other war-related problems had ruled out any large physical expansion during the war years. The only building projects to be completed during this period were a $175,000 addition to the North Avenue-Larrabee building in 1941 and the community boys' work building which was added to the Sears Roebuck Department. The following year more residence and recreation space was added at Austin, which had been granted a war priority to provide more housing for defense workers.

The North Avenue-Larrabee expansion represented another of the developing family traditions of the YMCA of Chicago. The department itself had been an outgrowth of the North Side Boys' Club, founded in 1908 with a $100,000 gift by Albert Keep in memory of his daughter, Lucy Keep Isham. Her hus-

296

band, Ralph Isham, had continued to be an interested supporter of the work at North Avenue. In his own will, Ralph Isham provided funds which his widow, Mrs. Mary Otis Isham—whom he had married after the death of his first wife—asked be invested in a new boys' work department and additional residence rooms. In 1955 the Board of Managers of the YMCA of Chicago passed a resolution changing the name of the department to the Isham Memorial YMCA, in honor of the many contributions to its development made by the Isham family. The change in name was scheduled to occur after the completion of yet another building addition in 1958.

Further attempts were being made to reach underprivileged boys on the near North Side through an outpost for boys established in 1944 by the Lawson YMCA. This program, conducted at first in a second-floor loft on North Clark Street and later moved to a rented store at 54 West Chicago Avenue, was designed to provide recreation for almost 1,200 boys who lived on a fringe of the downtown area with virtually no playground space. Support for the outpost also came from many of the business and civic organizations in the area. Another outpost branch established by Duncan at 3936 West North Avenue in 1953 was known as the Duncan-Northwest Outpost.

The only new department to be established during the war had been that at Grand Crossing-Chatham, where a YMCA was organized in 1943 after a year's work by the branch extension committee of Southtown and community leaders headed by H. B. Bentsen, C. N. Moorehead, E. B. Person, G. W. Samuelson, Mrs. N. A. Raiser and Mrs. R. V. Goodrich. Office space was taken at 7938 South Cottage Grove Avenue and a community program organized which strongly emphasized activities for youth that could be carried on through the churches, schools, and Park District field houses. The same year, the way was pre-

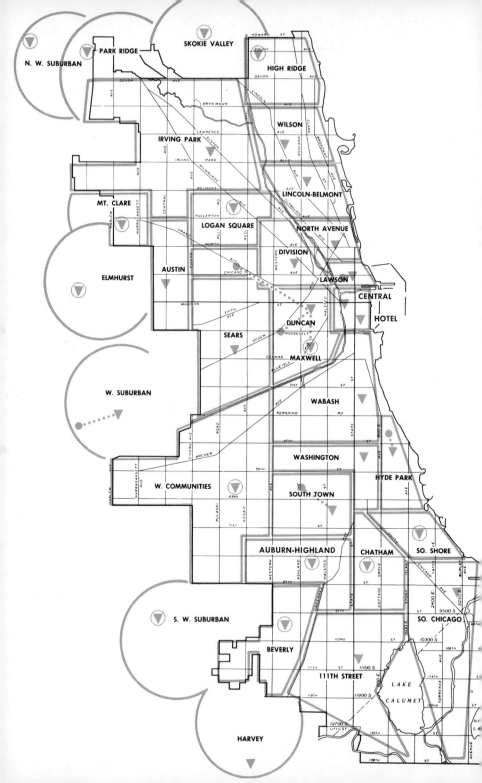

DEPARTMENTS of the YMCA of Metropolitan Chicago

The map on the opposite page shows the 32 departments of the YMCA of Metropolitan Chicago and the areas they serve. Triangles indicate major buildings, triangles within circles are community departments, and dots are branches or outposts.

AUBURN-HIGHLAND, 1155 W. 81st St.
AUSTIN, 501 N. Central Ave.
BEVERLY, 9916 S. Walden Pkwy.
CENTRAL, 19 S. La Salle St.
CHATHAM, 1021 E. 83rd St.
DIVISION STREET, 1621 W. Division St.
DUNCAN, 1515 W. Monroe St.
   Duncan-Maxwell Street Branch, 1012 W. Maxwell St.
   Duncan-Medical Center Branch, 1923 W. Ogden Ave.
   Duncan-North Avenue Branch, 3700 W. Grand
ELMHURST, 155 W. 1st Ave., Elmhurst, Ill.
GREATER LOGAN SQUARE, 3600 W. Fullerton Ave.
HARVEY, 178 E. 155th St. Harvey, Ill.
HIGH RIDGE, 2424 W. Touhy Ave.
HOTEL, 826 S. Wabash Ave.
HYDE PARK, 1400 E. 53rd St.
IRVING PARK, 4251 Irving Park Rd.
LAWSON, 30 W. Chicago Ave.
   Boys' Outpost, 54 W. Chicago Ave.
LINCOLN-BELMONT, 3333 N. Marshfield Ave.
MONT CLARE-LEYDEN, 2329 North Harlem Ave.
NORTH AVENUE-LARRABEE, 1508 N. Larrabee St.
NORTHWEST SUBURBAN, 1488 Miner St., Des Plaines, Ill.
111th STREET, 4 E. 111th St.
PARK RIDGE, 218 N. Northwest Highway, Park Ridge, Ill.
SEARS ROEBUCK, 3210 W. Arthington St.
SKOKIE VALLEY, 4419 Oakton, Skokie, Ill.
SOUTH CHICAGO, 3039 E. 91st St.
SOUTH SHORE, 1833 E. 71st St.
SOUTHTOWN, 6545 S. Union Ave.
   Ogden Park, 952 W. 59th St.
SOUTHWEST SUBURBAN, 5041 W. 95th St., Oak Lawn, Ill.
WABASH AVENUE, 3763 S. Wabash Ave.
WASHINGTON PARK, 5000 S. Indiana Ave.
WEST COMMUNITIES, 6235 S. Homan Ave.
WEST SUBURBAN, 31 E. Ogden Ave., LaGrange, Ill.
   Downers Grove Branch, 921 Curtiss Avenue, Downers Grove, Ill.
WILSON AVENUE, 1725 Wilson Ave.

pared for further growth on the South Side when the Board of Trustees acquired a piece of property at Seventy-first Street and Bennett Avenue as a site for the future building of the South Shore YMCA.

During the following year, a group of community leaders in Harvey, a suburb some twenty-five miles south of Chicago's Loop, were busy making plans for a new YMCA there. Two courses were open to them: They could form a YMCA independent of Chicago, or they could affiliate with the Chicago Association under the Metropolitan Plan. The Metropolitan Plan, conceived before Chicago had become a burgeoning complex of suburbs and superhighways, had not as yet been extended beyond the city limits. Evanston, Oak Park, and Glen Ellyn had YMCA's, but they were independent of the Chicago Association (although, of course, part of the same National Council of YMCA's). If Harvey decided to affiliate, its leaders would be hurling a new challenge at the Association—and for its part the Association would be setting a precedent for extending YMCA services to a major portion of the rapidly expanding metropolitan area forming around the great industries, railroads, and shipping docks at the southern end of Lake Michigan.

It was with a full knowledge of these implications that an agreement was reached in 1944 for the Harvey leaders to undertake the formation of a YMCA that would become the first suburban department of the Young Men's Christian Association of Chicago. Coincidence had a strange place in the location of this venture. The town of Harvey took its name from Turlington W. Harvey, who had himself been president of the Chicago Association for two periods from 1872–1874 and 1877–1879 and who had laid out the town and its principal streets.

When the new department was organized with Victor H. Rompel, later manager of the YMCA Hotel, as first executive secretary, the Chicago Association promised to furnish $200,000 toward a new building if $275,000 could be raised in Harvey. Volunteer workers headed by Campaign Chairman William E. McVey, later a U.S. representative, and Paul W. Soenksen, the first Board chairman, had raised a fund of more than $234,000 by the end of 1945. Unfortunately, construction was so long delayed by material shortages that prices rose far beyond the anticipations of the original estimate. When the building was finally dedicated in 1953, its total cost had mounted to $2,761,-360, of which $584,000 had been raised in Harvey from gifts of individuals and corporations. The series of fund drives necessary to launch such an enormous project had served an additional purpose of educating the public about the YMCA and awakening a lively interest in its objectives; when the department began its full program in the new building under Executive Secretary John O. Root, its initial roster listed more than 3,300 members. One of the Harvey members, Mrs. A. Myron Lambert, was to become the first woman member of the National Council of YMCA's.

Chicago was a city of many faces during these years. One face was turning toward the suburbs, where veterans returning from the war were hoping to raise their families in a new brick home bathed in sunlight and surrounded by a patch of green lawn. But there was another face to the city. It was the face that was turned inward, where nearly 300,000 rural workers brought north to work in Chicago's defense industries had swelled the city's Negro population from 90,000 in 1940 to almost 400,000 in 1945. At the vortex of all the currents created by this flooding tide of migrants was the Wabash Avenue YMCA, struggling bravely to accomplish a task far beyond the capacity of its limited resources.

The size of the problems at Wabash Avenue was ironically in direct proportion to the success with which it had served the community since it had first opened its doors in 1913. By letter and by word of mouth, the message had reached every county south of the Mason-Dixon line that there was no reason to be faint-hearted about taking a job in Chicago—"The Y will help you." To all who heard these words, the Wabash Avenue YMCA became a kind of port of debarkation where they could get job information, find a place to sleep, or locate their relatives. Sometimes they came by streetcar from the downtown railroad stations; others arrived in trucks owned by a more prosperous relative or purchased with pooled resources from a second-hand car dealer. They came in such numbers that on many nights there were not enough cots to go around. On these nights, Wabash Avenue could offer only a pillow and a step on the lobby stairs on which to sleep.

Overtaxed with transients and anticipating new problems that would arise as these rural people made the difficult adjustment to the city's patterns, the Wabash Avenue Board of Directors came to the Chicago Association with a bold proposition. They had surveyed their needs, they told the Board of Managers, and set $1,170,000 as the realistic estimate of what was necessary to provide more adequate services for this South Side area. They had agreed to raise $150,000 toward such a program in their own community, if the Association would undertake to raise the balance. More than $100,000 of the proposed goal was to be spent in providing more clubrooms for community meetings at the Wabash Y; another $30,000—a bequest to the Association by George R. Arthur, who had served Wabash Avenue as executive secretary for seventeen years—was to be used in enlarging the facilities at the department's summer camp, renamed Camp Arthur in his honor. The biggest share in the proposed fund—just over a million dollars—was the amount needed to erect a new YMCA building at Fiftieth and Indiana, which would serve that community as Wabash Avenue had served the district closer to the Loop.

The goal was a tremendous one, but the Board of Managers agreed to meet it. An immediate gift of $25,000 came from the Rosenwald Fund, then in the process of being liquidated in accordance with Rosenwald's wishes that his money be used for good purposes as quickly as possible after his death. This gift brought Rosenwald's program for enabling the Y to help Negroes to its full cycle in Chicago. The first gift had been to Wabash Avenue; subsequent donations of $25,000 each had gone to twenty-six other cities in ensuing years before this final gift to the new Washington Park YMCA on Chicago's South Side.

Although the Washington Park YMCA fulfilled Rosen-

A young Y member enters the water for the "flying fish" test that will qualify him for his water-achievement emblem.

wald's conditions as a department intended to serve a community almost entirely of one race, it was not set apart from any other department of the YMCA of Chicago. The Board of Managers made this clear on May 17, 1945, when it voted approval of an important declaration of policy with respect to minority groups prepared by a committee under the chairmanship of former president H. Fred Wuehrmann. This resolution declared it to be the policy of the Chicago Association that:

1. Participation by a member of the Association in any department or city-wide activity conducted under the Association's auspices shall not be denied because of race, color, or creed.

2. The patronage of restaurants, cafeterias, or soda fountains operated by the YMCA of Chicago shall not be limited on the basis of race, color, or creed.

3. Accommodations in YMCA residences shall be open to any member regardless of race, color, or creed, and especially when members of convention groups or delegations desire such accommodations.

4. An athletic team shall not be denied the right to participate in any league or tournament because any or all of its members are persons from racial minority groups.

The resolution went on to pledge that it is the desire of the Young Men's Christian Association of Chicago to work toward a more complete recognition of the rights and obligations of membership regardless of race, color, or creed.

The fund drive for the Washington Park YMCA developed into an unusual city-wide effort on behalf of a single department. Almost immediately, large contributions came from some of the city's leading businesses; among them were Sears, Roebuck and Company, Armour & Company, Swift & Company, and the International Harvester Company, each of which gave $50,000.

Other gifts of $15,000 from the Community Trust, $15,000 from the Wieboldt Foundation, and $10,000 from the Murphy Foundation swelled the fund. On the South Side, a group of canvassers moved steadily toward the $150,000 goal under the leadership of W. Ellis Stewart, first Negro member of the Board of Managers and chairman of the future plans committee of the Wabash Avenue YMCA, and A. W. Williams, chairman of the Board of Directors at Wabash. Again costs were rising, and before the project could be completed in 1951, the total budget had risen more than half a million dollars. For this reason it was necessary to erect the building without a gymnasium or swimming pool; priority was given to facilities that could meet the immediate community needs of a rural people seeking assistance in making the adaptation to city life. Two years later, a campaign for funds for a gymnasium and swimming pool to complete the $2,116,364 building was begun under Dr. T. M. Smith. This drive too became a city-wide project, with the other departments of the Chicago Association pledging supplemental funds of $100,000 toward the gymnasium and swimming pool— a practical symbol of the solidarity of purpose which has enabled the YMCA to set and achieve goals beyond the reach of a secular social agency.

The program developed at Washington Park under Executive Secretary O. O. Morris was a unique combination of Y traditions with the newest techniques of social service. The program for youth is, as it always has been, at the heart of any YMCA. This is augmented at Washington Park with a program for adults which begins with such fundamental tools as a class in "How to Write Your Name," for which the instructor is provided by the Board of Education. From this basic beginning, the program extends through a magnified spectrum of activities that includes meetings of university alumni and discussions of the great philosophers. Community service is emphasized in many ways. From noon on Saturday to Sunday night, the entire building is reserved for community meetings of "non-Y" organizations. From 1,200 to 1,500 people from the neighborhood stream into the Washington Park Department for these activities almost every week end; they are representatives of some 57,000 Chicagoans in the 500 South Side groups for whom the Y is meeting a need not filled by any other agency. In 1957, O. O. Morris left Washington Park to accept an appointment as an assistant general secretary of the YMCA of Metropolitan Chicago, the first Negro to fill a policy-making post in the history of the Association.

On the West Side, the Sears Roebuck Department marked the thirty-fifth anniversary of its establishment with the opening in 1946 of Camp Sears on Upper Scott Lake near Pullman, Michigan, where Division Street had already established Camp Channing. Farther to the west, a new department was added to the Association with the founding of the West Suburban YMCA by a group of citizens from the suburbs of La Grange, Western Springs, and Congress Park under the leadership of Harold M. Elliott, former president of the Illinois Area Council of the YMCA. Charles H. Stotz, a second-generation staff secretary whose father had been first secretary at the Sears Roebuck Department, was named to be executive secretary and undertake the organizing campaign at West Suburban. The same year Albert D. Farwell became president of the Association—continuing another family tradition.

During Farwell's administration, two South Side departments which had been organized during the worst years of the depression—South Shore and Beverly—were able to realize their plans for a building. In South Shore, Chairman Henry L. Porter of the Board of Directors and his group of fund-raisers reached the total necessary to erect the first section of a proposed million-dollar building. Construction of a building in sections represented a new approach made necessary by rising material and labor costs. Eugene B. White, director of the architectural and engineering department of the general offices since 1929, developed a series of plans which provided for the initial construction of a community or clubroom building on which such standard YMCA features as a gymnasium, swimming pool, and residence hall could be superimposed as funds became available. At South Shore, the first section to be constructed was a $216,000 youth center. Six years later the department dedicated a $555,200 addition which contained a gymnasium, swimming pool, and a business men's health center.

The Beverly Department acquired its building in 1949 from a group of high school students who had purchased a garage at 9916 South Walden Parkway, which they intended to use as a youth center under the name of the Beverly Youth Foundation. The commitments necessary to operate such a center proved so burdensome that the sponsors asked the YMCA to assume their assets and liabilities and integrate their program with that of the Y. With nearly $38,000 raised in Beverly and matching money of approximately $35,000 from the Chicago Association, the Beverly Department took over the building (plus a $5,000 mortgage) and remodeled it as the home of the Beverly community department of the YMCA.

One of the most active programs in the city during these years was that centering around the former Englewood Department—renamed Southtown—under the direction of Executive Secretary James F. McFarland. Southtown pioneered in developing a community extension program for boys and girls. The first of these was established in Auburn Park in 1936 with Harry A. Fischer as chairman of its Committee of Management. This community development, which later took the name of the Auburn-Highland branch, began a building campaign shortly after the war that culminated in 1949 in the erection of a $100,000 YMCA at the corner of Eighty-first and Racine. In 1951, as the branch continued to offer an increasingly diversified program of activities, Auburn-Highland was granted the status of a separate department.

Another department sponsored and nurtured by Southtown was the West Communities YMCA. Community work in this area, south of Forty-seventh Street and west of Bell Avenue, was started in 1936 under a community committee headed by Lambert Bere, and in 1950 the branch moved into a new building at 6235 South Homan. The following year, with a roster of more than 1,100 members, West Communities was made a separate department of the Chicago Association.

The third of the community extension programs established by Southtown was in Clearing, a predominantly industrial district on Chicago's Southwest Side. This program was not initiated until 1946, but by 1951 the Clearing branch was able to purchase and remodel a building for its own use at Sixty-fifth Street and South Major Avenue. The same year it cut its ties with Southtown and was recognized as a separate department.

In 1950 Albert Farwell was succeeded as president by Samuel L. Hypes, president of Wieboldt's and a son of W. F. Hypes, who had served in the same post from 1916–1926. Hypes asked the Association to undertake a basic self-examination, analyzing its purposes, techniques, and activities with a view to defining as freshly as possible what services the YMCA could best render to meet the needs of America at mid-century. As a result of this study, the Chicago Association urged its departments to re-emphasize six objectives in the next year's program. These were: (1) a more widespread lay leadership; (2) a more responsible and participating membership; (3) greater Christian emphasis "to encourage people to participate in the customs and beliefs of their own religious traditions"; (4) a world service program to help young people in other countries; (5) a program to reach more young adults, whose requirements had not been as specifically provided for as individuals in other age groups; and (6) an expanded public relations program to make people aware of the fundamental purposes of the YMCA. It was also in this period that a Board of Managers committee under Harold J. Nutting developed a program in conjunction with the Catholic Charities and the Jewish Welfare Board to re-establish a base of support for the USO, still needed because of the large number of boys and young men in the armed forces.

Hypes' successor in 1952 was Donald P. Welles, a Chicago banker who served as president during the period when many of the plans were being laid for suburban expansion and under whose administration the city-wide drive for funds for physical facilities at Washington Park was initiated. In 1954 Welles was succeeded by Colonel Clifford C. Gregg, director of the Chicago Natural History Museum. The election of Colonel Gregg marked the final stage in the reconciliation of the views of the Chicago Association with the National Council. Colonel Gregg had served on both area and national boards of the YMCA and on the executive committee of the National Board. In 1956 he was elected president of the National Council of YMCA's, the first member of the Chicago Association to hold this post.

The year 1950 marked the end of six years of planning for the organizers of the Greater Logan Square YMCA. As early as 1944, the future plans committee of the Board of Managers, under Jeffrey R. Short, had been surveying the neighborhood with a view to establishing a YMCA there. In March of 1951 an office was opened in a store-front location at 3435 West Fuller-

ton and work started with a combined fund of $14,000—
$9,000 of which was supplied by the Association. The balance
represented contributions of interested lay workers in the
neighborhood. The community quickly responded to the Y's
program, and in 1951 the Greater Logan Square YMCA was
granted departmental status.

On the far North Side, efforts to sustain a department in
Rogers Park had not been successful. After an extensive survey
under the direction of J. C. Aspley, then chairman of the Board
of Directors at Wilson Avenue, the project was given the new
name of High Ridge, made a branch of Wilson Avenue, and its
work extended throughout a wider area of the northern part of
Chicago. By 1951 High Ridge was able to raise $100,000 as its
share of a proposed $285,000 building and was again recognized
as a separate department. In 1954 it moved into its new community building at 2424 West Touhy Avenue.

The changing city severed one department from the Association in 1952 when the West Side Professional Schools building was demolished to make way for the Congress Street Ex-
pressway and the membership and program transferred to the
Duncan YMCA. The same year, however, the members of
Grand Crossing-Chatham Department (now called simply
Chatham) broke ground for a $295,000 building at Eighty-third
Street and Ellis Avenue, which was being erected to replace the
store front in which they had conducted their activities. It was
estimated that, when completed, the building would be serving
a neighborhood of more than 25,000 families.

The chief growth under Hathaway's leadership during the
1950–1955 period was in the suburbs. In 1951 the Mont Clare-
Leyden extension project had been established to serve both the
Mont Clare area within the city and Leyden Township, Elm-
wood Park, River Grove, and Franklin Park to the west.

CAMPS Operated by the YMCA of Metropolitan Chicago

Thirteen resident camps for boys, girls, and their families are operated by the various departments of the YMCA of Metropolitan Chicago, as listed below.

ARTHUR (Wabash Avenue), Dowagiac, Mich.
CHANNING (Division Street), Pullman, Mich.
CUTTEN (Southtown), Lake Villa, Ill.
DUNCAN (Duncan), Round Lake, Ill.
HASTINGS YMCA CAMP (Irving Park), Lake Villa, Ill.
MACLEAN (Austin), Burlington, Wis.
MARTIN JOHNSON (Hyde Park), Irons, Mich.
NAWAKWA (Southtown), Lac du Flambeau, Wis.
PINEWOOD (111th Street), Twin Lake, Mich.
RAVENSWOOD (Wilson Avenue), Lake Villa, Ill.
RODNEY KROEHLER YMCA CAMP (Irving Park), Hayward, Wis.
SEARS (Sears Roebuck), Pullman, Mich.
PALOS HILLS (Week-end, Overnight Camp), Lemont Township, Lemont, Ill.

The Irving Park Department was the scene of the organizing meeting for another suburban YMCA in 1952. A group of citizens from Elmhurst who met there to make plans for a YMCA in their suburb at first elected to take their charter from the Illinois Area Council of the YMCA and remain independent of the Chicago Association. However, the advantages of support from the Association were so many that this decision was later reversed and the Elmhurst group asked to be recognized as a department of the Chicago Association, affiliated under the Metropolitan Plan. When this was agreed to, offices were rented and a department organized with Alben F. Bates as first chairman of the Board of Directors. After a survey of 1,500 Elmhurst citizens, a decision was made in 1955 to plan a Y building tailored to the needs of the community. The estimated cost for the building was $930,000—of which one-third was to be furnished by the Chicago Association and two-thirds secured by subscriptions in Elmhurst.

Camping capacity was increased in 1953 when Mr. and Mrs. Delmar Kroehler donated a beautiful new country lodge and property worth nearly $100,000 on Couderay Lake near Hayward, Wisconsin, for the establishment of the Rodney Kroehler YMCA camp in memory of their son. At Hastings Lake, three different camps had grown up through the years—the Hastings Camp, operated by Irving Park (which also operated the new Rodney Kroehler camp); Camp Ravenswood, operated by Wilson Avenue; and Camp Cutten, which was a part of the Southtown Y program. Southtown also reorganized the camp at Lac du Flambeau which had been unused for a part of the period since it had been acquired; re-equipped as Camp Nawakwa, it offered family vacations in the North Woods at modest rentals.

In 1954 and 1955 the development of suburban departments was accelerated as the Board of Trustees under its president

Arthur B. Hall moved rapidly to acquire key sites for new department buildings in the suburban areas. The Northwest Suburban Department was founded in Des Plaines in 1954 to serve the communities of Des Plaines, Arlington Heights, Mount Prospect, Prospect Heights, Rolling Meadows, Palatine, and Wheeling. In 1955 it became apparent that the Clearing Department was not conveniently located for serving the many families moving into new homes at the southwest periphery of the city, and in its place a new Southwest Suburban Department was established with headquarters in Oak Lawn to serve the communities of Clearing, Palos Hills, and the greater Oak Lawn area. At the northern edge of the city, a Skokie community department was founded in September of 1955 to serve a population that had more than doubled in five years, increasing from 14,832 in 1950 to 33,398 in 1955.

Well-built, airy cabin at modern Camp Channing.

The year 1955 also saw the creation of a new suburban department in Park Ridge, a prosperous suburban community northwest of Chicago. This department, allowing itself one of the shortest establishment periods in the history of the Chicago Association, broke ground for a new $735,000 building just one year after the department was formally organized.

Park Ridge was the fourth suburban department to be established in two years. In recognition of the ever-widening circle of communities who were participating in the Association program, the Board of Managers on March 24, 1955, approved a change in the by-laws altering the name of the Association to

The Young Men's Christian Association
of
Metropolitan Chicago.

This change in name was both a new idea and an old one. It was new in recognizing the increasing role which the suburbs were taking in the affairs of the Association. But it was also a traditional idea, for it formally recognized the wisdom of the authors of the 1888 constitution, whose Metropolitan Plan had provided a framework for the growth of the Chicago Association.

Meanwhile, the West Suburban Department was giving an impressive demonstration of what could be accomplished by volunteer workers and members in these suburban communities. By 1953 the West Suburban program had grown so rapidly that it was necessary to establish a branch in Downers Grove. A building campaign, conducted by teams of enthusiastic volunteers in the western suburbs, was successful in raising $750,000 toward a new building. With a matching sum from the Board of Managers and the use of endowment funds for the residence halls, West Suburban was able to construct a building at 31 East Ogden in La Grange that represented a total cost of $2,759,164.

This futuristic cabin was designed by the Illinois Institute of Technology and erected at Camp Cutten.

The West Suburban building was formally dedicated in June of 1956 following a keynote talk by the pioneer automotive inventor, Charles F. Kettering, whose family had taken a leading role in the Y's campaign. Upon its completion, the West Suburban YMCA was the largest and most modern suburban department building in the world. Designed by Eugene B. White and his staff, it represented the architectural application of a quarter of a century's experience. Constructed of the newest building materials, with modern design and decor throughout (including a hanging staircase leading to the residences), the West Suburban building matched design with function in providing services for a twentieth-century suburb. Its swimming pool was constructed in the shape of an L so that the shallow waters for small children were efficiently separated from the boisterous activities of older brothers and sisters. Twenty years ago, different age groups would not have been using the pool at the same time; but for the modern suburb the facilities were tailored to the needs of the family unit as part of the YMCA's effort to permit the family "to play together—and to stay together." A series of meeting rooms of varying sizes made possible by flexible partitions represented the interests of the civic, women's, and business organizations who were also to be served by this suburban YMCA. In the dormitories, there were residences for young men, for young women, and for young married couples as well. Parking space comparable to that of a suburban shopping center was another part of the basic plan.

The opening of the West Suburban YMCA building was not a climax for the Chicago Association but rather a dramatization of a many-faceted development that outpaces any history which could be written about it. In physical assets and in mem-

West Suburban YMCA—largest and most complete suburban YMCA building in the world.

bership, the twelve years from the end of World War II up to the centennial year of 1958 had been a time of tremendous growth. Membership had increased from 84,000 (1945) to more than 114,000 (1956) "different members," while the number of departments was increasing from twenty-three in Chicago alone to thirty-two in Chicago and its suburbs. (Maxwell Street, formerly a separate department, was made a branch of Duncan in 1957, reducing the total for that year.)

In the midst of this tremendous development, Frank A. Hathaway retired as general secretary in 1954 and was succeeded by his associate general secretary, Lloyd L. McClow. This change in the chief administrative office of the Association was accomplished gradually; the fact that it made no perceptible change in the Association's program was itself a tradition of the office and a shared belief of both men that the best assurance of continuity in policy was to be found in developing volunteer leadership at the local, or departmental, level. Analyzing the growth of the YMCA of Chicago, Hathaway pointed to two factors as of primary importance. The first, he said, was "the distinctly Christian purpose" of the YMCA and the second was its form of organization which "widely delegates responsibility and control of department operations to leaders of local communities."

That Hathaway had been a successful administrator of such a philosophy is evident in the accomplishments of the YMCA of Chicago during the fifteen years he served as general secretary. Although the country had been at war for a third of that time, Hathaway had directed the establishment of sixteen community departments, branches, and outposts. Thirteen new buildings had been erected or acquired, and other new projects of renovation or modernization initiated that represented an investment of more than $15,000,000. Hathaway was always conscious that the effectiveness of the Y's membership was directly related to the efficiency with which it was served by the YMCA staff. He inaugurated an enlightened personnel program, including a death and disability plan for nonprofessional employees, liberalized vacation plans, and set up a supplemental retirement plan for secretaries over fifty-five years of age. He also arranged for job classifications and specifications for all regular employees which set standards of minimum and maximum wages.

Hathaway also made important contributions to the growth of the YMCA nationally. In 1943 he was named chairman of a staff "emergency services and debt reduction committee" of the National Council of YMCA's. Under his leadership, this committee raised more than a million dollars to help eliminate a national deficit and was instrumental in organizing a laymen's committee that secured another million dollars in funds to write off the National Council debt. He continued to be active following his retirement. After a year's service as consultant to the Board of Trustees of the Association, he was elected chairman of the Board of Trustees of George Williams College where he headed a development program to make it possible for the college to continue as a primary training agency for YMCA secretaries.

Lloyd L. McClow, the new general secretary, was a graduate of George Williams College who had been a physical director at Norfolk, Nebraska, and Bartlesville, Oklahoma, before joining the staff of the South Chicago Department in 1926. A specialist in teaching boxing and wrestling, he had been welterweight champion of Nebraska in 1919 and had developed a state championship team. He had written books on both boxing and wrestling that were widely used in YMCA's and other physical education departments. At South Chicago, he had pioneered in introducing women's and girls' work and later was promoted

Lloyd L. McClow
has been general secretary of the
YMCA of Metropolitan Chicago
since 1954.

to be executive secretary. In 1939 he had become the manager of the YMCA Hotel and in 1945 had joined the general office staff as assistant general secretary. With Hathaway's approaching retirement, McClow was advanced to associate general secretary and gradually assumed responsibility for the new projects which were pending at the time of Hathaway's retirement. McClow expanded the functions of the general secretary's cabinet to an even greater degree than Hathaway; committees were increased to include program specialists in addition to the executive secretaries who had traditionally been considered the only staff members eligible for cabinet committees. McClow fully shared Hathaway's views on the importance of lay leadership. Early in his administration, McClow began to push the expansion of the governing-member plan in the belief that it represented the best way "of expressing the YMCA's democratic ideals of management and of broadening the base of responsibility and support" for the Y's program. Leading members of the Association were also urging the development of a new concept of YMCA membership. Edward W. Emery, chairman of the Board of Managers' membership committee, and C. C. Robbins, a leader in the national membership movement as well as in the YMCA of Metropolitan Chicago, were successful in securing a wider acceptance of the governing-member plan as well as a sharp increase in the general membership. Robbins was also one of the outstanding spokesmen in the country in promoting the idea that YMCA membership was a service rather than merely the paying of a fee for the use of Y facilities. The effect of this approach was to add new vitality to the YMCA and make the various departments a more effective influence in their communities.

Members of the YMCA of Metropolitan Chicago in 1957—whether governing members, group leaders, or fund campaign workers—were pursuing their goals in communities widely separated by distance and by differences in age and interest. But their willingness to sacrifice time, effort, and money to the cause for which they worked was bound together by a common purpose. Whether raising funds for a new gymnasium or a chapel, whether acting as group sponsors for clubs that included their own children or functioning as advisors in a program to help underprivileged children from other areas of the city, all these volunteers were united by a knowledge that their purpose was the same. It was a purpose that had been well-expressed by Joseph S. Duncan—an earlier member of the YMCA whose personal interest and good works had done much to make the Y prosper.

"I have not been very much concerned about the praise of men," Duncan said. "What I have done, I have done because I wanted to do it. I am interested because I want to help young boys get started right. I get more value per dollar this way than by building a fountain or a public monument of some sort. I don't care for monuments. Money spent to help boys does more good and gives me more pleasure."

Duncan died in 1950, making a bequest to the YMCA of $1,125,000 so that his support could continue after his death. Few Chicagoans in 1957 could match this financial munificence, which brought Duncan's total contributions to more than $2,-225,000. However, more than 10,000 were following in Joseph S. Duncan's tradition as volunteers. What they were accomplishing is the climax of the first century of the Young Men's Christian Association of Metropolitan Chicago.

CHAPTER **15**

"The Dust of the Earth and the Breath of God"

WHEN THE Young Men's Christian Association of Metropolitan Chicago was founded in 1858, its purpose was stated as that of providing for ". . . the improvement of the spiritual, intellectual, and social condition" of the young men who were the dominant element in the population of Chicago at the time. As the city has changed in the ensuing century, this purpose has been broadened to meet new needs and new conditions. From the midpoint of the nineteenth century to the midpoint of the twentieth century, Chicago grew from a pioneer prairie town to a great metropolis at the center of an urban concentration of more than five million people. By 1957 it was the economic and industrial capital of midwestern America. The YMCA of Metropolitan Chicago has shared in this growth. Many of the same men who participated in building the great industries and business houses of Chicago have also had leading roles in linking the program and services of the YMCA to the many needs of a city grown to be a complex pattern of nationalities, cultures, races, and diverse economic interests.

These services of the YMCA are of a great variety. Whatever their nature, they are still motivated by the same purposes which led to the founding of a Young Men's Christian Association in Chicago a century ago. A membership pamphlet, issued within the last decade, echoes the feelings of Loring Wilbur Messer when he came to Chicago as general secretary of the Association. As Messer had done before them, the authors of the pamphlet recognized that the tools with which the YMCA worked sometimes obscured the one objective that has remained fundamental throughout its history. "To some people a Young Men's Christian Association is a building, a gymnasium, or a swimming pool; to others a place to sleep or to eat; to others a club, the center of their friendships; to still others a cause to which they devote much of their leisure and energy in an effort to make this world a more kindly, a more friendly place," the authors wrote in explaining the Y to new members. "Ideally and actually," they continued, "the Association is a world-wide fellowship of youth and youthfully minded men and women, united by a common interest. It is a fellowship that started with an idea—the idea that the principles by which Jesus lived would remake the world if translated into loving action. In Chicago and throughout the world, the YMCA has built buildings and operated gymnasiums and swimming pools and other program facilities only as tools to implement that idea, to provide ways and means for its members to spread a philosophy of life characterized by those principles by which Jesus lived."

The familiar symbol of the YMCA everywhere is the inverted red triangle. It was devised by Luther H. Gulick, an early leader in the physical work of the YMCA movement in North America. Gulick's apt description of the triangle's sym-

Official insignia of the YMCA.

bolism accurately defines the program of the YMCA of Metropolitan Chicago:

"The triangle stands, not for body or mind or spirit, but for the man as a whole," Gulick said. "The triangle, in symbolizing the man, also symbolizes the Association. Our work cannot be represented by the physical, plus the intellectual, plus the social, plus the spiritual, each one standing alone; for the relations that exist between them render each far more valuable than it would be by itself . . . and thus the total of our results is greater than the sum of the results in each department."

In 1895 this triangle was used as the basis for the official insignia of the YMCA. This insignia, which reflects through its various elements the purposes basic to the YMCA movement, is made up of four parts: (1) *A double circle*. One circle represents the unity of life; the other represents friendship among individuals. The rest of the emblem is placed within these circles. (2) *Chi Rho* (XP). These Greek letters are the first two letters of the word for Christ in the Greek language and served as an emblem for early Christianity. (3) *The triangle*. This is the central theme of the unity of men in spirit, mind, and body. (4) *The Bible*. The Bible lies open at JOHN 17:21, a verse which reads: *That they may all be one; as Thou, Father, are in me and I in Thee, that they also may be one in us; that the world may believe that Thou hast sent me.*

The programs offered by the YMCA of Metropolitan Chicago in its thirty-two departments center around this triangle of body, mind, and spirit, characterized by Gulick on another occasion as "a wonderful combination of the dust of the earth and the breath of God." The use of the word "Christian" in defining the purposes of the YMCA and in its official name does not exclude men and women from other faiths. Nor is YMCA membership restricted to any particular group of churches or denominations. Members of the Protestant, Roman Catholic, and Jewish faiths all are counted among the membership of the YMCA of Metropolitan Chicago. The basis for this interfaith and interdenominational participation was explicitly defined in a statement prepared by a committee under Dr. Rolland W. Schloerb in 1947 and given the official approval of the Board of Managers. The statement rejected any religious barrier to participation in the YMCA. Acknowledging that the YMCA was by its name committed to the pursuit of "Christian objectives," the authors of the statement reaffirmed the Y's traditional policy of encouraging any religious person to participate in the particular customs and beliefs of his own religious tradition. "A religious person expresses his religion by the way he lives and in everything that he does," the authors continued. "He is religious not only when he is in the church or synagogue but in the home, in his business, and at his play." In 1957 this policy was being successfully applied not only in Chicago but throughout the world. In India, almost 90 per cent of the 30,000 Y members in that country are Hindus. In Japan and in Ceylon, many Buddhists are counted among the membership.

To provide an atmosphere in which living in accordance with religious values can be emphasized, the YMCA carries on extensive programs of sports and athletics, club organizations, summer camps, and group activities for adults and young people with special interests.

When the YMCA of Chicago equipped a gymnasium for the first time in the third Farwell Hall, it did so that "Chicago youth might have a clean and comfortable place in which to exercise." This program has been expanded through a multi-million dollar investment in swimming pools and gymnasiums in twenty departments of the YMCA of Metropolitan Chicago, but its objectives remain very much the same. The Y's physical facilities permit young people and adults to learn basic skills from trained supervisors at a minimum of cost and encourage the appreciation of social values through games, sports, and team play. Departments which do not have a gym or a swimming pool

A handball court, such as this one at Division Street, is always busy.

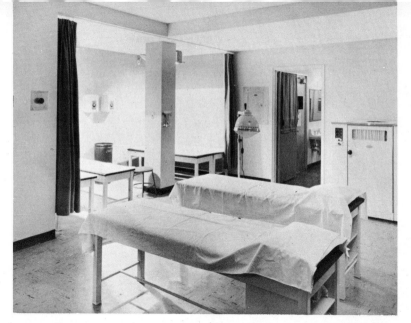

Fully-equipped health clubs for businessmen such as the one shown above at West Suburban YMCA are now to be found in many departments.

conduct their physical activities in outdoor parks or rented facilities. A major trend of recent years has been the development of coeducational and family athletic activities such as "family swim nights" and the Tiny Tot swim classes for children of preschool age. Businessmen's health clubs have grown in popularity with America's increasing health consciousness; many men in outlying sections of the city now enjoy facilities for relaxation and body-building which at one time would have required an expensive membership in a downtown club. The competitive aspect of Y-sponsored athletics is keen. In 1956, more than 2,400 boys, girls, and adults participated in city-wide tournaments in basketball, baseball, swimming, weight-lifting, wrestling, judo, volleyball, gymnastics, and handball. David C. Stubbs, metropolitan physical education director of the Association, was voted the Roberts-Gulick Memorial Award in 1957 by the Physical Education Society of the YMCA's of North

America for his contributions to the development of this program, particularly in its emphasis on the minor or "carry-over" sports which young people can learn and use in later life. Stubbs also played a leading role in the extension of the Y's Men's Club and Industrial Management Club program in the Chicago area.

The club program of the YMCA—designed to apply young people's energies to "purposeful activities"—is as carefully tailored to the capacities and interests of different age groups as its physical work. For children from six to nine, there are Indian Guide clubs for boys and Indian Princess clubs for girls. Both of these clubs require adult participation; no child may attend a meeting without bringing a parent to join in the traditional closing salutation (of the Indian Guides) of "Pals Forever."

Activities for Tri-Hi-Y girls include fashion shows such as this one at an Irving Park Hallowe'en party.

Indian Guide clubs
offer fathers a chance
to participate with their sons.

The Gra-Y clubs serve boys from six to nine and the Little Women clubs provide organized activities for girls of the same age. In junior high or upper elementary school, boys and girls are eligible for the Junior Hi-Y and Teen-Y, respectively.

The Hi-Y club for high school boys is the oldest of the Y youth clubs. The first high school YMCA was organized at Ann Arbor, Michigan, in 1876 and another at Ionia, Michigan, nine years later. In 1890 a club of high school boys was organized in the high school at Chapman, Kansas, but the name Hi-Y did not come into use until 1911 when a Pittsfield, Massachusetts, boys' club took the name of the Pi-Hi-Y. Today there are more than 11,000 Hi-Y clubs in America with 350,000 members. Of this number, more than 1,700 boys are members of 86 Hi-Y clubs in the Chicago area. The Tri-Hi-Y clubs for girls, established in 1939 and made a part of the National Hi-Y Fellowship in 1944, have more than 3,100 members enrolled in 125 clubs organized by the YMCA of Metropolitan Chicago. In addition

Boys in the Sky Valley day camp conducted by the Skokie Department make the acquaintance of a frog.

to an adult leader, each of these high school groups has a sponsoring committee of parents—another example of the Y's increasing efforts to stimulate mutual interest and closer ties within the home.

Summer camping under YMCA auspices has undergone many refinements since it was first inaugurated in temporary locations to permit city boys to become acquainted with the out-of-doors. The greater social mobility created by the automobile and a much higher average income have sharply altered the pattern of city living since the first summer camps were established.

Vacations in the family car have become routine; to a new generation of Americans the open meadows beyond the city streets are now commonplace settings for toll highways and billboards. Because of this change in living habits, camping is no longer considered primarily a means of exposing children to nature lore or permitting them a breath of nonindustrial air. Camping is rather planned as a unique "atmosphere of freedom" in which the young boy or girl away from home—often for the first time—learns self-reliance, self-discipline, courtesy, and respect for the rights of others with whom he or she may be living in close proximity during the camp period.

In the summer of 1957, the YMCA of Metropolitan Chicago was operating twelve resident summer camps and one week-end overnight camp (at Palos Hills) where five departments (Beverly, Hyde Park, 111th Street, Sears, Southtown) had constructed camp lodges. At Camps Channing, Nawakwa, Martin Johnson, and Pinewood, there are special camp periods for families who wish to spend their vacation together. For experienced campers in the older age group, camping activities have been extended to include long canoe trips in Canada (conducted by the Elmhurst Department), overnight hikes or horseback trips, the setting up of tepee villages and outpost camps, and other individually supervised experiences which supplement the normal in-camp program. All camps maintain a high level of trained supervision; at Camp Duncan, for example, there is one lifeguard for every ten swimmers during the camp swimming period. Corollary to the changing nature of the resident camps has been the increasing popularity of summer day camps conducted by the YMCA. More than twenty of these day camps, providing supervised activities in outdoor settings such as the beach, the parks, or the Palos Hills camp site, were being operated in 1957.

The "special activities" conducted by the departments of

the YMCA of Metropolitan Chicago in 1957 were as varied as the needs of the communities in which they were located. At Central Department, nearly 10,000 adults and young people enrolled annually in "Learning for Living" classes. The scope of the activities reflected the imagination and wide interests of the membership. A chorus of professional competence from the Irving Park YMCA, which assigned women members roles equally prominent with those of the men, made concert appearances with its own musical arrangements of popular, classical, and religious music. The West Suburban Department organized a 100-piece symphony orchestra. During the past ten years, the fifty- to eighty-member YMCA Hotel Oratorio Chorus has developed into a tradition, presenting Handel's "Messiah" each Christmas season.

The range of these specialized activities was easily discernible in a glance at the contemporary program at South Shore YMCA,

Members of YMCA Hotel's "Messiah" chorus symbolize the YMCA's emphasis on religious values.

A "Senior" member applies finishing touches to a portrait.

one of the community departments (without residence facilities but with a gymnasium and swimming pool). Members were offered a choice of courses in Spanish, German, or French, or could, if they wished, join in a discussion of Great Books under an outline prepared by the Great Books Foundation. Handicraft classes provided an opportunity for the development of such hobbies as ceramics, enameling on copper, leathercraft, painting, or figure sketching. Two courses in bridge, one of them for beginners, were offered to members, who also had their choice of four classes in dancing (including an advanced class in the currently popular Spanish-American dances of the rhumba, tango, samba and mambo). Camera clubs and Gavalier clubs to train both men and women in public speaking were typical of the program at many departments. An executive development course with a rotating panel of top businessmen kept the young businessmen who made up much of South Shore's population informed on the latest developments in management techniques. Many of these activities at South Shore and other departments were in the area of adult education. This reflected both an increasing participation in the Y by parents and the necessity of providing leisure-hour activities for the growing percentage of older people and retired workers in the population. At Hyde Park, Central, and Lawson, special groups of "Seniors" were organized to develop social contacts among elderly people and stimulate the awakening of new interests or hobbies that might ease the psychological fears of retirement.

A highly specialized kind of program is that represented by the Industrial Management Clubs, established in seventeen departments of the Chicago Association. The first of these clubs was organized at Duncan in 1912 to provide foremen and other supervisors from the West Side industrial area with an informal classroom in which they could discuss their problems, acquaint themselves with new developments in industrial and personnel practices, and hear talks by specialists in the field. Today these Industrial Management Clubs are made up of representatives of management on all levels, the program of each club being adapted to the economic status and aspirations of the particular community which the department serves. Nine of the clubs—those at Duncan, Elmhurst, Harvey, Mont Clare-Leyden, North Avenue-Larrabee, Sears Roebuck, West Communities, West Suburban, and South Chicago—are affiliated with a national organization of Industrial Management Clubs.

Although the noon prayer meeting with which the Young Men's Christian Association started in Chicago is no longer held, the YMCA still provides spiritual sustenance for Chicagoans through an adaptation of technology to religion that has brought the traditions of Farwell Hall as close to Chicagoans as their telephones. Known as "Inspiration," this round-the-clock service inaugurated in 1955 permits anyone to dial CEntral 6-2969 and hear a short devotional message or verse of scripture prerecorded on an automatic telephone. The message closes with a suggestion that the caller attend the church of his choice, evidence that the YMCA still considers one of its responsibilities to be that of helping build interest in the city's churches.

In all its specialized activities, the YMCA has sought to provide a specific answer to a well-defined problem. The most dramatic single application of this principle is the YMCA Hotel. For more than four decades the YMCA Hotel has been meeting an all-Chicago need by helping young people who are, in John G. Shedd's phrase, at "the doorway of city life." How much this help is needed was indicated in a 1957 survey of the "permanent" residents at the Hotel. It disclosed that nearly one-third of the residents were between the ages of twenty-two and twenty-six, and 81 per cent between the ages of eighteen and thirty-five. Represented in this number were guests from forty-two of the forty-eight states and twenty-eight foreign countries. A count of the transient guests would probably have revealed an even wider representation and higher proportion of young people, for about 1 per cent of the residents were retired persons who were staying at the Hotel because its program of activities had been expanded to meet their needs as well. More than half of the residents at the Hotel at the time of the survey had come to Chicago in search of a job. Some of them had found their first employment in the YMCA Hotel itself; there is always a small bulletin board behind the desk with a listing of the jobs available at the Hotel for the young man or young woman who arrives short of funds. Personal counseling and the aid of the loan fund are also still available to the newcomer. Students, many of whom work full time in addition to attending school, form a large proportion of the residents of the Hotel. Many are study-

Guests relax in a corner of the roof garden of the YMCA Hotel. Also on the roof are a shuffle-board court, ping-pong tables, and an area for sunbathing.

ing at nearby trade schools or colleges without dormitory facilities. Some are enrolled in trade schools varying from television and engineering to barber colleges and schools of floral design. Others are studying toward a degree at the University of Illinois Navy Pier division or at Roosevelt University. For music students, the Hotel provides five practice rooms equipped with pianos. All student rooms are equipped with desks and bookshelves. The guests also share in the privilege of a roof garden and of the Wilbur Messer Memorial Library, which is a recognized sub-station of the Chicago Public Library and keeps a current selection of more than five thousand books, magazines, and newspapers available to guests without charge.

These "residents" have not changed the nature of the Hotel or diverted it from the purpose for which Rosenwald wanted it used. From three hundred to five hundred new guests arrive at the Hotel on an average day. Even the residents stay only a relatively short while; more than 60 per cent in the survey had been in the Hotel less than a year. To serve these young people while they are new in the city, the Hotel spends approximately $50,-000 a year in furnishing programs to fill their spare hours and encourage the making of new friends. Every guest who expects to stay at the Hotel for any length of time is interviewed about becoming a resident member and is asked about the interests which she or he had before leaving home. The guest is then introduced to a member of one of the more than twenty volunteer committees or seventeen educational or cultural groups organized in the Hotel and is quickly assimilated into it. "We don't print anything here," a staff member at the Hotel remarked one night, "we just mimeograph because everyone and everything changes so quickly." During a week in the spring of 1957, for example, a guest might have started a course in French or Spanish, auditioned for an oratorio chorus, enrolled in a class in creative writing, joined groups for social dancing or the Club Latino for Spanish dancing, or tried figure sketching in the Dab 'n Draw club. In 1956, such activities as these attracted an attendance of more than 93,000. As with other phases of the YMCA program, Hotel activities are designed to aid in the objective of building Christian character. A vesper service has been held in the Hotel every evening since it was opened in 1916; the services in 1957 were being held in the recently remodeled and refurnished Dunbaugh Room where young people called out the numbers of their favorite hymns in a variety of accents that revealed how widely separated were the sections of America and the world from which they had come.

While the YMCA Hotel has continued to provide low-cost rooms for young people new to Chicago, the Y residences have attracted those who found the job for which they were looking and were established in the city. In 1957 there were more than 7,000 beds available in the Hotel and seventeen departmental residences throughout Chicago and the suburbs—at Austin, Division Street, Duncan, Harvey, Hyde Park, Irving Park, Lawson, Lincoln-Belmont, North Avenue-Larrabee, 111th Street, Sears Roebuck, South Chicago, Southtown, Wabash Avenue, Washington Park, West Suburban, and Wilson Avenue. The special needs of modern suburbia are reflected in the fact that two of the three departments with residences for families—Harvey and West Suburban—are located outside the city limits of Chicago. The third department with family residences is Washington Park, located in a section of the South Side without adequate housing for its rapidly increasing population. As is the case with the Hotel, these residences are considered more than a place to stay; they also have a planned program of activities intended to provide an atmosphere "most favorable for Christian living and character development." All these residences provide reciprocal benefits. For the young people who live in the dormitories, the privileges of the swimming pool, gymnasium, and social programs sponsored by the department are available. The revenue from rents and the return on the endowment funds invested in the building, in turn, are utilized to expand the number of services which the department is able to render its community.

The multiplicity of services of which these programs are a part has taken the YMCA of Metropolitan Chicago to a position of world leadership. Not only is Colonel Clifford C. Gregg president of the National Council of YMCA's, but Lloyd L. McClow, the general secretary, is president of the world federation of Associations of YMCA Secretaries. In its centennial year, the Association begun so hopefully by Cyrus Bentley and others is the largest YMCA in the world. It has expanded to thirty-two different departments with eight branches and outposts and thirteen summer camps. Eighteen of the departments are major YMCA buildings with complete gymnasium, swimming pool, and residence facilities. The YMCA Hotel (which is administered as a department) remains one of the ten largest hotels in the world in number of rooms. Fourteen departments are community YMCA's. Some are in compact buildings of modern design with clubrooms, craft shops, youth canteens, and office space for trained staff members who supervise well-organized programs for all ages. Others carry on as best they can in rented storefronts and other improvised quarters. The outposts and branches carry on year-round activities under YMCA supervision in parks, schools, and other buildings.

During 1956, the last year for which complete figures are

Neighborhood basketball competition at the South Shore Department.

Learning a craft—modeling in clay at the Hyde Park YMCA.

available, there were 114,549 different members enrolled in the YMCA of Metropolitan Chicago, of which more than 33,000 were women and girls. An attendance of more than 3,000,000 was recorded at group events conducted under YMCA supervision. Total attendance at YMCA functions of all kinds amounted to more than 10,000,000. There were more than 4,500 program groups with registered enrollment organized under the auspices of the YMCA of Metropolitan Chicago. Supervising this program was a professionally trained staff of 242 full-time YMCA secretaries and more than 2,000 other employees. The cost of operating the YMCA for a single year was more than $13,000,000.

Nearing the end of its first hundred years, the YMCA of Metropolitan Chicago could accurately be listed among the "great enterprises" of a city of great businesses and industries. Its net assets were in excess of $26,000,000. More than 33,000 people contributed directly to its support. It received additional funds from the Community Fund of Chicago and the suburban Community Chests of Oak Lawn, Bedford Park, Elmwood Park, La Grange, Western Springs, Hinsdale, Brookfield, Palos Township, Des Plaines, Clarendon Hills, and Riverside.

The assets and size of the YMCA of Metropolitan Chicago, of course, were of importance only as they contributed to the realization of its purposes. "All this physical property has no meaning unless the mind and spirit really function," Theodore V. Houser, president of the Association in its centennial year, told a meeting of lay leaders. "The YMCA deals with the very practical objective of improving the daily lives of people," he said. "In the YMCA we have a vast field which is neither individual nor church nor state, wherein individual people of a free society can co-operate and work together on matters for the

A meeting of lay leaders and professional staff workers from the YMCA of Metropolitan Chicago. Newton Farr, chairman of the Centennial Committee, is in the center at the head of the table.

common good. The YMCA is unique in being such a vehicle and in being so adaptable in its wide variety of programs to the needs of so many different groups. . . . This implies the voluntary acceptance of obligations and the sharing of responsibilities for the common good."

This "voluntary acceptance of obligations" is basic to the organization of the YMCA of Metropolitan Chicago. More than 6,500 men and women give of their time to serve on its official boards and committees. The Association has grown on the principle that the management of a department should be the function of the local community and its leaders and that authority should be decentralized as much as possible. The program and activities of each department are determined by its members and Board of Directors. Each department also prepares its own budget and decides upon its own method of financing within the broad policies set by the Association's Board of Managers.

To provide continuity in these departments, the YMCA is continually training future members for its own staff and laymen for its boards and committees. In this group are the individuals who will probably be leaders in their communities as well as in the YMCA. Such leadership training begins in simple ways—a staff member invites one or two boys to help set up some gymnasium apparatus; others are taught to lead a squad of their own age or are given the responsibility of planning a meeting or a tournament. Members serve on the gym floor, in the pool, in the classroom, and at dances. There emerge from these activities, year after year, young men and women qualified for leadership and trained for it. Within the past two years, the need for such training was more formally recognized in the organization of "Fishers of Men," a plan developed by the YMCA of Metropolitan Chicago to attract more lay leaders to YMCA boys' work.

President Houser, in describing the role of this lay leadership said, "The YMCA of Chicago is a very impressive organization—impressive in the size of its investments and net worth—its plant and facilities—the magnitude of its operating budgets—the size of its operating personnel—and the unique place it occupies in the affairs of this great city. It is unique in the impressive degree to which it utilizes the services of its nonprofessional, nonpaid friends to carry on its activities. You have here no entrenched bureaucratic group actively soliciting funds and directing the expenditure of such funds into whatever channels seem appropriate. Instead, you have a local and dedicated staff and administrative organization with the over-all policy of the institution determined by private citizens, motivated by no other inter-

Young people from the Irving Park YMCA on an outing at Camp Hastings. The boy in the background wears the insignia of "senior leader," one of the programs through which the Y is developing new leadership for the future.

est than giving of their time freely to support activities worth while to many people—youngsters and adults. You have the determination of programs controlled by similar groups in each department, each serving its local area, and you have such programs carried out to a considerable extent by the voluntary efforts again of nonpaid, nonprofessional people."

In any analysis of the reasons for the extraordinary growth of the YMCA of Metropolitan Chicago, the quality of this nonprofessional leadership must be given as a primary cause. From the beginning of the YMCA in Chicago as an entirely volunteer group under Bentley, Farwell, and Moody, and continuing with the men enrolled by the professional staffs under Hemingway, Messer, Parker, Hathaway, and McClow, the YMCA has always been identified with outstanding leaders in the community. These men and women—already successful in other fields and working together through the YMCA for the achievement of a common objective—have proved to be among the most dynamic forces in the growth of the city and its wide-spreading suburbs.

CHAPTER **16**

"Our Business Is to Create"

IN ITS centennial year, the YMCA of Metropolitan Chicago is a conspicuously successful example of the adaptation of a social institution to its public environment. The growth of the Association during its first century and the acceptance it represents were achieved in a period of great social fluidity when the habits, social relations, economic status, and leisure-time interests of the American family were undergoing a series of rapid and radical transformations. The YMCA and other organizations dependent upon voluntary public support had to keep pace with these developments or perish. In the face of these changing necessities, many public-spirited citizens who set up organizations of high purpose found their resources and imagination unequal to the task and had to disband. The YMCA of Metropolitan Chicago not only survived but flourished, maintaining its basic religious purpose but altering its methods as the situation might demand.

In 1957, as it plans for its centennial, the YMCA of Metropolitan Chicago is continuing to look for new ways to translate its purposes into contemporary terms. "The virtue of our cause is not enough," General Secretary McClow said in commenting upon new program activities. "We are living in an age of the yearly model—in cars, in clothing, and in many other things; the housewife is now being offered each year a new model kitchen. Modern industries are spending billions of dollars in research, not only to provide the public with new conveniences but also to meet the competition of others in their field. . . . We, too, are competing against those who attempt to lead people into activities which are negative," he said. "Our business is to create constructive and interesting programs with a Christian emphasis that will win people to us by offering more attractive programs than the influences to which we are opposed."

Some of the approaches that are evolving reflect a response to the need of a particular neighborhood—whether it be the "inner city" where blight and delinquency are street-corner companions, or the suburbs where a wave of new families has overtaxed the recreational and service facilities available. Other new YMCA activities are projected through many neighborhood departments to meet the common needs of a great metropolis. Many of these courses—such as "Lose Weight the Y's Way" for women, the city-wide swim campaign or the recently organized Teen-Y charm course for girls—may seem frivolous when considered separately; yet when evaluated as part of a planned effort to bring normal social contacts to more people, they may be seen as an important tool in preventing the personality disintegration that is frequently a by-product of the stresses of urban life. By conducting simultaneous courses in many departments, the Association is able to have an impact that its separate units functioning independently could not achieve. "We are learning how to use our strength," McClow explained in outlin-

Ideas for tomorrow—members of a Y Inventors' Club discuss their projects with adult advisors.

ing the reasons for planning these varied city-wide activities.

As is implicit in its name, the Young Men's Christian Association is most sensitive to the needs and problems of young people. In this role it seeks to provide what it describes as "purposeful" activities which will provide a socially beneficial outlet for their extraordinary energies. Two recent programs—one of them originated by the YMCA of Metropolitan Chicago—illustrate how the adult leadership of the Y is able to supply the needs of the everchanging interests of youth. These are the new Inventors' Clubs and the University of Good Government, founded in 1942.

The Inventors' Clubs had their origin in an informal dinner conversation between George Forsyth, a Chicago inventor, and General Secretary McClow. Forsyth, expressing his concern over the shortage of creative scientists and engineers in a modern society so dependent upon technology, asked McClow if the Y could not provide a program to stimulate young people's interest in these fields. McClow discussed the problem with members of his program committee and staff, who developed the idea for the Inventors' Clubs in a series of subsequent meetings.

With the support of a contribution from Forsyth, the first Inventors' Clubs were established to stimulate creative thinking in young people, primarily between the ages of fifteen and twenty-one. This was a formidable assignment, for both Forsyth and the YMCA leaders were aware that creative thinking could not be forced into existence. It could, however, be encouraged. Through group work and discussion of ideas—"brainstorming" as a popular word of a few years later was to describe it—young people were stimulated to express their own ideas in drawings and in models. Forsyth originally intended that the members should exchange ideas in the field of the social sciences as well as working on experiments in the physical and biological sciences. The difficulties of dealing with exact terms in the former field and the different areas of interest represented by social thought and the principles of mechanics soon resulted in the evolution of a program centered almost entirely around inventions and their application.

Inventors' Clubs hold regular meetings, devoted both to experimentation and to learning about the techniques and regulations involved in preparing and registering new inventions. Lecturers discuss the latest processes and techniques developed by science and encourage the members to ask questions about them. Each member of the club has one or more projects on which he is working. He is expected to keep an accurate diary of his work—and to conscientiously record any suggestions made toward the invention by another member. If anyone develops a patentable invention, he or she is entitled to all the royalties or benefits accruing from it (subject only to the jurisdiction of the parents). Every Inventors' Club has a patent attorney advisor who has been delegated by the Patent Law Association of Chicago to help with technical problems, but who disqualifies himself from acting as legal counsel or profiting in any way from club inventions. Many patentable ideas have already come out of these clubs, but this physical accomplishment is not regarded by the YMCA as of primary importance. Dr. Frank Lerman, in speaking of the clubs, expressed the viewpoint of the YMCA leadership when he said, "Perhaps one in ten or twenty will find the training of the Y Inventors' Club program of direct professional help to him as a future inventor, research scientist, or development engineer. However, the other nine or nineteen will have been trained to think clearly and creatively and to put their new ideas into practice."

The Inventors' Clubs are a functioning example of the manner in which the YMCA programs have traditionally originated. The idea or objective may be suggested by any member; the professional staff then uses its experience to provide a program through which that objective can be achieved.

While the Inventors' Clubs have been developing skills in the fields of industrial science and engineering for young people, the University of Good Government has proved to be a successful training ground in government and social thought. Each year about 250 high school boys and girls from Chicago area Hi-Y and Tri-Hi-Y clubs are elected to participate in the University of Good Government. These delegates serve as representatives of their clubs in meetings with public officials, model legislative sessions in the chambers of the City Council, and in other contacts with men in public life. The delegates give regular reports to their clubs so that their impressions of politics and government on a day-to-day level are shared by many thousands of students in the Chicago area. During the course of the year, each club prepares a bill to be introduced in the Youth Legislature, held during a two-day period of spring vacation in Springfield. At the Springfield meeting, the delegates meet in the halls of the state legislature, elect their own state officials, and consider the bills introduced by each club under regular rules of parliamentary committee procedure and debate. Upon their return to Chicago, the apprentice legislators are feted at a special Youth Citizenship luncheon attended by the leading civic and business figures of Chicago.

Another project in which teen-agers take a prominent role is the annual World Service drive for funds to support YMCA work overseas. The purpose of this overseas YMCA program is

Members of the University of Good Government take their places in the chamber of the state House of Representatives at Springfield, Illinois.

primarily one of "helping people to help themselves." In particular, the YMCA is trying to develop an indigenous leadership in
countries where the lack of such training has made it impossible
for a free and responsible government to function effectively.
Another special interest of the YMCA of Metropolitan Chicago
was the rebuilding of the YMCA of Kassel, Germany. Of the
$400,000 required for this building, the members of the YMCA
of Metropolitan Chicago pledged themselves to raise $80,000,
or 20 per cent of the total. To help raise the needed funds for
this and other projects, Y members sell refreshments at football
and basketball games, peddle candy mints, model hats, have
special weigh-in programs (at a penny a pound), and in many
other ways muster up aggregates of money sufficient to buy a
trampoline for a Y building in Asuncion, Paraguay, or help pay
for a YMCA for boys at a railway station in Madras, India
(toward which Chicago contributed $10,000).

A major project—and problem—of the YMCA in recent
years has been the maintenance of the Y's program in Chicago's
"inner city." This is the area surrounding the central business
district where light industry, warehouses, and other commercial
activities have expanded into neighborhoods that were formerly
residential. With the movement of population away from these
communities, the houses and apartments that remain have in
many cases been converted to substandard housing for unskilled
workers and their families or a newly-arrived migrant population. As this change took place, the demands on the eleven
YMCA departments located in this section of Chicago increased
as the sources of support dwindled. In 1956 it cost $1,906,822
to operate these eleven departments. With the aid of almost two
thousand volunteer Y member-workers, the departments served
more than a million and a quarter persons. At one department the
cost per boy or girl was more than $50 per year; yet these same

boys and girls could afford no more than $6.00 to $10 per year in membership fees. Even with help from contributors and the Community Fund, it was necessary for the Association's Board of Managers to make supplementary appropriations of $358,347 to make YMCA services available in these areas which for a period of ten or twenty years have no prospect of attracting a population with sufficient resources to support the full work of a department.

One of the most difficult problems to be faced in these blighted sections of the city is that of the "youth gangs," tightly organized groups of boys who drift at random through the shadow-world of the slums with the possibility of violence or major crime never more than a step or two behind. The changing city was a spawning ground for delinquency as well as progress—in a single year more than 15,000 complaints about juvenile misbehavior were made to Chicago law-enforcement officials. This was the situation in 1955 when the Board of Managers acted to assume responsibility for turning back the rising rate of delinquency. A committee, appointed to find a way of withdrawing these boys from their gang organizations and dealing with their problems as individuals, recommended that specially trained workers be hired to seek out such boys "in their natural habitat—the vacant lot or the street corner." In general, these Y workers were to become parts of the gangs, find the causes that drove boys into them, and seek means of diverting them toward a normal life.

Two workers were assigned to a "pilot project" for the purpose of testing various techniques of breaking down the gang loyalties. Their assignment was dangerous as well as difficult; almost every gang included at least one or two narcotics addicts whose behavior might at any moment become irresponsible. Even in the face of such hazards, these men are achieving results

A hitch in time—
an instructor takes a tuck
for a young pugilist
at Sears Roebuck Department,
one of the eleven "inner-city"
YMCA's.

nearly as remarkable as those of Dwight L. Moody at his North Market Hall mission. One staff worker reduced the gang disturbances in his section from twelve the summer before to only one during his first few months of association with the boys. A baseball team was organized and a former tavern cleaned up and outfitted as a club where boys off the street could drop in for recreation. Another worker, assigned to an area with many narcotic problems as well as racial tensions, found gangs which sometimes had as many as three hundred members; he was working with a gang of sixty-five.

The program which these "youth gang" secretaries followed was based in good measure on the advice of the Y's founder, Sir George Williams. "Don't argue with a young man who has lost God," Williams once advised a friend. "Take him out to supper." By finding jobs for gang members, encouraging them to return to school or providing means for them to pursue their natural interests, specially trained Y staff members in mod-

Mothers and children participate together in the Tiny Tot swim program at the Harvey Department.

ern Chicago were able to chip away at the edges of the gangs and reclaim those boys who were not too deeply involved. To seek out and help more of these boys who are not approachable through a departmental program, the Association's Board of Managers in 1957 set a centennial year goal of half a million dollars for additional secretaries to work on the youth-gang problem until such time as the city had finished the rebuilding and conservation program through which it hoped to eliminate the living conditions that produced much of the delinquency.

Not only the inner city, but the development of new cities around the periphery of Chicago required new methods. The old idea that a YMCA should be at the center of town, for example, has shifted as the new suburban families look for their YMCA in an area with easy access to transportation and plenty of space for parking the family car. In Park Ridge and in Des Plaines, the new building sites are at the edge of the community. At Park Ridge, the swimming pool is not tucked away in an isolated part of the building but is an integrated and visible part of the decor of the lobby. But the greatest innovation of the Y's centennial year in Chicago is the new department planned for the suburban communities of Oak Lawn, Garfield Ridge, Clearing, Scottsdale, Hometown, Palos Park, Worth, Palos Heights, Chicago Ridge, Evergreen Park, Orland Park, and Argo-Summit, served by the Southwest Suburban YMCA.

The impetus for this new approach came from an executive conference around the department's centennial goals. An outdoor swimming pool—the first such Y pool in the Chicago area—was promised by the Association if the communities participating

Family activities are emphasized at suburban YMCA's. Here a member of a YMCA pre-school day nursery lets himself go on the big slide.

in Southwest Suburban would raise $100,000 to establish a combined outdoor-indoor program. In addition, the Association's Board of Managers pledged funds to match those raised in the community. The result was one of the fastest money-raising campaigns in the Association's history. Within sixty days, $100,000 had been raised toward the eventual $320,000 cost and construction ordered on a T-shaped outdoor swimming pool that would be the nucleus of a unique group of YMCA facilities on a six-acre tract near Ninety-fifth and Cicero. Near the pool, a refrigerated outdoor ice-rink is to be constructed whose special asphalt surface can serve in the summer as volleyball, basketball, or tennis courts. Although the pool is originally to be out-of-doors, eventual plans call for it to be sheltered under a modern

Plan of the Southwest Suburban YMCA, showing the transparent aluminum and plastic shell planned to permit year-round swimming in the outdoor pool.

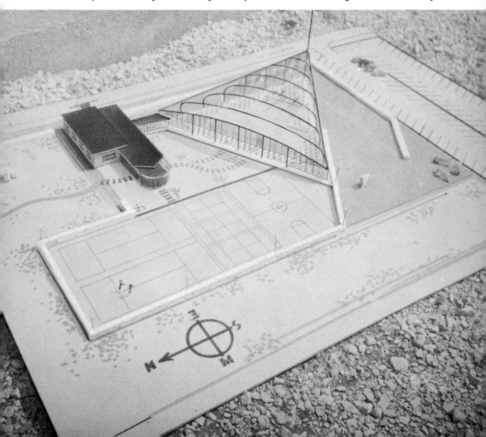

shell of glass and aluminum that will permit year-round swimming. The entire conception of the Southwest Suburban facilities is new to YMCA's in the Midwest. Outdoor athletics—with only a minimum investment in a headquarters building—have permitted the establishment of a YMCA program in a community much earlier than would otherwise have been possible. In addition, the extension of the plant over a large acreage of land with adjacent parking facilities is a development feasible only in suburbs so new that large sections of property are still available.

All of these developments represent a planned effort by the YMCA to match its growth with that of Chicago, described by *Fortune* magazine in a contemporary article as "the most exciting city in the United States." In his annual report for 1956, General Secretary McClow asserted that "the present size and scope of the program are indications that we have met some of Chicago's most vital needs and that its citizens have recognized this by responding generously to its support." As an illustration of this support, McClow cited the fact that the buildings owned by the YMCA of Metropolitan Chicago would form a structure twice the height of Chicago's Prudential Building if they were all combined on a similar site.

The centennial year in 1958 offered the same challenge to McClow as the 50th Anniversary campaign had presented to Messer half a century earlier. Nearly four years before the official anniversary of the Association on March 22, 1958, informal discussions were being held to originate ideas for observing the event in a manner that would result in a further extension of YMCA services. Early in 1955, committees were appointed to begin active planning for the celebration. Other committees were formed to direct the raising of an $8,000,000 Centennial Fund that would furnish the financial means for launching an aggressive program looking forward to the second century.

Speaking at the pre-centennial annual meeting in January of 1957, President Houser traced the outlines of this expanded program. "In my mind, the Young Men's Christian Association must more and more serve as a most useful agency within the boundaries of Christian concepts and precepts for the improvement of the civic and social problems that beset our city," he said. "We must continue our strategic work with youth in both the 'inner city' and the greatly expanding suburban areas, because youth is our country's strength for the future and we are bound to both for the continued betterment of mankind. As we progress along these lines we will merit a broader and broader base of support from all people of all races and creeds, from corporations and everyone interested in building a better Chicagoland."

The specific means by which the YMCA hoped to achieve these objectives were outlined by General Secretary McClow as a complete re-examination of program, a greatly increased endowment, and a new analysis of the Association's structure to make the Chicago Association "as highly efficient an organization as the modern techniques of management can produce." The re-examination of program, he said, should result in a "re-tooling" of YMCA services to meet the specific needs of Chicago and thus provide a "cutting edge" that would thrust the Y program into an ever-increasing number of communities and involve a continually growing number of individuals in its efforts for social and individual betterment. The second objective—that of greatly enlarging the endowment—was necessary to stabilize the YMCA services in the needy sections of the city where such work could only be sustained by endowment income. The third goal—that of providing maximum efficiency—was a pledge to Chicagoans that if they would give generously to the Centennial Fund, their gifts would continue to be used to produce a

Theodore V. Houser,
Centennial-year president
of the YMCA of Metropolitan
Chicago.

"maximum result" in pursuing the objectives which the YMCA
is trying to achieve.

To head the hundreds of committees and teams of laymen
who were to participate in the centennial observance, the Board
of Managers named two former presidents of the Association.
They were Newton C. Farr, chairman of the Centennial committee, and Donald P. Welles, designated chairman of the Centennial Fund committee. Both men immediately matched their
personal commitment with substantial gifts to the Fund, Farr
making a contribution of $50,000 and Welles one of $25,000.
Another early gift to the Fund of $250,000 was from Sears,
Roebuck and Company, one of the great business firms that has
been for more than forty years a bulwark of the "great enterprises" undertaken by the YMCA. Three vice-chairmen—
Robert E. Brooker, Edward W. Emery, and C. Virgil Martin—
were also chosen to assist in the campaign, and L. W. Stratton
was named to direct the drive for departmental special gifts.

"Building for the future."

Special anniversary observances were also planned by the Centennial Events committee headed by Wayne A. Johnston, president of the Illinois Central Railroad. They included the Festival of Youth on November 15 and 16, 1957; the 100th Annual Meeting on January 23, 1958; and the Centennial Program Pageant on March 22, 1958. All the meetings were set for the International Amphitheatre, permitting more than 10,000 YMCA supporters and members to participate in each of the functions.

At the heart of the centennial planning is the Centennial Fund campaign, for it is through the funds raised in this drive that the YMCA of Metropolitan Chicago is basing its hopes for the future. As a result of this campaign the YMCA hopes to be able to modernize worn-out buildings in the "inner city" as well as to provide support for new YMCA's in the suburbs. Other plans call for the launching of new program activities (such as a "This Is Your Day" program for young mothers which permits them to bring their tots to the Y while they enjoy a day of planned recreation), expansion of the staff for helping hard-to-reach boys caught up in youth gangs, aiding a rehabilitation program at George Williams College (which continues to provide much-needed personnel for undermanned Y staffs) and the raising of Chicago's share of World Service funds needed to construct YMCA buildings overseas.

As the YMCA of Metropolitan Chicago made plans for these centennial year activities with the theme of "Serving Youth . . . That Youth May Serve," it could look back on a hundred years in which it had more than fulfilled the expectations of the early editorial writer who said he believed it was destined "to accomplish much good in our city." Facing a new century, it could rightfully claim its place as a great enterprise devoted to the public good.

AUTHOR'S NOTE

THE YMCA of Metropolitan Chicago is fortunate in having a well-organized and complete set of historical records. The ready access of these documents and publications in the vaults of the Association was of great value in the preparation of this history.

In addition, the author is particularly indebted to Herman A. Stotz and Ralph Wendling Cooke for preparatory research which they did following their retirement as executive secretaries. The chapter on the first YMCA of Chicago is largely based on an unpublished manuscript by Stotz; material relating to the development of the general secretary's authority and the dramatic kick-off luncheon of the 50th Anniversary Campaign had been outlined in other manuscripts by Cooke, who has also been most helpful in checking the accuracy of the twentieth-century period of this history and contributing personal reminiscences of the personalities involved. John E. Peel, assistant general secretary and veteran comptroller, invested many hours in assuring the correctness of the financial statistics that form a part of this history and its appendices. Robert W. Sellen, who served as a research assistant at a critical moment in the history, and Kirk W. Fraser, who performed many services in collecting photographs, also rendered valuable aid.

A special debt is owed to the Public Relations Committee of the Board of Managers and its chairman, Dale Cox, and to the assistant general secretaries in charge of public relations, Robert T. Magnuson and Howard H. Kustermann, for giving the author a completely free hand to present this history as he felt it should be written. Warren E. Thompson, as the special representative of the committee for the centennial history, was a stimulating and cordial collaborator in evaluating material suggested for inclusion. My appreciation also is due Frank A. Hathaway and Lloyd L. McClow for their close perusal of the manuscript and the time which they were willing to devote to providing a complete historical record.

EMMETT DEDMON

APPENDIX I

The Young Men's Christian Association of Metropolitan Chicago, 1957

BOARD OF TRUSTEES

BOARD OF MANAGERS

APPENDIX II

GENERAL OFFICE EXECUTIVES

LLOYD L. McCLOW, *General Secretary*

Assistant General Secretaries

JOHN E. PEEL, *Comptroller*

DANIEL A. SHAEFER,
Business Administration

HENRY L. SISTRUNK,
Communities, Expansion

JOHN O. ROOT, *Program Services*

ALFRED C. ROGERS,
Personnel Services

ROBERT T. MAGNUSON,
Public Relations and Development

GERALD L. HEYL,
Membership and Centennial

O. O. MORRIS,
Special Developments

CALVIN F. SCHAEFER,
Properties and Insurance

EUGENE B. WHITE, *Architectural Services*

LOCAL DEPARTMENTS

Location	Chairman	Executive Secretary
Auburn-Highland	John C. Telander	Roger A. Treloar
Austin	Orville R. Radebaugh	Archie G. Beck
Beverly	Malcolm Campbell	William J. Wilson
Central	Charles S. McCoy	Bruce M. Cole
Chatham	Frank Hagerty	Thomas J. Curtin
Division Street	Henry G. Hartmann	Walter S. Bell
Duncan	Wade O. Meloan	Charles E. Allen
Maxwell St.	Dr. Joshua M. Brown	Milton O. Carter
Medical Center	Paul H. Hassell	Richard E. Sweitzer
North Ave.	Christ Brix	Peter F. Sorensen
Elmhurst	Dr. David L. Olinger	L. Keith Boys
Greater Logan Square	John M. McGregor	L. Aumund Andre
Harvey	Dr. H. C. Drummond	Ivan C. Smith
High Ridge	Frank L. Haas	Joseph B. Field
Hotel	Dr. Wm. H. Barnes	Victor H. Rompel

Appendix

Location	Chairman	Executive Secretary
Hyde Park	J. Gibson Brown	John L. MacBean
Irving Park	W. H. Lerch	William S. Miller
Lawson	James J. Kingham	O. W. Bauer
Boys' Outpost	Dr. Carl V. Shipley	George Hamaishi
Lincoln-Belmont	A. B. Anderson	James A. Evar
Mont Clare-Leyden	Ruelle Caldwell	Edward J. Rohmann
North Avenue-Larrabee	Samuel A. Culbertson, II	John W. McDole
Northwest Suburban	Thomas M. Blake	Charles McClellan
111th Street	E. J. Beezhold	Robert H. Freitag
Park Ridge	Robert D. Bjork	William G. Kuntz
Sears Roebuck	John Todd	Chester A. Hall
Skokie Valley	Philip E. Eddy	M. Marvin Lotz
South Chicago	Gen. Horace F. Wulf	W. Stewart Friend
South Shore	Frank W. Mezek	Burton L. Wiese
Southtown	Cameron A. Urquhart	Harold L. Lotz
Ogden Park	Henry Bledsoe, Jr.	John H. Bell
Southwest Suburban	William E. Cairnes	Robert M. Williams
Wabash Avenue	Eugene W. Wood	James E. Gleason
Washington Park	Arthur B. Knight	Walter F. Worrill
West Communities	Anthony C. Duvall	M. H. Johnson
West Suburban	Stanley W. Anderson	Charles H. Stotz
Downers Grove	Wayne Guthrie	George A. Georgandas
Wilson Avenue	Winard G. Olsen	J. Dale Litney

PRESIDENTS *of the*

Young Men's Christian Association of Metropolitan Chicago, 1858–1957

CYRUS BENTLEY	1858–1859	HENRY M. HUBBARD	1894–1900
JOHN V. FARWELL	1859–1861	JAMES H. ECKELS	1900–1903
J. H. HOLLISTER	1861–1862	EDWARD P. BAILEY	1903–1911
BENJAMIN F. JACOBS	1862–1863	WILLIAM P. SIDLEY	1911–1916
EDWIN S. WELLS	1863–1864	W. F. HYPES	1916–1926
H. W. FULLER	1864–1865	WILLIAM FRANCIS	1926–1932
DWIGHT L. MOODY	1865–1869	GEORGE B. McKIBBIN	
C. M. HENDERSON	1869–1871		1932–1935
TURLINGTON W. HARVEY		JOHN S. BROEKSMIT	1935–1938
	1871–1873	NEWTON C. FARR	1938–1940
N. S. BOUTON	1873–1874	JEFFREY R. SHORT	1940–1942
JOHN V. FARWELL	1874–1876	H. FRED WUEHRMANN	1942–1945
TURLINGTON W. HARVEY		JAMES F. OATES, JR.	1945–1947
	1876–1878	ALBERT D. FARWELL	1947–1950
E. G. KEITH	1878–1881	S. L. HYPES	1950–1952
JAMES L. HOUGHTELING		DONALD P. WELLES	1952–1954
	1881–1884	CLIFFORD C. GREGG	1954–1957
JOHN V. FARWELL, JR.		THEODORE V. HOUSER	1957–
	1884–1894		

PRESIDENTS OF THE BOARD OF TRUSTEES
of the YMCA of Metropolitan Chicago

T. M. AVERY	1868–1869	ALBERT L. COE	1896–1901
CHARLES G. HAMMOND	1869	JOHN V. FARWELL, JR.	1901–1944
WILLIAM L. LEE	1869–1883	WILLIAM P. SIDLEY	1944–1948
H. E. SARGENT	1883–1890	JEFFREY R. SHORT	1948–1954
SILAS M. MOORE	1890–1896	ARTHUR B. HALL	1954–1956

JOHN S. BROEKSMIT 1956–

GENERAL SECRETARIES *of the* Chicago Association

DWIGHT L. MOODY   *Librarian and City Missionary—without pay*   1861–1866

WILLIAM W. VANARSDALE
Agent of Executive Committee, Board of Managers   1866–1872

ANSON T. HEMINGWAY
First officially designated General Secretary   1878–1888

LORING W. MESSER   1888–1923   FRANK A. HATHAWAY 1939–1954

WILLIAM J. PARKER   1923–1939   LLOYD L. McCLOW   1954–

VETERANS *of the* General Secretary's Cabinet

In the first one hundred years of the YMCA of Metropolitan Chicago, only forty-four men employed by the Association qualified as Veterans of the Cabinet of the General Secretary. All were employed by the YMCA of Metropolitan Chicago for fifteen years or more and during their service were members of the Cabinet of the General Secretary for ten years or more. Many of their names appear in this history. The full list follows:

GLENN D. ADAMS
DR. R. A. ALLEN
GEORGE R. ARTHUR
PETER C. ATKINSON
PERCY BAINES
ABRAHAM BOWERS
MURRAY BREWER
WILLIAM COOK
RALPH W. COOKE
MERLE E. DENNIS
A. S. EDDY
JAMES D. ELLIS
PAUL C. FOSTER
MAURICE F. GOGLE
WALTER T. HART
FRANK A. HATHAWAY
LOUIS H. HEIN
ANSON T. HEMINGWAY
JACOB A. HILLER
LUCIUS C. HOLLISTER
S. O. HOUSER
ABIJAH JARMAN

ARTHUR J. LARSON
GROVER P. LICHTENHELD
GEORGE M. MARTIN
RICHARD A. MASKE
JAMES F. McFARLAND
LORING W. MESSER
JOHN L. NELSON
WILLIAM J. PARKER
J. GOODWIN PERKINS
H. S. PRINCE
A. J. REED, JR.
FRANK M. ROCKWELL
C. B. ROUSE
WILLIAM T. ROWE
EDWARD W. RUEHRWEIN
CHARLES C. SHEDD
FRED J. SPROWLES
HERMAN A. STOTZ
WILLIAM W. VANARSDALE
JAMES C. VYNALEK
A. C. WILLIAMS
HARRY T. WILLIAMS

MEMORIAL FUNDS and TRUSTS June 30, 1957

In addition to funds established by bequests, the Association holds certain trusts and memorial funds which it administers for the purposes specified by the donors.

Year	Fund, Donor, and Purpose	Amount
1901–1907	ALUMNI ENDOWMENT FUND Alumni of Professional Schools. Maintenance of Student Work ....$	1,715.95
1912	PRINCETON FOUNDATION FUND Cyrus McCormick, Jr. To promote Good Citizenship	5,000.00
1916	ELI B. AND HARRIET B. WILLIAMS FUND Hobart W. Williams. Charitable and Educational Purposes	90,000.00
1928–1932	MR. AND MRS. JOSEPH S. DUNCAN Duncan Department Endowment Fund. Support of Camp Duncan and Duncan Department	231,311.14
1935	JOSEPH S. DUNCAN Joseph S. Duncan Fund. Work with Boys and Younger Men by the Duncan Department.	91,200.00
1935	MRS. KATHARINE ADAMS WELLS General Endowment Fund. General Association Purposes	77,000.00

Year	Fund, Donor, and Purpose	Amount
1936–1938	WILLIAM P. SIDLEY FUND William P. Sidley. Current Purposes ...	5,000.00
1936	CYRUS H. McCORMICK FUND Cyrus H. McCormick. General Association Purposes	250,000.00
1936–1941	EDWARD C. JENKINS LOAN FUND R. T. Miller, Jr. Small loans to Young People in Temporary Financial Distress and Scholarships	30,000.00
1937	E. J. BUFFINGTON General Endowment Fund. General Association Purposes	5,000.00
1938–1947	ALBERT DICKINSON FUND A Friend. Washington Park ...	8,253.02
1938	ALBERT DICKINSON FUND Miss Katherine Boyles. Washington Park ...	1,000.00
1940–1956	ERI HULBERT WYANT FUND Dr. A. R. E. Wyant. Such Association purposes as the donor	

Year	Fund, Donor, and Purpose	Amount	Year	Fund, Donor, and Purpose	Amount
	may direct	18,976.42		gartner. Southtown for religious purposes	5,500.00
1941	JOSEPH S. DUNCAN GENERAL FUND Joseph S. Duncan. Purposes approved by the Board of Managers	68,500.00	1945–1948	WALTER HALLSTEEN SCHOLARSHIP FUND Robert A. Ilg. Work with Boys of Irving Park	3,007.00
1942	CHARLES HENRY CHAPPELL FUND Mrs. May L. Owings. Work with Young Boys	30,580.34	1945	GENERAL ENDOWMENT FUND Poor and Company. General Association Purposes	1,000.00
1942–1944	ALBERT DICKINSON FUND A Friend. Washington Park ...	381.91	1947–1956	JAMES N. SEMPLE FUND Contributions of Friends. To help send boys of Division Street Department to Camp Channing	4,318.33
1943–1944	WILLIAM J. PARKER FUND John V. Farwell. Outpost Work and Work with Boys and Girls .... Balance in Fund.....	139,270.41 260,651.15	1947	ANDREW MACLEISH General Endowment Fund. General Association Purposes	4,551.59
1943–1949	ANDREW DOLE MEMORIAL FUND Mrs. Mary Hooker Dole. Duncan Department. Balance in Fund.....	11,900.00 21,900.00	1948–1956	RALPH W. OLMSTEAD FUND Mrs. Jannette P. Olmstead. Austin	4,500.00
1943	DIVISION ST. DEPT. ENDOWMENT FUND A Friend. Division Street Department	5,000.00	1949–1956	JAMES C. VYNALEK FUND Friends and Relatives. Washington Park ...	8,918.00
1944	JOHN V. FARWELL FUND John V. Farwell. Original Gift .... Balance in Fund..... Unrestricted	74,800.00 44,331.56	1949	C. T. B. GOODSPEED FUND C. T. B. Goodspeed. Washington Park ...	4,515.63
1945–1948	HARRY W. BAUMGARTNER FUND Mrs. Harry W. Baum-		1950	TOMMY SIMPSON CAMP FUND Friends and Relatives. Camp MacLean	575.00

Year	Fund, Donor, and Purpose	Amount	Year	Fund, Donor, and Purpose	Amount
1951–1956	HERMAN M. KOELLIKER FUND Gifts from Friends. Division Street Department Camp Channing	50,795.56		To send worthy children to Camp Sears..	3,000.00
	Balance in Fund.....	56,004.56	1955	ROBERT MALCOLM FUND Relatives and Friends. Duncan Department.	1,313.15
1952	HELEN BAKER PARKER FUND Mrs. Parker's Husband and Children. Association Purposes.	15,000.00		Balance in Fund.....	4,621.64
			1955–1956	MR. AND MRS. JEFFREY R. SHORT FUND Relatives and Friends. To send worthy children to Camp Arthur	2,000.00
1952	FREDERICK AND WARREN PARKER FUND Mr. and Mrs. William J. Parker. Association Purposes.	15,000.00	1955	FRANK JUDSON FUND Relatives and Friends. Sears Roebuck	520.00
1954	HERMAN A. STOTZ FUND Relatives and Friends. Historical Research Projects	654.50	1955–1956	MARION MASKE GIBBS MEMORIAL FUND Relatives and Friends. High Ridge	1,838.00
1954–1956	MRS. MARY G. WAGNER ENDOWMENT FUND Mr. and Mrs. Percy E. Wagner. Central for special purposes	7,500.00	1956	WARD BECK MEMORIAL FUND Archie G. Beck. Austin Department—Camp MacLean	50.00
1954–1956	MR. & MRS. JAMES STORKAN FUND Gift of Robert S. Storkan in Honor of the 60th Wedding Anniversary of His Parents.		1956	SOLON G. KOCLANES Austin Department Boys' Work	100.00
			1957	MR. AND MRS. ABRAHAM BOWERS MEMORIAL FUND For benefit of foreign students	100.00

Year	Donor	Amount
	General Endowment Fund	
1889	John Crerar ......$	50,000.00
1899	James Craigmile ..	500.00
1899	Marshall H. Cone.	1,000.00
1899	Leonard Gould ...	12,500.00
1900	Silas B. Cobb......	5,000.00
1901	John Quincy Adams	10,000.00
1901	George Scott	10,000.00
1904	Henry J. Willing.	5,000.00
1910	Mrs. Ellen Sage...	1,000.00
1910	Thomas Murdoch ⅓ of residuary estate	815,084.42
1912	Arthur D. Wheeler	1,000.00
1913	Kenneth Barnhart	5,000.00
1913	Miss Martha S. Hill	10,000.00
1916	Thomas Templeton	50,000.00
1916	Henry Schoellkopf	1,000.00
1918	George A. Rollins.	4,000.00
1919	Charles S. Holt...	1,500.00
1919	Harland Grant Beatty 1/10 of trust estate.	660.36
1920	James R. Chapman.	5,000.00
1921	Leverett Thompson	5,000.00
1922	Francis W. Parker.	1,000.00
1923	Mrs. Nettie F. McCormick	100,000.00
1924	George M. Clark..	2,000.00
1925	Charles F. Grey 4/27 of ½ residuary estate	151,095.07
1926	William J. Watson 1/10 income from trust estate	
1926	Mrs. Elizabeth J. Ward	10,000.00
1927	Ernest A. Hamill.	10,000.00
1927	Edward Hillman .	1,000.00
1927	Arthur B. Jones...	10,000.00
1928	Anna Josephine Greeley	1,000.00
1930	Frank H. Millard.	10,000.00
1930	Alfred T. Martin.	1,000.00
1930	George H.	

Year	Donor	Amount
	McCammon	10,000.00
1930	Albert E. Cross (30,230.17 received to date)	75,000.00
1931	Miss Jessie Galbraith Templeton 1/10 of residuary estate	23,397.45
1931	Frank O. Dryer ¼ of residuary estate	1,350.17
1932	Miss Mary Templeton 1/10 of residuary estate	21,919.14
1932	William C. Miller ⅛ of residuary estate	2,352.62
1932	Martin A. Ryerson	10,000.00
1932	Howard H. Hitchcock Securities $10,000 (face value) $4,300 (market value)	
1933	Fred B. Jones......	23,500.00
1936	Mrs. Marion C. Van Dusen in memory of her father, Myron J. Carpenter	100.00
1936	John W. Hirst....	5,000.00
1941	Henry Schoellkopf, Jr.	419.78
1942	Harry P. Weber 2/16 of residuary estate .... ¼ contingent interest in trust estate (Not Yet Payable)	27,290.29
1944	Clifford W. Barnes 2½% of net income from the Clifford W. Barnes Foundation. Fund held by the Chicago Community Trust.	

Year	Donor	Amount	Year	Donor	Amount
1930	HARRY BERNARD LUSCH Held by Harris Trust & Savings Bank. Income distributed by Chicago Community Trust.			**Bequests Not Yet Payable**	
			1955	JANET H. HENNEBERRY 5% of residuary estate (Not Yet Payable)	
1942	MISS AUGUSTA E. LEHMANN	5,000.00	1955	FRANK W. PORTER..	100,000.00
			1956	VICTOR A. BECKMAN 111th Street	1,000.00
1945	MRS. ALICE CHAPIN MAY .... (paid on account: $1,875.88)	2,500.00	1956	MRS. FANNIE F. CROSS	25,000.00
			1956	ALBERT A. HENRY West Suburban Building Fund	5,000.00
1946	JAMES A. COX....... Placed in the Clara M. Cox and James Alfred Cox Endowment Fund. Total received from gifts and bequests $17,024.02.	7,018.02	1956	WILLIAM J. KALISH Hyde Park	1,000.00
			1956	NOAH VAN CLEEF Hyde Park and South Shore. Amount not known.	
1949	THOMAS A. RUTHERFORD 5% of a $10,000 Trust Fund	572.10	1957	MRS. JOHANNA M. LERCH 3% interest in 50% of the Residuary Trust after certain direct bequests and 40% contingent interest in two Life Trusts. Solely for the benefit of the Irving Park Department.	
1949	JOHN J. MCINERNEY.	100.00			
1952	CHARLES F. GREY...	2,000.00			
1955	PHILIP B. GALE..... 1/100 part of residuary estate. Placed in the Bernadine D. Gale Memorial Fund.	14,787.24	1957	CHARLES H. CRAM 10% interest in the Residuary Estate for the benefit of the West Suburban Department.	
1956	MRS. NETTIE A. BARNES	5,000.00			
1957	WILLIAM LIDDELL..	2,000.00	1957	NOAH L. KRATZ.... Income to be used for current expense.	3,000.00
1957	MISS BESS P. EELS..	2,000.00			
1957	MISS EMMA B. KLEIN .... 18% of Residuary Estate	27,436.59	1957	MISS ADAH F. WHITCOMB $1,000 and an interest in the Residuary Estate	
1957	GEORGE P. ROSE.... One-third interest in Residuary Estate	54,540.12			

Year	Donor	Amount	Year	Donor	Amount

Bequests Subject to Life Trusts

1908   MRS. CHARLOTTE E. COE
¼ of residuary estate.

1936   CYRUS HALL McCORMICK
15% contingent interest in residuary estate.

1937   RALPH ISHAM
¼ of trust estate. Subject to a life trust. For the benefit of the North Avenue Larrabee Boys' Club.

1947   DR. JAMES GRAYBEAL
⅓ of trust estate. To be used for the benefit of the Southtown Department.

1949   ALBERT MATHESON
$1,000 from Trust Fund subject to special conditions.

1950   FRANK D. WILSON
⅙ of Trust Estate subject to special conditions.

1955   BENJAMIN J. BROXTON
½ of residuary trust. To be used for the benefit of the Wabash Avenue or Washington Park Departments, or both.

1955   EDWARD PAGE SMITH
$5,000 subject to certain Life Trusts. To be used for the benefit of the Central Department.

1955   W. ELLIS STEWART

$20,000 subject to certain Life Trusts. To be used to create a Trust Fund to finance Memberships for Boys and Girls in "Y" Activities and Camps.

Special Endowment Funds

1873	JAMES L. REYNOLDS Reynolds Fund. Support of a female city missionary	10,000.00
1901	HUNTINGTON W. JACKSON Purchase books for library	1,000.00
1909	LUCY KEEP ISHAM FUND Albert Keep North Avenue Larrabee Boys' Club..	100,000.00
1917	CHARLES F. KIMBALL Held by the First National Bank of Chicago. Provide memberships for young men.	
1925	BURTON JOHNSON FUND Miss Florence Johnson. Benefit of the employes of the C. & N. W. Railway..	10,000.00
1925	AARON B. MEAD Support of a female city missionary	1,000.00
1937– 1955	WILLIAM T. WESTGATE Y.M.C.A. Hotel Loan Fund	7,259.20
1940	L. WILBUR MESSER LIBRARY FUND Elizabeth Garcelon

Year	Donor	Amount	Year	Donor	Amount
	Messer. Professional Library	4,848.39	1922	MRS. ANN M. SWIFT Hyde Park	10,000.00
1941	JOHN M. RYAN Employment Office	1,000.00	1923	EMMA F. BLOOM 111th Street	500.00
1941– 1956	JOSEPH S. DUNCAN Duncan Memorial Fund in honor of Mr. Duncan's mother, Mary E. Duncan, and the mother of his wife, Belinda C. Yockey. Duncan ...	1,235,950.84	1927	ANDREW P. HUMBURG Central	200.00
			1928	HORACE L. CROFT Wabash Avenue ...	5,000.00
			1928	OLIVER M. ZEIS Southtown	2,982.11
1947	FREDERICK AND HELEN BAKER MEMORIAL FUND Mrs. Helen Baker Parker. Preferably work among the people of the Negro race.....	5,000.00	1931	FRANK K. HOOVER Hyde Park	20,000.00
			1931	JOHN N. DOLE Duncan	2,000.00
			1931	DR. HORACE M. STARKEY FUND Mrs. Emily Starkey Central	500.00
1954	MISS KATHERINE BOYLES Albert Dickinson Fund. Washington Park ..	100.00	1934	EDWARD V. PRICE Washington Park Department	27,178.99
			1934– 1946	AMBROSE V. POWELL FUND Mrs. Hannah B. Clark Powell. Hyde Park	9,179.65

Department Endowment Funds

Year	Donor	Amount	Year	Donor	Amount
			1935	WILLIAM W. CRAIG 111th Street	205.41
1909	N. B. HOLDEN Income from $1,-000.00 trust fund held by the First National Bank of Chicago. Duncan.		1935	ROBERT TEMPLETON Duncan Boys' Work	17,389.36
			1946	HARRY W. MIXSELL Washington Park (On Account)	1,200.00
			1946	RALPH W. OLMSTEAD Austin	500.00
1910	MRS. SARAH A. HAWLEY Hyde Park ....$	23,886.00	1949	CHARLES E. STROHM Medical Center	495.00
1914	H. M. HOOKER Duncan	10,000.00	1950	ANDREW DOLE MEMORIAL FUND Mrs. Mary Hooker Dole Duncan	10,000.00
1916	CHAS. D. ETTINGER Hyde Park	5,603.88			
1916	OSCAR F. LENGACHER Central	1,000.00	1950– 1951	C. T. B. GOODSPEED Washington Park ..	3,200.81
1916	EDGAR H. NICHOLS Southtown	2,500.00	1950– 1954	WILLIAM J. NOBACH Duncan	15,988.00

Year	Donor	Amount	Year	Donor	Amount
1951	RAPHAEL P. MARSHALL South Shore	1,664.62	1957	MRS. LULA L. MILLS Harvey	2,000.00
1952	LIZZIE K. SCHERMERHORN W. Irving Schermerhorn Estate. Hyde Park	5,000.00		**Special Funds**	
1952	SANDY W. TRICE Wabash Avenue ...	1,000.00	1920	JOHN H. HEWITT Expended for High Ridge Dept. Site...	28,000.00
1952	FRED A. GROW Southtown	2,500.00	1925	VICTOR F. LAWSON Used for the construction of new de-	
1953	PRESLY M. HERON Duncan	5,000.00		partment buildings .	3,590,570.90
1953	JAMES V. PARKER Hyde Park	2,500.00	1931	MRS. MARY E. WOLFE Mary E. Wolfe Loan Fund.	
1953	BENJAMIN STRAUSS Irving Park	1,000.00		Benefit of residents of Duncan Department	301.89
1954	MRS. FANNIE WEDELES Executor of the Estate. South Shore	1,000.00	1941	GEORGE R. ARTHUR Camp Arthur	30,533.43
1955	ROBERT MALCOLM Duncan	3,310.49	1947	MICHAEL GALLAGHER Southtown Building Fund	4,976.01
1955	NAOMI H. GIBSON MEMORIAL FUND George H. Gibson Harvey	2,500.00	1949	WILBUR F. BUDD Southtown Building Fund	500.00
1955	MRS. GLADYS F. BADGER ⅓ of Residuary Estate. For the benefit of the Irving Park Department Tri-Hi-Y.		1951	PAULINE E. RUETTINGER Gymnasium Fund of Washington Park	500.00
			1957	MRS. IDA A. BAUMGARTNER .... To apply on purchase of electric organ for Southtown Department.	1,000.00
1956	CHARLES F. HASELTINE Hyde Park	1,000.00			
1956	CHARLES W. HOFF Hyde Park	1,000.00		**Life Income Gift**	
1956	SIGMUND WEISS Division Street	250.00	1956	JOHN C. ASPLEY Wilson Avenue	10,000.00

APPENDIX VI

METROPOLITAN CENTENNIAL EVENTS

Event	Place	Date
1. Centennial Youth Festival	Conrad Hilton Hotel and International Amphitheatre	November 15–16, 1957
2. 100th Annual Meeting	International Amphitheatre	January 23, 1958
3. Centennial Program Pageant	International Amphitheatre	March 22, 1958
4. Centennial Woman's Luncheon	To be selected	October 15, 1958

NATIONAL CONFERENCES AND EVENTS

1. North American Association of Secretaries Business Administration Conference	Morrison Hotel	November 10–13, 1957
2. National YMCA Handball Championships	Hyde Park YMCA, Lawson YMCA, and Town Club	March 22–29, 1958
3. Annual Meeting of National Council of Industrial Management Clubs	Conrad Hilton Hotel	May 8–10, 1958
4. National Council of YMCA's	Conrad Hilton Hotel	May 23–25, 1958

Index

Index

Field, Marshall, 41, 95, 166
Filbey, Emery T., 293
Finney, Chas. G., 24, 116
First Presbyterian Church, 27
Fischer, Harry A., 307
Fleming, Robert H., 200
Forgan, James B., 219
Forsyth, George, 347, 348
Fort Donelson, 44, 46
Fox, Dr. G. George, 229
Francis, William P., 231, 271
Friedeman, William F., 224
Fuller, Henry Weld, 55
Fuller, Melville W., 55

Gary, Judge Elbert, 227
George Williams College, 120, 209, 318, 361
Gibbs, O. C., 60
Gilkey, Rev. Charles W., 222
Gilliland, Walter D., 293
Goodrich, Mrs. R. V., 297
Goodspeed, Chas. T. B., 207, 255
Grant, Gen. U. S., 51
Gregg, Col. Clifford C., 309, 338
Gulick, Luther H., 323-325

Hahnemann Medical College, 62, 142
Hall, Arthur B., 313
Hamrin, S. A., 293
Hansel, John W., 120
Harmony Hall, 20
Harper, William Rainey, 118
Harper's Weekly, 129
Harris, Albert W., 137
Harris, N. W., 165, 185, 197, 200
Harris Trust & Savings Co., 165, 185
Hart, Walter T., 107
Harvey, Turlington W., 74, 300
Hathaway, Frank A., 250, 264-267, 282, 310, 317-319, 344
Havelock Guards, 48
Hawley, Sarah E., 168
Heald, Henry T., 293
Heavenly Tidings, 63, 82
Hemingway, A. T., 83-85, 87, 88, 90-92, 96, 99-101, 103, 344
Hester, Mrs. Harriet, 286
Higinbotham, Mrs. Harlow, 126
Hiller, J. A., 227
Hinsdale, Henry W., 52
Holden, Charles N., 134
Holden, Charles R., 134
Holden, William H., 134
Hollister, Dr. J. H., 55

Holmes, John, 277
Hopkins, C. Howard, 77
Hotchkiss, Prof. Willard E., 191
Houghteling, James L., 88-90, 92, 93, 98-100, 103, 105, 123, 219
Houghteling, Mrs. James, 126, 156
Houser, Theodore V., 277, 341, 342, 358
Howser, George T., 91, 92
Hubbard, Henry M., 123, 143
Hutchins, Chauncey, 28
Hypes, Samuel L., 289, 308
Hypes, W. F., 219, 231, 308

Illinois Steel Co., 132, 166
Industrial Management Club, 328, 334
Insull, Samuel, 95, 200
International Harvester Co., 166, 226, 304
Inventors' Clubs, 347, 348, 349
Isham, Elizabeth, 126
Isham, Lucy Keep, 173, 296
Isham, Mary Otis, 297
Isham, Ralph, 297

Jacobs, Benjamin F., 46, 50, 55, 58, 72, 79, 126
Jenney, William LeBaron, 124
Jevne & Almini, 124
Johnson, Martin, 238-239
Johnston, Wayne A., 361
Jones, Arthur B., 200
Jones, David D., 70, 141
Jones, Mark, 246

Keep, Albert, 173, 296
Keep, Mrs. Albert, 173, 175
Keith, E. G., 122, 123
Kelley, William V., 219
Kettering, Chas. F., 315
Kimball, Curtis N., 165
King, Simeon W., 126
King, Tuthill, 46, 52
Knowles, Malcolm S., 295
Kohlsaat, Judge C. C., 165
Kroehler, Mr. & Mrs. Delmar, 312

Lambert, Mrs. A. Myron, 301
La Salle Club, 134, 135
Lawson Memorial Library, 244
Lawson, Mr. & Mrs. Iver, 244
Lawson, Victor F., 95, 164, 199, 241, 242
Lerman, Dr. Frank, 349
Loucks, Charles O., 230
Loucks, Vernon R., 256
Lowden, Gov. Frank O., 93
Lundquist, Simon, 227

379

Index

Quincy YMCA, 21
Quayle, Robert, 138

Raiser, Mrs. N. A., 297
Reed, Andrew J., 261
Reeves, Floyd W., 279
Remy, G. Vern, 263
Rice, Dr. Nathan L., 33
Robbins, C. C., 320
Roberts, G. F., 229
Rock Island RR, 96, 138
Rockwell, Frank Malaby, 56, 57, 81, 82
Rompel, Victor H., 300
Roosevelt, Pres. Theodore, 172
Roosevelt University, 292, 294
Root, George F., 93
Root, John O., 301
Rosenthal, Benjamin J., 200
Rosenwald Fund, 303
Rosenwald, Julius, 160, 164, 182-184,
    186, 189, 195, 197-199, 222, 336
Routson, W. E., 203
Rumsey, Dr. L. A., 263
Rush Medical College, 142

Samuelson, G. W., 297
Sanitary Fair, 50
Sankey, Ira, 76
Schaefer, Daniel A., 283
Scherer, Bert, 92, 93
Schloerb, Dr. Rolland W., 325
Schroeder, Carl A., 236
Scully, John E., 85
Searle, Dr. G. D., 239
Sears, Roebuck & Company, 160, 172,
    182, 304, 359
Secretarial Institute & Training School,
    149
Senate, 93
Shedd, John G., 158-160, 163, 197, 198,
    200, 219, 335
Sherman, Gen. William T., 51
Shiloh, 47
Short, Jeffrey R., 282, 309
Sidley, William P., 204
Sistrunk, Henry L., 263
Sites, Fred, 227
Sloan, Daniel, 129-130
Smith, Byron L., 123
Smith, Edwin Burritt, 107
Smith, Dr. T. M., 305
Soenksen, Paul W., 301
Soldiers' Home, 51
Sparling, Dr. Edward J., 281, 290, 292,
    293
Starkey, Dr. Horace M., 107

Stewart, W. Ellis, 305
Stone, Rev. Luther, 18, 20
Stotz, Charles H., 306
Stotz, Herman A., 208
Stratton, L. W., 359
Stuart, Harold, 277
Stubbs, David C., 327, 328
Sudler, Carroll H., Jr., 287
Sullivan, Ed, 205
Sunday, W. A. (Billy), 93, 114-116
Swift & Co., 304
Swift, Mrs. Gustavus F., 199

Taft, Pres. William Howard, 188
Taylor, Prof. Graham, 156
Tegtmeier, Wm. F., 224
Templeton, Thomas, 159
Thomas, Gen. George Henry, 47
Thomas, Lowell, 167
Tilghman, J. H., 186
Titsworth, A. D. & Co., 25
Townsend, G. B., 91
Trumbull, Sen. Lyman, 93
Tucker, Leroy, 188

Underwood, P. L., 58
U. S. Christian Commission, 46, 48, 50,
    51, 63
U. S. Sanitary Commission, 46, 47, 51
United States Steel Corp., 227
University of Chicago, 142, 192, 294
University of Good Government, 347,
    349, 350
University of Illinois College of
    Dentistry, 142

Vanarsdale, W. W., 82, 83
Verness, Levi, 44

Wadsworth, E. S., 52
Wallace, Andrew, 227
Wanzer, William B., 224
Ward, Samuel Dexter, 20, 21, 126
Wardell, W. R., 90
Washington, Booker T., 186
Watchman, The, 82, 83
Watchman of the Prairies, 17
Weidensall, Robert, 95, 98, 120
Welles, Donald P., 309, 359
Welles, Edwin S., 27, 55
Wentworth, Mayor John, 15, 16, 24
West Market Mission Sunday School, 55
Western Secretarial Institute, 99, 120
Wheeler, Harry A., 164
White, A. Stamford, 164
White, Eugene B., 307, 315

Index